Beyond Baja Legends

From Beautiful Baja to Mainland Mexico

By Greg Niemann

SUNBELT PUBLICATIONS
CHULA VISTA, CALIFORNIA

Beyond Baja Legends: From Beautiful Baja to Mainland Mexico

Sunbelt Publications, Inc.
 First edition 2025

Edited by Jennifer Redmond
Cover and book design by Nichole Groschup-Black
Project management by Deborah Young
Printed in United States of America

Please direct comments and inquiries to:

Sunbelt Publications, Inc.
664 Marsat Ct., #A
Chula Vista, CA 91911
(619) 258-4911, fax: (619) 258-4916
www.sunbeltpublications.com

28 27 26 25 4 3 2 1

Library of Congress Cataloging-in-Publication Data

Names: Niemann, Greg, 1939- author.
Title: Beyond Baja Legends: From Beautiful Baja to Mainland Mexico/ by Greg Niemann.
Other titles: Tales from Beautiful Baja to the Mainland
Description: First edition. | Chula Vista, CA : Sunbelt Publications, Inc., 2025. | Includes bibliographical references and index.
Identifiers: LCCN 2024041759 | ISBN 9781941384725 (paperback)
Subjects: LCSH: Baja California (Mexico : Peninsula)--Description and travel. | Baja California (Mexico : Peninsula)--Anecdotes. | Baja California (Mexico: Peninsula)--Social life and customs. | Baja California (Mexico : Peninsula) --History. | Niemann, Greg, 1939-
Classification: LCC F1246 .N55 2025 | DDC 972/.2--dc23/eng/20241206
LC record available at https://lccn.loc.gov/2024041759

All photographs are by the author unless noted or in public domain.

This book is dedicated to my son Steven V. Niemann, and to the heartfelt memory of my daughter Annalies J. "Bucky" Niemann (1964-2024). Both were introduced to the wonders of Baja California at very young ages.

Acknowledgements

Photos of Bascom A. Stephens came from Niemann Family archives. Stephens' hand-drawn map of the gold fields came from the *Los Angeles Tribune* (1889). Map of Tijuana by Sharon Crockett (1930); Map of Mexicali from Imperial Irrigation District (1920).

Much information and some photos came from books by John Steinbeck, Erle Stanley Gardner, William Walker, and Jack Smith; Smith photo from the *Los Angeles Times.* Photo of Steve McQueen from SCORE International; Photo of Mazatlan Hurricane by Greg Niemann, courtesy *Los Angeles Times.*

Some of the photos were taken by Leila Niemann; the remainder are by Greg Niemann.

I thank *Baja Bound Insurance* for publishing many of the book's stories in their monthly newsletter under their Travel Guide (Baja Adventures). Also, I want to thank the *San Clemente Journal* for publishing a number of these articles.

I am also indebted to the reviewers who wrote such glowing tributes about the stories in this book.

Lastly, this book would not be a reality without the fine efforts of the team at Sunbelt Publications. I single out Lisa Gulick (CEO), Debi Young (Production Manager), Nichole Groschup-Black, and my friend and outstanding editor Jennifer Redmond.

Table of Contents

How Baja Beckons

Author at Pyramid Resort Baja Bookfest 2011

Introduction

As author of two earlier books about Baja California: *Baja Fever* (Mountain N' Air Books, La Crescenta, 1998), and *Baja Legends* (Sunbelt Publications, San Diego, 2002), I have often been asked about my next Baja book.

Since *Baja Legends* was released, I've written and published three non-Baja related books. And even though I've also written numerous travel, adventure and historical articles, until now I had not attempted a third Baja book.

Now in its sixth printing, *Baja Legends* has been a perennial seller, both in print and Kindle versions. Even today, over 20 years later, I am still being asked to give presentations about the book. That's the kind of draw the intriguing peninsula of Baja California has on people.

In the years since *Baja Legends* was published by Sunbelt, most of the articles I have written were about Baja California for web and print magazines. A number of those articles, some truncated and edited, are included here. I also looked at a few old stories from my Baja books that needed to be updated, added to, and rewritten. And, of course, I wrote new stories specifically for this book.

Thus, the narratives and tales about Baja included here span a lifetime of travels across the border, as well as research on some more interesting history of the peninsula.

While some of the stories have been updated, others did not lend themselves to it. You might be tempted to think, "It's not like that anymore," so I recommend you look at the date the story was written. Some of the stories in this book were little changed from the original but might include a brief update as an "Update note" at the end.

I've tried to arrange the chapters in a somewhat chronological and also a loose geographical order.

The book starts off with stories called **"How Baja Beckons"** in which some historical adventures are presented with more recent forays into Baja, illustrating how people through the years have succumbed to Baja Fever.

The stories in the next section **"Narratives from Baja Norte"** mainly take place in the northern state of Baja California. The next set of stories, **"Memos from Mexicali to San Felipe"** are from locations also in the northern state but on the gulf side. The third set **"Tales from Baja Sur"** are adventures and tales from the state of Baja California Sur.

In this book, I am going beyond Baja to also add a few narratives from Mainland Mexico, which I label **"Beyond the Peninsula."** Then the book closes with stories about Mexican holidays and culture, called **"Sampling Mexican Culture."**

I hope many supporters of *Baja Legends* and *Baja Fever* enjoy this new book, knowing that many of you can relate to much of it.

For you readers new to the Baja California experience, welcome and enjoy *Beyond Baja Legends*. Hopefully you too can appreciate how Baja can call out, beckoning visitors like the seductive sirens did Ulysses. You will learn and understand what many call Baja Fever, the phrase that became the title of my first book.

Catching Baja Fever

An acquaintance who knew I was a Baja buff once commented that she and her husband had gone down to Baja California the previous summer. "We had a great time," she admitted, and then added, "but it sure was nice to get back across the

View from La Unica on the Sea of Cortez

border to the good old U.S. of A."

Obviously that couple was not afflicted with what I call Baja Fever. To those who have this chronic disease, the comfort is crossing the border going south. I will concede that it is nice getting the car into high gear on the wide, multi-lane U.S. freeway after leaving the border congestion, but I am saddened each time I cross north, not relieved.

I know I'm back in a land where precious minutes and seconds are all-important, where material goods and status mean more than character and family and friends. Where I know I'll be busy just managing my daily affairs.

Going south has always been great therapy for me, especially before I retired. After a busy week in the business world I would cross the border and immediately start slowing down. My heart would start beating slower in Baja. My attitude began mellowing. Within a day my self-regulatory watch would be put in a drawer until we had to leave. It's easy to lose track of time in Baja, even lose track of days, because you're not compelled to count.

The slower pace of Baja offers a sense of timelessness, and those who can forsake the commuter traffic, or jump off the corporate merry-go-round long enough to enjoy it rarely regret it. The wife of one manager we took to our Baja house marveled for years afterward that she had never seen her Type-A husband as relaxed as he was that weekend.

John Steinbeck described the feeling well in his *Log From The Sea of Cortez* when he acknowledged, "The matters of great importance we had left were not important....Our pace had slowed greatly: the hundred thousand small reactions of our daily world were reduced to very few."

Baja is unique

Baja is unique – even to the rest of Mexico. There are more American tourists and expats, and a greater influence from them, especially in the border region where the dollar is widely used and English is widely spoken.

There is more desolation in Baja. And there is a greater feeling of remoteness, of being apart from mainland Mexico.

Early tribes of those peoples who crossed from Asia to populate the Americas had lived in Baja California and left their legacy in artwork on the walls of obscure caves in distant mountain valleys. The confines and harshness of the narrow peninsula had entrapped them, and they and their descendants eked out livings in a difficult land.

Then by the 1600s Europeans arrived on the peninsula, some seeking gold and land to conquer, while others sought heathens they could convert to their religion. While the gold mostly eluded them, the padres found plenty of indigenous habitants as they established a chain of missions from the tip of Baja all the way up to northern California's San Francisco area.

From 1697, when the first permanent settlement in the Californias was established at Loreto, the next 100 years saw Spanish padres and soldiers conquering and taming the barren and sparsely settled peninsula.

After Mexico won its independence from Spain in 1821, Baja California remained a remote Mexican territory. America tried several times to wrest the peninsula form Mexico even requesting it as one of the spoils of the Mexican/American war. However, Mexico remained adamant and never yielded ownership of the Baja peninsula.

By the late 1800s numerous groups, including English, French, and Russians, established small colonies in Baja. Several fortune seekers and renegade Americans also tried to inhabit and/or take over Baja.

The hostile takeover attempts all failed and for that the Baja buff is lucky. Then again, would a different ownership have developed the Baja peninsula any sooner? Probably not. Only recently has rapid progress made any headway.

Max Miller, in his 1943 book *Land Where Time Stands Still,* noted, "Progress is a debatable subject; but certainly material progress has come slowly and in small measure to Lower (Baja) California. The contrast between its primitiveness and the glittering man-made works of California is sudden and sharp. One is thrown into the past."

Tourist dollar fuels economy

Today the tourist dollar has created a wealth not imagined by the Mexicans and early settlers and fortune seekers. The growth, especially in the extreme north and south, spearheaded by American and Canadian tourist dollars has made the two peninsular states among the wealthiest per capita of Mexico's 32 states.

Snowbirds from not only Canada, but Washington, Oregon, and other northern U.S. states have been busy, especially in the last 20 years or so, establishing winter homes in places like Loreto, the East Cape area, and the once small village of Todos Santos.

Todos Santos is now a quick jaunt from either La Paz or the Los Cabos region via newly widened paved roads. That town has seemingly tripled in size every time I've seen it. It's hard for me to believe that when I was there in the mid-1970s the rough dirt road from Cabo San Lucas was hard to follow as it was sandy and went through private ranches. And once we arrived in the old sugar-cane town there were only two small inns and a couple of rustic thatch-roofed, dirt-floor restaurants.

Baja is one of earth's last outposts, certainly the only one accessible to so many people. It abuts directly against one of the most affluent and populous states of the most influential country on this planet. Nowhere else in the world is there such a collision of cultures, values, and lifestyles.

Today (2024), more than fifty million people legally cross between San Diego and Tijuana annually, making the San Ysidro border crossing the busiest international border in the world. That's about one million people a week!

Being right next door to California, those who cross in either direction whittle away at the differences between the two countries. The Mexicans learn our way of life and we are foolish if we in turn cannot learn from theirs. We have much to gain.

For decades visitors to Baja California have noted the graciousness, friendliness, and helpfulness of their hosts.

In his 1948 book *The Land of Shorter Shadows,* famous mystery author Erle Stanley Gardner commented, "Baja is a most interesting territory, and it is a friendly territory. Many of the people there don't have the individual wealth that we have in the United States. But they do have the dignity of men who are making an honorable living, who are close to nature and who have priceless integrity of character. Their poverty is only as to material luxuries....I hope to go back there next year for a longer stay."

Like so many of us, Gardner returned many times. He ended up penning eight books about his Baja explorations.

Cortés Colony is Baja's First Settlement

It was conquistador Hernán Cortés, the conqueror of Mexico, who personally went on to Baja California in 1535 to establish the peninsula's first settlement, brief though it was. After claiming Mexico for the Spanish crown in 1519-21, and Honduras (1524-25), Cortés continued to lead expeditions for Spain in the New World.

Hernán Cortés

The further westward explorations of Cortés and others was driven by, and enhanced by, some fantastic stories and myths.

Throughout history, few subjects have fired up man's imagination more than the prospect of instant riches. And if you throw in a legend about beautiful women, you've got a box office hit. In the case of "California" in the early 16th century, you've got the ingredients for the intrigue that surrounded that mythical "island."

Following the discovery of great wealth in Mexico and Peru, the Spaniards were willing to believe anything. Fancy was so attractive it became fact.

The popular Spanish novel *Sergas (The Exploits of) de Esplandian* told about Amazon women of "beautiful robust bodies" on an island where gold was the only metal. The unknown land had to be out there somewhere, and Mexico became filled with adventurers who sought it, further spreading tall tales. Even Hernán Cortés was taken in by the myth and wrote the King of Spain that he would seek its truth.

In addition, an old European legend about seven cities of gold in a place called Cibola was resurrected by Cabeza de Vaca and his handful of men who wandered lost for eight years throughout what is now the Southwest United States. They claim to have seen the cities shimmering in the sunlight from a distance. Resolute adventurers searched for both legends over the next century and eventually settled for the realities that the seven cities were yellow clay Indian pueblos, and that the "island" of California had neither Amazons nor the riches they sought. Nor was California an island. They also searched for a "northwest passage" that would expedite ships heading to the Orient. It took them a long time to dispel the stories yet many died trying, and Cortés was involved in these pursuits.

Enamored by the stories, Cortés sent ships to seek the land inspired by legend, that mythical "island of riches" that became California. In 1532 his first two ships didn't get far, landing back on the Mexican mainland on the east side of the gulf (Gulf of California). One ship turned back in a storm and the crew of the other, commanded by Cortés' cousin, were all killed by natives on the mainland.

He sent two more ships late in 1533 but they got separated and the first one returned to Acapulco. The other ship, the "Concepcion," was commanded by another Cortés relative, Diego Becerra de Mendoza who was not well liked. The crew mutinied, killing him in his sleep and establish the Basque pilot Fortun Jimenez as commander. They stopped on the mainland coast north of Acapulco and sent Becerra's sympathizers ashore and set about fleeing to the north.

A storm blew the fugitives west by mistake into what is now La Paz, making them the first Europeans to set foot on (Baja) California. Unfortunately, most of the men didn't live to tell about it as local Indians killed Jimenez and 20 of his men.

The 18 survivors fled, sailing back across the gulf only to fall into the hands of Cortés' arch-rival Nuño de Guzman. Most were killed, but at least one escaped to relate to Cortés the tale of the landing in the new "island" to the west where there were many pearls. One historical report indicated there were two surviving seamen who told Cortés that there was "good evidence of pearls."

Thus the actual discovery of California by Europeans was an ignoble result of treachery, storms, mistakes, mutiny and counter-mutiny, all shrouded in violence, perpetrated by both the fugitive visitors and those whose homes and cultures, primitive as they may have been, were endangered.

Cortés Colony Short Lived

After hearing about the pearls and potential wealth in this "island" to the west, Cortés was encouraged. He used his own money, took three ships, a total of about 500 Spaniards who would establish a settlement, and set out to colonize the new land.

They crossed the gulf and on May 3, 1535, the party landed in what Cortés named Santa Cruz, the northeast corner of La Paz Bay, on what they called the Isle of Pearls.

The Cortés party found evidence of the earlier Jimenez landing and giving credence to the reports, also found pearls in great abundance, at least 30 pearl oyster beds. It appeared, however, that most were deep and would require diving, but they still began what would be a centuries-long pearl industry.

From the start, Cortés had problems supporting the colony. Not only were they harassed by attacks from the native Guaycura, but they found the land too arid to support them. Cortés had the ships return to the mainland to pick up additional colonists and supplies, but they had such bad luck that only one returned, and without any provisions at that.

Cortés himself took off back to the mainland with the remaining ship, only to discover that both vessels had run aground on the coast of Sinaloa. One, they were able to release, but the other was severely damaged upon a reef. Using the one ship able to sail, they also had a hard time getting supplies.

To further complicate matters, the pilot died on the journey back to the colony, so Cortés himself had to take the wheel. When they finally returned to Santa Cruz (La Paz) they discovered 23 of the colonists dead from starvation and a few others soon died from gorging themselves when food arrived.

The colony built a church and housing but could not sustain themselves from the land nor count on consistent supplies. Cortés abandoned the colony and the last of the colonists returned to the Mexican mainland in 1536. Cortés spent a fortune on this year-long enterprise and had nothing to show for it other than a few nice pearls, including one that was allegedly valued at 5,000 ducats, however much that totaled considering that at the time each ducat contained 3.5 grams of gold. Cortés was to get another expedition as he still wanted to find the lost city of Cibola gold legend and the fabled "northwest passage" strait. In 1539, before he returned to Spain, he sent Francisco de Ulloa north along the mainland coast from Acapulco in search of Cibola. Their three small ships made it to the Colorado River delta but they did not determine if it was a river or a strait to the South Sea (Pacific Ocean).

They sailed down the western shore, rounded the cape of San Lucas, and went as far north as Punta Baja which they named Cape Disappointment, "a fitting term for Cortés' last exploration" said one historian. They discovered neither gold, nor riches, nor did they confirm whether Baja was an island. The Gulf of California was renamed the Sea of Cortéz in the conquistador's honor. The former Governor of New Spain and leader of the expedition that caused the fall of the Aztec Empire, Hernán Cortés died in Spain in 1547. While he had some disappointments himself, all of his explorations provided enlightened information and data for those who followed him. He conquered mainland Mexico and Honduras, but as many visitors have learned through the years, Baja California proved to be a challenge.

Walker's Army Overthrows Baja (1850s)

William Walker

The most infamous American to set foot in Baja California was likely William Walker, a diminutive southerner who went there to establish his own country which he called the Republic of Lower California.

An unlikely warrior, Walker was born into a distinguished Tennessee family on May 8, 1824. One of his maternal uncles was a U.S. Senator and founder of the still viable *Philadelphia Enquirer.* A child genius, Walker graduated from the University of Nashville at the top of his class at age 14. By the time he was 25, he had degrees in both medicine and law and was legally allowed to practice as both a doctor and lawyer. He also worked as a publisher and journalist.

At heart, however, Walker was a restless adventurer. While still a teen, he went to Europe and studied at both the University of Edinburgh and the University of Heidelberg before receiving his medical degree at the University of Pennsylvania – all before the age of 19! He also spent time in New Orleans and San Francisco.

Although standing only 5'2", Walker still had a commanding presence and the charisma of later-day televangelists. He was also fearless. While working as editor of the *San Francisco Herald* in January 1851, Walker was shot in the thigh in a highly-publicized duel with a notorious gunfighter.

It seems that medicine, law, journalism, and travel were not enough for the visionary Walker. He dreamed big and set out to conquer much of Latin America, starting in Mexico!

Taking over Baja California

In 1853, he first sought a grant from Mexico to create a colony in Sonora which would serve as a fortified frontier, providing protection from Indian raids. Mexico refused.

Undaunted, he began recruiting American supporters of slavery and the Manifest Destiny doctrine. His plans then expanded from that proposed buffer colony to establishing an entirely independent Republic of Sonora.

But first he decided to conquer Lower California (Baja California); once the peninsula was secured, he planned to advance on Sonora. In October 1853, Walker sailed from San Francisco with 45 men to take over Lower California.

He and his army, mostly young southerners like himself, stopped in La Paz where they captured the governor, hoisted their own flag, and proclaimed their land the Republic of Lower California. Mexican forces gathered against him, and after one skirmish Walker fled to Ensenada where he proclaimed himself "president of his new republic" and applied the laws of the State of Louisiana, which included legalized slavery.

Word of his daring attack had spread in the United States and a large number of Americans thought Walker's project was a great idea. Volunteers lined up to join the expedition.

Even though his army was bolstered with 230 more volunteers, he was attacked by Mexican forces. There were a few fatalities, but Walker and his men were able to fight off the attempts.

After a U.S. government ship came to Ensenada to persuade Walker to leave, he marched his army south and relocated his "capital" in the old mission town of San Vicente.

In March 1854, he lost most of his troops to suffering, thirst, and desertion as he tried to cross the desert to realize his original dream, that of capturing the mainland state of Sonora. He returned to San Vicente to learn most of the small force he left there had deserted, and those who did not were killed by the Mexican army. In May, he and the remainder of his troops fought their way back to the United States.

He was captured crossing the border and was tried by an American jury for conducting an illegal war and violating neutrality laws. In that era his filibustering project was popular, especially in the southern and western United States, and the jury took only eight minutes to acquit him.

Released, but not reformed, he focused his eyes on even bigger targets. William Walker formed a new army and headed for Central America.

President of Nicaragua

Within a year Walker was back in action in Nicaragua which had one tremendous advantage before the Panama Canal was built. Most shipping went through Nicaragua by sailing up the San Juan River from the Caribbean, across Lake Nicaragua and then a short overland trip through Rivas to the Pacific. At the time Nicaragua was involved in a civil war, one party based in the city of Granada and the other in Leon. Walker was approached by the Leon faction—which was losing—and he rushed to Nicaragua with some 60 well-armed men. Upon landing, he was reinforced with another 100 Americans and almost 200 Nicaraguans. His army marched on Granada and captured it in October 1855. Because he was already considered supreme general of the army, he had no trouble declaring himself president. In May 1856, U.S. President Franklin Pierce even officially recognized Walker's Nicaraguan government.

Walker had made many enemies in his conquest, including shipping magnate Cornelius Vanderbilt, who controlled the route across the isthmus. As president, Walker revoked Vanderbilt's rights to ship through Nicaragua. Vanderbilt was understandably enraged and sent soldiers to oust him. Vanderbilt's men were joined by those of other Central American nations who feared that Walker would take over their countries too.

Walker had overturned Nicaragua's anti-slavery laws and made English the official language, which angered many Nicaraguans. In early 1857 the Costa Ricans invaded, supported by Guatemala, Honduras, and El Salvador, as well as Vanderbilt's money and men. Walker's army was defeated at the Second Battle of Rivas.

A Hard Man to Kill

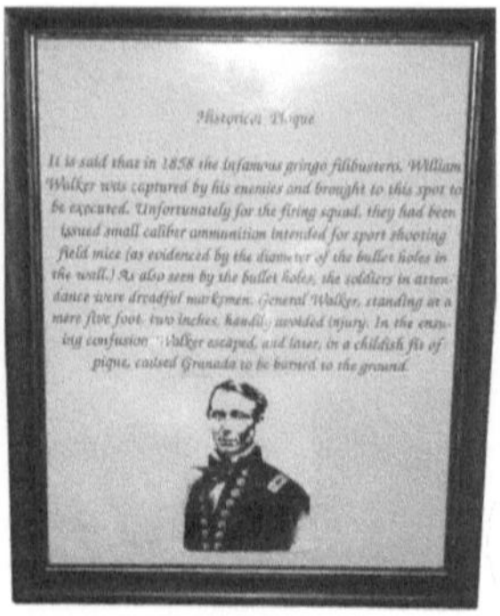

I had previously written about William Walker and his pursuits in Baja California and also was aware that he went on to Central America. Yet when I visited Nicaragua a few years ago, I was still surprised at his legacy there.

Sitting in an old, colonial restaurant in Granada, I noticed bullet holes in the wall behind me surrounded by clippings, artifacts including an old set of handcuffs, and a photo of the infamous Walker.

Fascinated, I looked over the exhibit. One Historical Plaque read:

> *It is said that in 1858 the infamous gringo filibustero William Walker was captured by his enemies and brought to this spot to be executed. Unfortunately for the firing squad, they had been issued small caliber ammunition intended for sport shooting field mice (as evidenced by the diameter of the bul-*

let holes in the wall.) As also seen by the bullet holes, the soldiers in attendance were dreadful marksmen. General Walker, standing at a mere five feet, two inches, handily avoided injury. In the ensuing confusion, Walker escaped, and later, in a childish fit of pique, caused Granada to be burned to the ground.

I question the veracity of the above report primarily because of the wrong date (It was in December 1856 when Walker was run out of Granada and had his men burn most of the old colonial city down.), But the rest of the story could be true because Walker to that point had lived a very charmed life.

Finally defeated in 1857, Walker returned to the states and was greeted as a hero in the south. He practiced law and wrote a book about his experiences titled *The War in Nicaragua.* A bachelor, he did plan to marry once but his fiancée died of yellow fever.

His restlessness prevailed, however, and he returned to Central America hoping to resume his presidency. He landed in Trujillo, Honduras, and was quickly captured. In September 1860, at the age of only 36, Walker was executed by a Honduran firing squad. Walker's filibusters had a significant positive impact on southerners, and it is said his example helped inspire the Confederacy. By contrast, Latin Americans saw the defeat of Walker and his armies as a source of pride. In Nicaragua, September 14 is San Jacinto Day, celebrating a decisive 1856 victory against Walker and "U.S. arrogance in general." In Costa Rica, April 11 is celebrated as a national holiday to commemorate Walker's defeat at Rivas. In Mexico, the combative Walker is well known. I even noticed an historical lesson about him in a Baja California third-grade primer.

However, William Walker is a little-known figure in American history, evidenced in 1988 when President George H.W. Bush selected a new ambassador for El Salvador. He didn't make any points in Central American as the name was, totally by chance, William Walker.

Baja Settlers and Prospectors (1880s)

Some of the early chroniclers of Baja California were not impressed with the peninsula—they lambasted everything from the indigenous people to the paucity of water, and what they considered the land's barren nothingness.

Then there were those who went overboard in extolling undeserved merits to everything, painting a seductive picture so glowing and inviting that it bordered on deception. By the mid-1880s, the hype offered by reporters and writers made the peninsula of Lower (Baja) California seem larger than life.

For example, an Ensenada newspaper in 1888 reported that a sheaf of wild oats sent from Baja's El Sauzal measured four feet in length and contained so much grain that "immense fields of them go to waste for want of stock to eat them."

Americans north of the border heard tales about Baja's "ideal climate, great natural mineral wealth, good tillable land for orchards, tall forests and abundant water, even with rivers to float the logs out of the mountains." That these unfounded legends and unrealized fantasies were able to thrive illustrates the remoteness of the land.

By the late 1880s some Americans, especially Southern Californians, had taken to looking south across the border, many having become convinced there was more abundant and fertile land with endless possibilities, compared to the U.S.

Consider these alluring comments about Baja California from Bascom A. Stephens in his 1889 book *The Gold Fields of Lower California*:

> "...The boundary line (U.S. – Mexico) does not change the climate and resources. Nature had not placed an oasis on the American side and a desert on the Mexican side. Alta California was once a part of Mexico. The same mountains that are towers of strength to Southern California are the eternal fastnesses of the peninsula. The same balmy breezes blow softly amid her pines and waft the fragrance of her orange blossoms inland.
>
> "The same characteristics of soil, climate and products exist south of the boundary line as north. It is a land of sunshine and silver, of fruits and flowers, of grain and gold, of gems and jewels, of the walnut and wine, of the olive and the orange, of banana and tobacco, of fish and fowl, of grand possibilities and certain probabilities of development."

Provocative Propaganda

If the aforementioned sounds like provocative Chamber of Commerce propaganda of the sort that might lure people to migrate, it should. In the late 19th century many books and pamphlets were published to attract thousands of Americans to settle in Southern California, and later by extension, Baja California, and Bascom A. Stephens was the author of several of them. He was also Secretary of the Historical Society of Southern California, a reporter for several different Los Angeles newspapers, city editor of the *Tucson Daily Citizen*

Bascom A. Stephens and grandson, A.H. Niemann, Jr. (the author's father)

(1882), and publisher of the *Pomona Progress and Independent* (1886-87).

Stephens married in 1878 and had three children, one of whom (Minerva Stephens Niemann) was my grandmother. Yes, this newspaperman who wrote such glowing fantasies about Baja California was in fact my great grandfather. It appears he was also a company hack for the International Company.

International Company to Develop Baja

Between 1880 and 1889 the Mexican government granted several large concessions of land to foreigners to develop. The largest of these in Baja became the International Company of Mexico, managed and financed by Americans.

The International Company chose the two finest ports in the northern part of Lower California and set about to develop the area. The company offered future colonists lots of 6 1/2, 25, and 50 acres at attractive terms. The capital of the district since 1882, Ensenada was but a rancho before 1887 when it was being developed by the International Company.

Due to effective touting of the area that led to colonization mostly by Americans, by January 1888 Ensenada had a population of 1,375, of whom only 28 percent were Mexican.

Gold Fever!

Gold had been known in Baja California for over a century and there were a few profitable mining diggings. Not missing a trick to help colonize their 20,000,000-acre land holdings, the International Company had been widely advertising the mineral wealth of Baja. Initially the unexciting gold reports were secondary to the Baja land offerings.

But a frenzied gold boom began immediately after February 23, 1889 when an Indian named Rafael Lopez showed up in an Ensenada store with a 10-ounce placer nugget he took from the Santa Clara mining area in the mountains southeast of town.

By this time the land boom up in Southern California had stalemated and thousands of Californians were out of work and becoming desperate. They were ripe to be infected with Gold Fever. Within weeks, thousands of prospectors invaded Baja, 3,000 from San Diego alone.

On one single day at the height of the boom, 600 prospectors left Los Angeles by train to San Diego and the Baja gold fields. The boom was not only hyped by many who claimed to have found gold, but also fanned by the flames of favorable reports from the first reporter on the scene, *San Diego Union and Bee* correspondent Captain James Edward Friend. Other reporters quickly joined Friend. They wrote about the number of miners arriving each day and the bounty of those finding gold.

Both San Diego and Ensenada were booming, with merchants happily outfit-

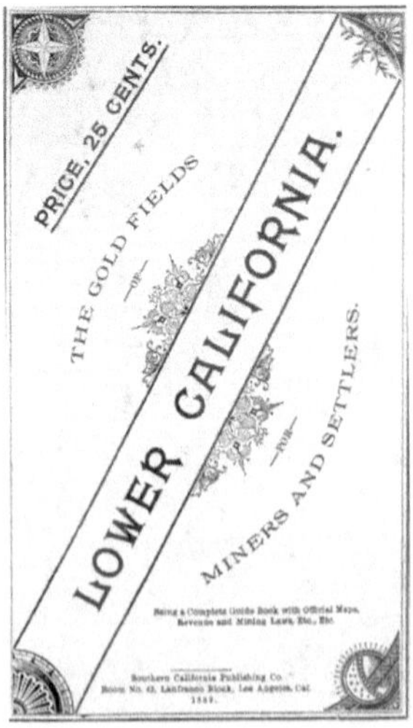

BAS Gold Field Book. 1889 (Huntington Library)

ting the argonauts. It was a heady time for the thousands who sought their fortunes, and they seemed to revel in and be energized by the tiniest rumor. Fantasies and exaggerations abounded; that 10-ounce nugget grew with each retelling,

While there was gold to be found, most prospectors were disappointed and the exciting placer strikes had all but petered out by the end of March. Many men lingered on in Mexico, some working the quartz mines at nearby El Alamo.

Stephens was extremely quick, especially for 1889 technology, in getting his 48-page book out to the miners by March 9. The first part of the book includes maps, directions, and several reports from Friend and other San Diego reporters.

Another part of the book is about mining—mining laws, equipment needed, etc. That material would have already been prepared by Stephens and lifted from his earlier (1884) book *Quijotoa Mining District Guide Book,* outlining that Arizona gold strike in which he also took part.

However, much of the book includes information for settlers, maps of the San Quintin area, and verbiage about colonization and Mexican Revenue Laws. This part appears to be direct propaganda for the International Company.

The International Company

About the company, in the book Stephens said, "The International Company of Mexico was organized in 1885. Among its members were E.T. Welles, L.R. Huller, and George Sisson. Its concession has been turned over to new management with B. Scott, Esq. of Ensenada as general manager. It has a concession for all the public domain on the peninsula north of the 28th parallel...

"By its efforts flourishing colonies exist at Ensenada, Colnett and San Quintin. A railroad coast survey has been made between San Diego and Ensenada."

In describing the routes to the mines, Stephens notes two ways, overland or steamer. He reported that the International Company made three trips each week from San Diego to Ensenada with their two steamers.

He also listed Ensenada rainfall figures from 1878 to 1888 noting an average of 22.69 inches per year. This is reported from the daily record by Col. D.K. Allen, Land Inspector for the International Company. Those numbers appear to be a gross exaggeration as Ensenada currently averages less than half that, around 10 inches per year.

Despite the best propaganda efforts of the International Company and their two steamships, they were having trouble attracting quality colonists to help settle their property. There was also a negative report by a Mexican inspector, alleged poor management, and many Mexicans were raising doubts abouts foreigners' settling in Baja. The company decided to bail out.

The English Take Over

On May 11, 1889 the International Company sold their interests to an English firm headquartered in London. Now called the Mexican Land and Colonization Company, they began paying outstanding bills and developing Ensenada.

A subsidiary English company, the Lower California Development Company, took over 160,000 hectares (almost 400,000 acres) in San Quintin and promised to settle 1,000 colonists there. They began to dig wells and create irrigation. They set about dredging the harbor and building a pier. They built a flour mill and exhibited machinery that they said was to start the construction of a Yuma-San Quintin railroad.

The enterprise failed, however, as much of this fanfare was a charade to attract investors. Neither this railroad, nor the San Diego-Ensenada line was ever built, even to this day.

There were 200 English colonists who did emigrate to San Quintin but they were further devastated by drought. Despite the prodigious amounts of rainfall reported, nature showed just how fickle she can be—between the years 1892 and 1896 not one inch of rain fell in either Ensenada or San Quintin.

English Cemetery in San Quintin

Ultimately it was the harshness and unpredictability of Baja California that thwarted the efforts of these settlers. It seems propaganda could feed mining frenzies, create desire, attract settlers—but it couldn't make rain!

The Filibuster of 1890

In a clandestine 1890 meeting, a few San Diego conspirators reviewed their plot to seize Baja California. Smug in the anticipated success of establishing their new "Republic of Lower California," they had already written a draft of the constitution and designed a colorful flag. With resources secured by the Mexican Land and Colonization Company (often referred as the English Company) they felt their chances to wrest the Baja Peninsula away from Mexico were better than earlier attempts.

Following the Mexican-American War (1846-1848) California was split and the present international border was created. As war spoils were divvied up, Mexico ceded California (Alta) and parts of Texas and New Mexico to the U.S., but managed to keep Lower (Baja) California.

The expansionist-minded U.S. however, wanted Lower California. It took a firm counterproposal in the Treaty of Guadalupe Hidalgo negotiations to save what is now "Baja California" for Mexico.

Following the war, Mexico was forced to sell the southern parts of Arizona and New Mexico to the U.S. in 1853-54 (Gadsden Purchase).

Lower California, with an 1851 population of only 7,000, was neglected by Mexico yet grew to over 20,000 by 1866.

There were several attempts to "take over" Lower California. A war veteran named Joseph Moorehead landed with troops in La Paz in 1851. He was defeated. So, eventually, was the infamous William Walker who made that storied takeover attempt in 1853. (See "Walker's Army"above.)

Then there was Henry Crabb, a former California state senator who led 69 men into Sonora in the 1850s. They were defeated and the vast majority executed, including Crabb, whose head was reportedly preserved in a jar of alcohol and displayed as a warning not to invade Mexican territory.

There were official attempts as well. In 1859, U.S. President James Buchanan sent minister Robert McLane to Mexico to negotiate purchasing several Mexican provinces including Lower California. Even after the negotiations were confined to Lower California alone, Mexican President Benito Juarez refused to sell.

In 1881 President John Garfield, through Secretary James G. Blaine, again approached Mexico on her willingness to sell the Peninsula.

Also in 1881, trailblazer John C. Fremont, at the time territorial governor of Arizona, proposed to the U.S. Government that Lower California be cordoned off as a reservation or asylum for the warlike Apache Indians.

Conspirators knew the history

Those San Diego conspirators finalizing their 1890 takeover plans were fully aware of the long-standing sentiment that the U.S. should get Baja California. After all, they were mostly journalists who had spent much of the previous decade writing inflammatory editorials and articles pushing for a takeover.

The journalists wanted to break away from Northern California influence, grab Baja, and include it in a new state of "Southern California."

Following is an example of the secessionist mindset at the time as reported by Captain John E. Janes in his San Pedro newspaper in 1883: "I hope to see the day when Southern California will become a state and Los Angeles the capital. Lower California we must have; it belongs naturally to Alta California. The Peninsula in the hands of the Mexican government is worthless to them, and always will be.... The government of this country must buy it, or we will have to take it for our own protection."

Janes was a convincing character whose rhetoric did incite others to action. In July 1888, Colonel J. E. Mulkey organized a secret society called "The Order of the Golden Field" with the sole purpose of claiming Lower California. The plan was exposed and the "society" was disbanded. Mulkey later joined the 1890 plot.

Yet it was Colonel Janes himself who "let the cat out of the bag" about the Filibuster of 1890 and uncovered the conspirators.

The Filibuster of 1890

There was considerable precedence, thus, for those 1890 conspirators and their filibustering scheme. They were mostly Southern Californian newspapermen anxious to capture Lower California, set up an independent government, and ultimately annex it to the United States.

Newspaperman B. A. Stephens

Imagine my chagrin to learn that one of the key figures in this shadowy scheme was my great-grandfather Bascom A. Stephens—the same newspaperman who penned several books including 1889's *Gold Fields of Lower California.*

In full disclosure, the *San Diego Union* on May 21, 1890 carried a story about the aborted filibuster, naming names, and citing details of the planned takeover. It highlighted my ancestor's involvement in the initial exposé:

> "...about six weeks ago B.A. Stephens arrived in San Diego from Los Angeles and formed an editorial connection with the *Informant* newspaper. Stephens is well known to Southern California newspapermen as one who has written a good deal in favor of the Annexation of the Peninsula and it is believed that he was fully cognizant of the Mulkey scheme. Stephens came to San Diego on the invitation of Augustus Merrill, editor of the Informant, and immediately upon his arrival was informed by Merrill of the details of the plan to take the peninsula.
>
> "Merrill told Stephens that the Mexican Land and Colonization Company had pledged $100,000 to support the scheme and that other money would be raised by individuals who had interests that would be served by the annexation."

The *Union* report further stated that Merrill introduced Stephens to prominent journalist Walter G. Smith, then editor of the *San Diego Sun,* who confirmed Merrill's statements and solicited Stephens' involvement.

Along with real estate speculator "Colonel" Edward Hill, the principals met the next evening, April 8, 1890, at the posh, only two-year-old Hotel del Coronado. It was revealed that $25,000 immediate cash from private parties including $5,000 from Hill would be refunded out of the $100,000 the English Company had pledged.

During that and subsequent secret planning meetings held in both San Diego and Ensenada, it was brought out that the English Company, with the exception of its President Sir Edward Jenkinson, was in favor of the scheme because they felt their huge Baja land concession was almost worthless under Mexican rule.

The conspirators were working through the English Company Manager Major Buchanan Scott of Ensenada, and Company Treasurer Mr. McQuilter.

The conspirators' planning was notably detailed, including how to "take" the Peninsula and organize the new government.

They decided to fill the English Company warehouses with arms, ammunition, and provisions and then bring a large number of American "laborers" (read troops) into Mexico. On a certain night a grand fandango was to be given at Ensenada's Hotel Iturbide overlooking the harbor, to which all Mexican officials would be invited. The conspirators would get them all drunk, bribe the Captain of the Guard, and on a given signal begin the revolution by overpowering the guards.

The English Company offered the use of two steamers (the *Manuel Dublán* and the *Carlos Pacheco*) for shuttling colonists and supplies into Baja for the revolutionists.

Along with the design of a new flag each new department head set about to organize his function.

Walter G. Smith, the *Sun* editor, was to be the President of the new Republic, with the militaristic title of Governor-General. A former member of the New York legislature, he wrote a Declaration of Independence for Lower California and even read his inaugural address to the group.

Flag of the Republic of Lower California, 1890

The Commanding General was to be Merrill, a former member of the Grand Army and editor of the *Informant,* who drew up a plan for the military establishment of the new government.

Bascom A. Stephens was to be the Secretary-General. He wrote a draft of the Constitution for the Republic of Lower California, but to date I have been unsuccessful in locating a copy.

Ranford Worthing, who was to be Treasurer-General, read an elaborate finance plan including details of printing money. Col. Edward Hill was to be War-General. C.A. Harris, a Baja landowner, was named Surveyor-General. Three other Cabinet posts (Attorney-General, Postal-General and Industrial General) were unfilled, presumably to be occupied by supportive Mexicans.

Janes was planning an independent foray to take Lower California but was talked into joining the San Diego newspapermen. However, he harbored suspicions that the others were surely to profit monetarily and were cutting him out.

Back in San Pedro, Janes wrote enough hints about the filibuster that both Smith and Merrill went to visit him and request his silence. Their visits were reported in the *San Diego Union* and leaks about the filibuster were feared.

Their fears were grounded as the *San Diego Union* got wind of the entire plot and exposed it in the May 21 edition, thus forever making a moot issue as to whether or not the fandango caper would have worked.

The next day the *San Francisco Chronicle* outlined the entire folly and included biographies of the conspirators. Editorials in both papers called for the U.S. government to do something to those who openly defied the treaty relations between Mexico and the United States.

During the hectic days following the divulgence, there was a lot of finger-pointing, with Janes accusing the other conspirators and vice-versa.

Smith was challenged to a duel by Mexican Colonel Manuel A.C. Ferrer for what he claimed an insult to Mexico. The duel never took place.

The Mexican Land and Colonization Company (The English Company) of course denied any involvement, although Manager Scott was on the next boat to England. Lower California Politico Jefe (Governor) Luis Torres displayed a willingness to work with the new company officers, and his belief that the filibustering conspiracy was “limited to a very few, irresponsible adventurers” helped Mexico’s President Porfirio Diaz determine that the case was closed.

While the filibuster caused a lot of generalized excitement in Mexico City, President Diaz told an Associated Press correspondent that he placed little importance in the movement. He knew the United States Government would not allow the neutrality to be violated, and the Mexican Government would protect her territory.

Thanks to the gracious attitudes of Governor Torres and President Diaz none of the conspirators was jailed for his involvement.

U.S. Secretary of State Blaine apologized to the Mexican government on behalf of the U.S President, and responsible journalists across the country berated their fellow newspapermen for their hare-brained scheme.

Stephens’ daughter Minerva (Niemann) was a carefree 8-year-old when all this was going on and fortunately didn't have to see her dad carted off to jail, or worse – see his head in a jar. She was such a sweet and mild-mannered Grandma, it's hard to imagine her dad as an international conspirator.

Finding Real del Castillo (1998)

It was back in 1998, and my timing for an adventure into Baja California's northernmost mountains could have hardly been worse. The punch of violent rainstorms

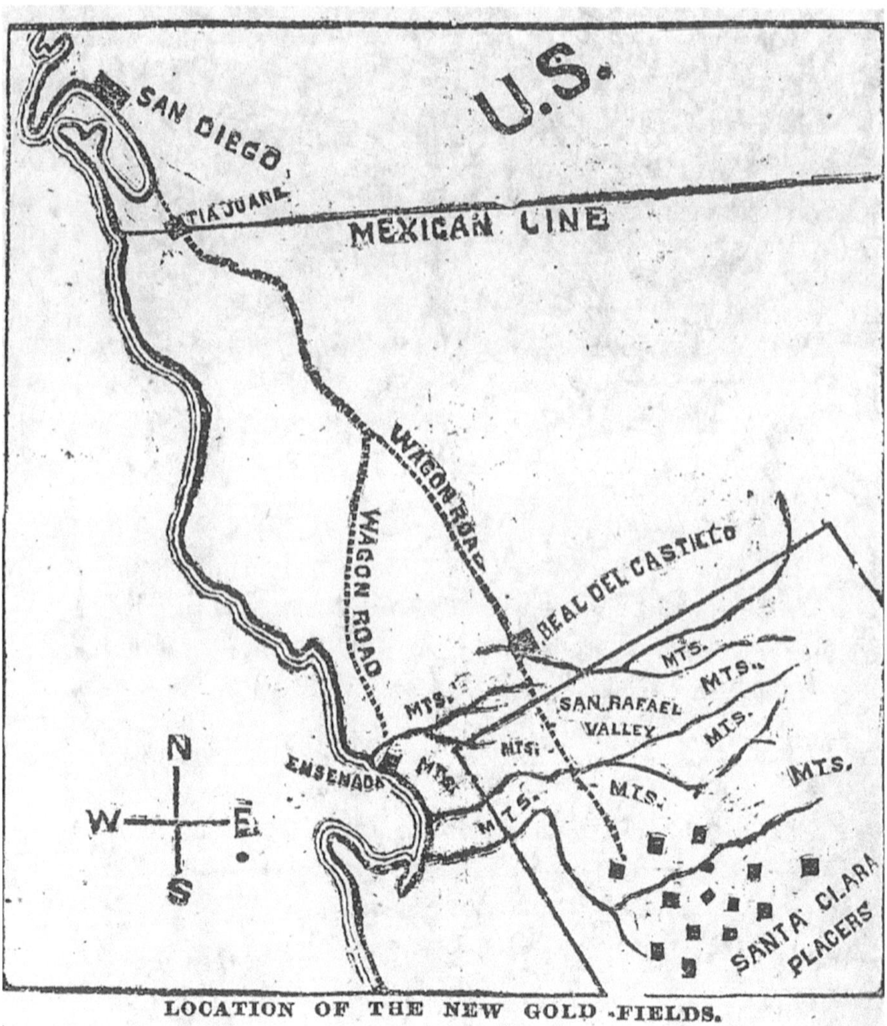

Map of the New Gold Fields, Los Angeles Tribune, March 7, 1889

spawned by the warm El Niño current had just left thousands of nearby Tijuana residents homeless. Many people lost their lives in onslaughts of mud and water during the seemingly endless February rains.

March 3 dawned bright and sunny and the horrors of the rains were fading with the sunshine of six warm days in a row. With the improved weather, the sirens of the Sierra Juarez called to me.

From my Cantamar base, I loaded up my 2-wheel drive Ford Explorer, pored over several maps, and headed off to visit the old mining town of Real del Castillo.

The muddy, potholed streets of Ensenada served as a premonition I chose to ignore. After all, adventure travel requires optimism. In some of us, sometimes, that optimism spills over and becomes downright foolhardiness. Call it whatever, I pressed on.

Highway 3 winds up out of the Ensenada suburbs into the mountains. Potholes, which are always a Baja hazard, were of legendary size and number all along the 160-mile highway to San Felipe and the gulf. Mud cascaded onto the highway, and in parts the macadam road had actually been washed away, leaving only a single lane.

After 25 miles, the winding road descended into a broad fertile valley. At just over 2,000-foot elevation, the 18-mile long by 6-mile-wide valley is called the Valle de San Rafael, the Valle del Real del Castillo, or the Valle de Ojos Negros, take your pick.

Here fertile green farms and pastoral ranches checker the landscape, broken only by the common Baja fencing—three strands of barbed wire wrapped around intermittent mesquite branches. The cows here, unlike their scrawny kin in the wilds to the south, are stocky and appear well-fed. In fact cattle have been grazing there since 1798 when padres from the Santo Tomás mission brought 800 head to graze, making the valley a major mission subsistence area.

I stopped at a grocery store in the village of Ojos Negros to confirm directions to Real del Castillo, once the most important town and for 10 years the capital of Baja California.

Most people had never heard of the place, but after gold was discovered there in 1870 by Manuel del Castillo, a mining boom was set off creating a bustling settlement of about 1,500 people within two years. It became so important that by 1872 it had replaced Santo Tomás as the capital of the Baja California Norte district and remained so until 1882 when the capital was removed to Ensenada.

It was a later (1889) gold boom a few miles to the south around El Alamo that prompted Bascom A. Stephens to pen the book "Gold Fields of Lower California." Old maps in his book show the major route from San Diego going through Tijuana, south to the Guadalupe valley and then up through Real del Castillo.

No current map or guidebook shows a road going through from Guadalupe to Real del Castillo even though I knew a trail had to go up through a canyon nearby.

The previous summer a rancher on the northwest Guadalupe side confirmed to me that his canyon was indeed the one the miners used over 120 years previous. That day I hiked partway up to a tumbling waterfall with a cool, clear pool, and to the "Agua Caliente" that gave the canyon its name. I enjoyed immersing myself in the steaming small pool of natural hot water, imagining dusty, tired argonauts heading south with big dreams. Did they stop to enjoy the thermal water? Or did the dream of a bonanza preclude such foolishness?

Convinced of the route, I planned to see this former boomtown at the top of the canyon for myself.

So, on that winter day at the Ojos Negros abarrotes (grocery store), I encountered an elderly woman who knew the area's history well. She lamented that most of the Real del Castillo buildings had fallen down through neglect and then pointed out the road that leads north along the valley's western flanks to the old mining capital.

The only paved road in the valley is Highway 3 from Ensenada to San Felipe. The rest are dirt, flat farm roads which after heavy storms became mud, with occasional bogs and quagmires.

Thus the entire eight-mile trip out to Real del Castillo became an obstacle course. Many muddy pools had to be skirted, detoured around or slowly driven through. The rains had left rivulets across the road so that even seemingly fast flat sections required utmost caution.

At one section a small crew was shoveling dirt into an especially nasty hole where half the road had eroded away. It seemed like trying to win a war with a pea shooter to me. One worker confirmed that Real del Castillo was only "cinco minutos" away, just over the crest ahead where the valley ended.

From the crest I could see a meandering river below. On its banks rose a flat townsite with just a few buildings remaining. I pulled out an old photo of the town and matched it up with the distant hills and mountains. Yup, this was it all right.

Ahead I initially balked at fording the river, now swollen from the rains. After visually sizing up the water's depth, I quickly drove across, reaching the town's center on a flat plateau.

A couple old buildings remained. I walked to one with signs indicating it was a museum, but it was empty and showed no signs of showcasing anything but dust. About 100 yards away, across the flat barren field, was a large old building with a tin roof. But what caught my eye was a huge sign above the door that in bright orange lettering said "Saloon."

Thinking it to be a business establishment, I approached and hallooed my presence. I could hear soft, gentle music in the background, a contrast to the fast tempo of the "Ranchero" music so often heard in rural Baja. A petite and pretty Mexican woman of indeterminate age came to the door and at her heels a charming little girl about six years old.

"No, it's not a saloon," she said. They just liked the sign.

Yes, she said, the well-fed stream that now wound around her house and descended into the nearby canyon behind was the old miners' road. As we were talking, an older looking man with a white beard strode up to the house from across the field.

"Mi esposo," she said, telling me it was her husband who was approaching. As he neared I could see he was younger than his white beard at first indicated. "Me llamo Enrique Lenchione," he said in introduction. "Y esta es mi esposa Rachela. Y nuestra hija, Rachelita Sesena," he added proudly, indicating their daughter. "Con mucho gusto," I replied politely, and told them I was a writer interested in the history of Real del Castillo.

They seemed proud to be sitting on a piece of such significant terrain, the closest building to the head of the canyon from which the miners had emerged. They had their own stories, how half of their house was a holdover from the 1870s.

Rachela went in and brought out a treasure she'd found behind the house, an 1872 American dime, again confirming that Americans came this way back then. Rachela also presented an article in an American newsletter apparently written during the 1970s about Real del Castillo. It was her only copy and I was wishing I had a portable fax machine, but returned it to her after I read it, and translated as much of it as I could for her.

Then she brought out a large sheet of parchment paper upon which was printed a copy of the town's incorporation in 1870. Titled "Acta De Instalacion del Pueblo y Real del Castillo," it states how the dignitaries got together on October 2, 1870 and set out to establish the town.

"Es un regalo," she offered, explaining the copy was a gift for me. I gratefully accepted and remembered to give them a few items before leaving.

The importance of the old mining town of Real del Castillo had dwindled for the past 120 plus years and the one-time capital had dissolved to an almost barren plateau.

Visions of those ambitious travelers who established the town, pumped up with the optimism of striking it rich, are omnipresent. To tread the town is to feel their presence. One of them even lost a new dime that would link the place in history to the present.

Even without that history, friendly people like the Lenchione family make heading into rural Baja, specifically a small village like Real del Castillo, a warm place to visit.

John Steinbeck's Baja Adventures

John Steinbeck, California's most prominent gift to the world of literature, was yet another American attracted to the wilds of Baja California. Even before the Nobel Prize winner went on his epic 1940 trip into the Sea of Cortez, he felt an affinity with our neighbors to the south.

The Forgotten Village

Steinbeck's love for Mexico, paired with his desire to write a movie without any Hollywood involvement led to the documentary *The Forgotten Village.* The film, directed by Herbert Kline and Alexander Hammid, and narrated by Burgess Meredith, was produced in 1940. Steinbeck's empathy with living conditions in American migrant camps and Mexican farm laborers led to the movie which depicts a clash between traditional Mexican village life and encroaching modernism.

The initial reaction to the movie was shocking. The New York State Board of Censors called the movie "indecent," the "indecency" consisting of an off-camera childbirth scene, and a scene of the mother nursing the infant. But Steinbeck pointed out: "In the picture there is no nudity. No suggestiveness and no actual birth is shown. The indecent fact which seems to have upset the board is that childbirth is painful in primitive communities where there is no medical care, not only painful but dangerous." The movie was finally released in late 1941, impressing critics. Steinbeck would always be proud of *The Forgotten Village.*

The entire movie is available today on Youtube.

While the movie was under production, Steinbeck had the opportunity to explore Baja California in depth, thanks to his good friend, the biologist Edward F. Ricketts (Better known to readers as "Doc" in Cannery Row and other books.)

Ed "Doc" Ricketts

In the 1930s and 1940s, Ed Ricketts was a big influence on Steinbeck, who had also studied marine biology while at Stanford University. They took brief excursions together along the California coast to collect biological specimens which Ricketts sold for a living. For years, Ricketts made numerous trips from Canada to Baja California which resulted in his book *Between Pacific Tides* (1939—Stanford University Press).

Ricketts made several trips to Baja California beginning in 1925. He mentions finding numerous octopus: "Between Tijuana and Ensenada we have found octopuses very numerous in April, May, and December, in several different years.

In December 1930 they were so abundant that one could count on finding a specimen under at least every fourth rock overturned."

In March of 1931 Ricketts, with noted Swedish biologist Torsten Gislen and their wives, went to Baja California in Ed's modified Packard. They mention exploring the kelp forest, sea caves, and tide pools around the Halfway House, and also the bay and estuary at Ensenada. In 1936 Steinbeck accompanied his biologist friend on an auto excursion to the Halfway House area.

Sea of Cortez: A Leisurely Journal of Travel and Research

Ricketts planned a grand trip around Baja California and into the Sea of Cortez to collect marine invertebrates and invited his writer friend. Steinbeck's Pulitzer Prize winning novel *The Grapes of Wrath* had just been released and the publicity-shy novelist was anxious to get away.

In March 1940, the duo (along with Steinbeck's first wife Carol, skipper Tony Berry, engineer Tex Travis, and two crewmen, Sparky Enea and Tiny Colleto) left Monterey on the historic trip aboard the leased sardine boat *Western Flyer.*

The resulting 1941 book T*he Sea of Cortez: A Leisurely Journal of Travel and Research* (Viking Press) was co-authored with Ricketts. Well annotated, the 598-page book contains numerous color and black and white photo plates of the various specimens collected. The reminiscences, musings, and philosophy throughout are pure Steinbeck at his best.

The Western Flyer

The author followed it up with *The Log from the Sea of Cortez,* which also includes a bonus profile of Ed Ricketts. The Log itself is exciting, thoughtful, and revealing. For example, Steinbeck wrote, "We said, 'Let's go wide open. Let's see what we see, record what we find, and not fool ourselves with conventional scientific strictures. We could not observe a completely objective Sea of Cortez anyway, for in that lonely and uninhabited Gulf our boat and ourselves would change it the moment we entered.'"

The literary sage also noted brighter skies and a brilliant ocean once south of the border. He wrote: "Below the Mexican border the water changes color; it takes on a deep, ultramarine blue—a washtub bluing blue, intense and seeming to penetrate deep into the water; the fishermen call it 'tuna water.'"

The expedition circled the cape, stopping at the tuna cannery in Cape San Lucas (Not much town in 1940), and went collecting up the peninsula side of the gulf. They stopped in La Paz, Loreto, San Lucas Cove, and up past Bahia de los Angeles, collecting and annotating as they went.

They recruited a little help in La Paz. After paying a few little boys for gathering, Steinbeck noted: "The population of small boys at La Paz is tremendous, and we had business dealings with a good part of it. Hardly had we returned to the *Western Flyer* and begun to lay out our specimens when we were invaded. Word had spread that there were crazy people in port who gave money for things a boy could pick up on the rocks. We were more than invaded—we were deluged with small boys bearing specimens. They came out in canoes, in flatboats, some even swam out, and all of them carried specimens."

Later, while moored at Puerto Escondido, Steinbeck and Ricketts were invited by a few locals to head into the rugged Sierra de la Giganta for an overnight camping trip. Aboard mules and then scrambling afoot, they explored a steep boulder-filled canyon. Even though today called Tabor Canyon, many people still refer to the idyllic setting as Steinbeck Canyon and today is a favorite hiking destination for Loreto area tour groups.

Steinbeck wrote, "After a short climb we emerged on a level place in a deep cleft in the granite mountains. In this cleft a tiny stream of water fell hundreds of feet from pool to pool. There were palm trees and wild grapevines and large ferns, and the water was cool and sweet. This little stream, coming from so high up in the mountains and falling so far, never had the final dignity of reaching the ocean."

They crossed the gulf, visited Guaymas on the mainland, and then returned to Monterey after a six-week trip that filled numerous specimen jars and uncovered a wealth of information, including 35 new marine species.

"The Pearl"

In La Paz, Steinbeck was intrigued by the pearl industry and heard heart-breaking tales about the difficult lives of the pearl fishermen. The industry and the setting led to one of Steinbeck's most famous stories, *The Pearl* (Viking Press—1947). *The Pearl* became a movie with both English and Spanish versions (*La Perla*).

In addition to the aforementioned books, years later crewman Sparky Enea came out with a book, *With Steinbeck in the Sea of Cortez: A Memoir of the Steinbeck/ Ricketts Expedition.* (Sand River Press—1991). It's an eye-opening account from a different point of view. Enea also brings the readers up to date from the aftermath of the trip to his publishing. He mentions, "When we docked in Monterey in the morning, it seemed as if everyone was there to meet us. The dock was full of people."

He adds, "But we didn't need another party. We were just getting back from a six-week party in the Sea of Cortez."

The group talked about another trip back to Baja California but World War II came along, Steinbeck and Carol divorced in 1941; he remarried in 1942, moved to New York, and the camaraderie began to dissolve.

A huge shock came in 1948 when Ed Ricketts' car, apparently stalled on the railroad tracks in Monterey, was struck by the Southern Pacific Railway's Del Monte Express. He died three days later, just three days shy of his 52nd birthday.

Word of his friend's death numbed Steinbeck. The author, then living in New York, returned to the lab and, like other grieving friends, retrieved some personal items, including their correspondence.

In a 1951 tribute, Steinbeck explained why Ricketts' death had such a searing impact on him and so many others: "He was different from anyone and yet so like that everyone found himself in Ed, and that might be one of the reasons his death had such an impact. It wasn't Ed who had died but a large and important part of oneself."

Another account of the Ricketts/Steinbeck journey to Baja was published as recently as 9 years ago: Kevin M. Bailey, *The Western Flyer* (University of Chicago Press, 2015).

About Baja, Steinbeck later commented, "Trying to remember the Gulf is like trying to re-create a dream...There is always in the back of our minds the positive drive to go back again. If it were lush and rich, one could understand the pull, but it is fierce and hostile and sullen. The stone mountains pile up to the sky and there is little fresh water. But we must go back if we live, and we don't know why."

Unfortunately, Steinbeck who died in 1968, never returned to Baja.

"Unexplored" Baja Lures Adventurers

Marquis McDonal in 1967

As a schoolboy in the 1920's, Marquis McDonald was intrigued by explorers and dreamt of possible adventures. While still a young man, he began to realize those dreams, riding freight trains from coast to coast, and traveling to far-flung places like Alaska, Okinawa, Saudi Arabia, and Afghanistan.

Returning to Visalia, CA following a two-year construction stint in Saudi

Arabia, he was antsy to get on the road again and knew where he wanted to go. He'd been thinking about Baja California since grammar school when he noticed his geography book featured the word "Unexplored" emblazoned over a map of "Lower California."

In 1949-50, McDonald was able visit that intriguing "unexplored" peninsula. It worked out that a former co-worker in Arabia, Glenn N. Oster from Long Beach, CA was available to accompany him. No stranger to adventure, Oster had been shot down twice over Germany during WWII and spent time in a Nazi prison camp.

Fascinated by the Spanish missions established in Baja California from 1697 to 1834, they determined to set out upon a quest—to locate, annotate, and photograph each mission, hopefully becoming the first Americans to visit *all* the Baja mission sites.

They diligently researched previous Baja explorations and were especially inspired by the author Arthur W. North, whose adventurous trek down the peninsula in 1908-1910 resulted in the very fine book, *Camp and Camino in Lower California.* North's travels took him to most of the missions, but not all.

In late autumn 1949 the enlightened and determined young men set off in a Jeep intent on finding and visiting all 37 missions and visitas (satellite missions) from the territory of Baja California Norte to the tip of the territory of Baja California Sur. (Those territories did not achieve Mexican statehood until 1952 and 1974, respectively).

Marquis McDonald wrote about their trip, and almost two decades later his book *Baja: Land of Lost Missions* (The Naylor Company, 1968) was published.

Surprising correspondence

I learned of their adventure via a friendly and quite unexpected letter from the author. In the 1980s I had studied much about Baja and had written numerous articles including a series on the missions. I was still pleasantly shocked in late December 1987 to receive a letter addressed to me at the Baja Times, an English newspaper based in Rosarito Beach.

The letter from a Marquis McDonald postmarked Olympia, WA read:

> *"Dear Mr. Niemann. A friend has kindly sent me some copies of the 'Baja Times' with some of your great articles on the missions.*
>
> *"In 1949-1950 a friend (Glenn Oster) and I spent many months by Jeep, horse, mule and afoot searching out all the old missions and sites. I then wrote a (not widely distributed) book, 'Baja: Land of Lost Missions,' published by the Southwest publisher Naylor of San Antonio Texas. (A regional publisher).*
>
> *"I still have all the photos we took on this trip – mostly 2 ¼ x 2 ¼ color transparencies. If you know of anyone, or any group or organization that would find them of value, or would preserve them, I would be happy to contrib-*

ute them, gratis of course.

"I loved Baja, and needless to say, our trip was to us at least, a great adventure, although pretty rough under those relatively primitive conditions. It would quickly kill me now.

"Best regards and Happy 1988. Marquis McDonald."

I answered right away, thanking him for the kind letter and letting him know that I would appreciate receiving the photos and would take care to preserve them. I also asked to purchase a copy of the book as I had not come across it to date.

He replied: "I am enclosing a copy of my Baja book (It is virtually impossible to buy one and long out of print) – a gift!"

McDonald Book

He went on to mention that Glenn Oster was still living and included his Torrance, CA address. About Oster, the humble McDonald wrote, "If there was any hero on our trip, he deserves the credit (but would never claim it!). All I could do most of the time was hang on!"

As to the photos, it seems he had just sent them to a friend to copy them to videotape. Then he could forward them to me.

They never arrived and later McDonald wrote again stating that he had asked the individual to just forward them to me. We played a lot of letter tag and in one letter to me said, "His son tells me that he has been down to Cape San Lucas. I'm sure you'll eventually get the photos."

To make a long story short, the 185 photos today are well preserved. They are at UC San Diego, where the Images of Marquis McDonald are in the Special Collections and Archives section, along with those of Baja explorers Harry Crosby and Howard Gulick.

The Adventure

McDonald learned Spanish from phonograph courses and could read it well. He said it was still hard for him to understand the locals. Oster did not speak Spanish at all, but he proved invaluable doing most of the driving. McDonald was the photographer.

They were glad they had 4-wheel drive as even north of Ensenada they needed it, getting stuck several times looking for the Guadalupe mission site. Even with 4-wheel drive, many times on the trek they had to backtrack due to impassable roads.

Trying to climb a steep mountain near the Valle de Trinidad, the Jeep slipped into neutral and started rolling down, flipping over two times before teetering on the brink of a deep chasm. They jumped out, uninjured, but the Jeep sustained a lot of damage. Luckily, it still ran so they limped into Ensenada and got it repaired.

Trying to get to Mission San Pedro Martír, they found they could not get there from Meling Ranch, and Mrs. Meling told them of the more southern route but advised that they could not make it that winter. That, and other missions that would be impassable until spring, made the young adventurers change their plans.

Originally, they expected to visit all the missions going south, take the ferry from La Paz to mainland Mexico and continue down the Pan-American Highway all the way to South America.

They realized that idea was out. To accomplish their primary objective of visiting *all* the missions, they would have to visit some heading back north.

They were surprised to see many of the northern adobe missions just piles of debris. Their first stone church encountered, San Borja, was especially a delight. McDonald wrote, "Although San Xavier (Javier), San Ignacio, and Comondú are usually considered to be the three outstanding missions, Glenn and I felt that San Borja, though never completed, should rank second only to San Xavier, and certainly equal to San Ignacio."

They found Loreto, "the Mother of the Missions" was missing its bell tower; a new one was added in 1955.

Knowing they would be driving back north gave them more options, but all of the roads were a challenge. They traveled mission to mission down the old road, occasionally taking off on side roads, and hiring guides, horses, and mules to reach many destinations. Roads were onerous or non-existent. For example, they left Loreto on mule-back in the wee hours of the morning, went up the rugged trail cut into the rocks and finally arrived at San Javier at three in the afternoon.

On their return trip, they finally made it to their last mission site in the northern mountains. Camped nearby, McDonald wrote, "...beside a hot fire, we fell asleep jubilant that at last we had conquered the jinx and our nemesis, San Pedro Martír."

After driving over 6,000 miles, with many more afoot and in the saddle and not arriving home until late spring 1950, McDonald concluded, "We felt, with some justifiable pride, that we were undoubtedly the only Americans, at least, to have visited all the known missions of Lower California; and we had discovered a few unknown ones for good measure."

The adventurous pair did what they set out to do. As my last communication with the modest author was almost 35 years ago, I lost touch with the pair. If they are still alive they'd be approximately 100 years old.

Baja beckoned to them and they explored the "unexplored" peninsula and completed their quest. Their knowledge helped make the "lost" missions more accessible to those who followed. They answered the call of Baja and in the process of their "great adventure" they were humbled by the still difficult terrain trod by those who came before them.

First Summits of Baja's Highest Peak

Picacho del Diablo (Devil's Peak), at 10,157 is the highest mountain on the Baja California peninsula and looms like a jagged tooth across the flat desert west of San Felipe. Alternately called Cerro de la Encantada, or La Providencia, the massive peak in the Sierra de San Pedro Mártir has long attracted mountaineers.

While Baja has beckoned adventurers for years, Picacho del Diablo has long-standing appeal to mountain climbers. Some of the early ascents, both from the eastern and western routes, were accomplished by an elite bunch, climbers noted far beyond Baja.

Picacho del Diablo looms over Valle San Felipe.

The first recorded and accepted ascent was in 1911 by topographer, cartographer and prospector Don McClain, who made a solo climb of the north peak (at 10,157 it is just a few feet higher than the south peak) from the western high plateau.

McClain first descended the Colorado River to San Felipe on a skiff, searching for placer mines. From there he hiked to the San Pedro Mártir range and the La Grulla area at the 9,200-foot level. To summit Picacho del Diablo from that escarpment he then descended a steep ridge and made his way up the northwest side of the Picacho del Diablo traversing huge granite blocks:

"I was able to thread my way with difficulty between these large rocks making use of some rather airy handholds and working my way over hard snow onto the east face of the summit ridge." (It was the higher north summit and McClain stated he put his business card into a thin tin tobacco box and placed a flat rock on top of it).

McClain was an outdoorsman who had worked for the U.S. Geological Survey, the U.S. Forest Service, and the National Park Service. In the Angeles and San Bernardino national forests he revised the maps and supplied numerous place names still used today, including Kratka Ridge, Charlton Flat, Mt. Williamson, Mt. Lukens, and others.

An elite group of mountaineers

Norman Clyde

The second ascent, and the first to the south summit, was attained in 1932 by an elite Sierra Club group led by Norman Clyde, considered the greatest of all Sierra mountaineers. His group was made up of Bestor Robinson, Glen Dawson, Nathan Clark, Richard Jones, and Walter Brem.

Norman Clyde (1885-1972) was a writer/photographer who became world renowned for ascending more than 1,000 peaks in his lifetime, including at least 200 first ascents! He was also known by fellow climbers for the baggage he carried (axes, shovels, cast iron cookware, even volumes of classical literature (in Greek and Latin).

He lived in the Big Pine area of the Eastern Sierra and was often called upon to locate lost climbers, the most famous instance being his discovery of the body of Walter Starr, Jr. among the crags of the Minarets in 1933.

The name of Norman Clyde endures well beyond Baja as Norman Clyde Peak, at 13,861 feet, is one of the highest in the Sierra Nevada. It is on the main ridge of the Palisades with Norman Clyde Glacier on its north face, feeding the headwaters of Big Pine Creek. Clyde Minaret, Clyde Spire, Clyde Ledge, and Clyde Meadow are some other Sierra wilderness features that now carry his name.

Those who joined Clyde on the second ascent were also well-known outdoorsmen: Mountaineer Bestor Robinson (1898-1987) was an environmentalist, attorney, inventor, and a long-time leader of the Sierra Club. He was a law partner of Earl Warren, later governor of California and Chief Justice of the U. S. Supreme Court.

Glen Dawson (1912–2016) was an antiquarian bookseller, publisher, environmentalist, and mountaineer; along with Clyde, Dawson was part of the first group to scale the steep eastern face of Mt. Whitney. His father, Ernest Dawson (1882–1947), was also a climber, antiquarian bookseller, and served as Sierra Club president from 1934-1937. Dawson's Book Shop also published Clyde's account of his historic Baja climbs.

Nathan Clark (1906-1993) participated in High Sierra trips of the 1930s and early 1940s. In addition to being chairman of several club committees, he was a member of the Sierra Club Board of Directors for sixteen years, serving as president from 1959 to 1961.

Richard "Dick" Jones (1912-1995) was an active Sierra Club member for 14 years (1933-1947) and was one of the fourteen charter members of the Ski Mountaineers.

Walter "Bubs" Brem, in 1931, along with fellow teenagers Jules Eichorn and Glen Dawson completed the first ascent of Matthes Crest in Yosemite. For that challenging rock formation, the teens introduced rope climbing to Sierra Club members.

Sierra Club ascent, 1932

For the second ascent of Picacho del Diablo the Sierra Club group also climbed from the west. They left Meling Ranch and crossed over to the high point of the eastern escarpment (now known as Blue Bottle). The route to the summit looked deceptively simple to them (descend 1,500 feet into the notch and climb up the ridge to the summit). But it wasn't simple at all.

This veteran climbing group spent all day scrambling up a ridge serrated by five deep clefts. The sun was setting and their food and water was almost gone. They had a "go or no-go" decision to make. They decided to hike off the ridge in search of water. They would retreat and try the next day if none could be found. But they found a small pool about 1,000 feet below the ridge. They bivouacked and attained the summit the next day.

They returned two days overdue, but had summited both peaks, and realized a much greater respect for Baja's highest mountain.

Henderson tries from the east

The summit had been now reached twice, both times from the west. No one had successfully conquered the peak from the eastern desert. A couple of attempts were made in 1934 and 1935, both by the same adventurer/writer, Randall Henderson, who finally succeeded in 1937.

Henderson (1888-1970) was an Army pilot in WWI and was the first pilot to ever land in Las Vegas. Known as "Mr. Desert," in 1937 Henderson became the founder, publisher and editor of *Desert Magazine,* which he established in a barren cove in the Coachella Valley. He and his brother Cliff Henderson would give birth to the city of Palm Desert, California, on that desert site.

While *Desert Magazine* and the city of Palm Desert went on to achieve national prominence, Henderson sold the magazine in 1958 to continue his explorations. The Randall Henderson Trail is one of several tributes named for him and he was made an Honorary Life Member of the Sierra Club in 1947.

In his book *On Desert Trails* (Westernlore Press, Los Angeles, 1961), Henderson reveals his Baja adventures: "The high adventure of my Baja California exploration was the ascent of Picacho del Diablo.

"Malcolm Huey and I attempted to reach this summit in 1934, but we had underestimated the climbing difficulties. Our route was up Providencia Canyon, which seemed to provide the most direct route to the peak, 15 miles away."

They were accompanied by noted El Centro attorney Harry Horton (1892-1966) and his friend W.J. McClelland, Imperial County Clerk, both familiar with Baja. Hiring a local guide named Juan, they were able to get their two "desert jalopies" with big tires across the desert to the base of Providencia Canyon. The group then spent a day scaling or detouring around waterfalls, wading pools, and bucking heavy brush, reaching only the 3,500-foot level before turning back in the morning.

A year later Henderson and Huey, this time joined by Wilson McKenney and Paul Cook, both of Calexico, made a second attempt. On the second day they camped at the 7,000-foot level, and the third day explored possible routes only to be turned back due to lack of time after they realized the summit was separated from them by a deep chasm.

Undeterred, in April 1937 Henderson made another attempt of Picacho del Diablo and was finally successful. This time he joined forces with a fellow Sierra Club member, the esteemed mountaineer Norman Clyde who had already led that successful 1932 ascent. Clyde wanted to try it from the "other side." Henderson noted that Clyde, as usual, carried an enormous 60-pound pack and ice axe.

After he and Clyde summitted, Henderson later wrote: "....we reached the top late in the afternoon on the third day, and stood on the one point on the peninsula where it is possible to view both the Gulf of California on the east and the Pacific Ocean, where the sun was setting in the west."

They bivouacked in a sheltered cove near the summit and spent two days return-

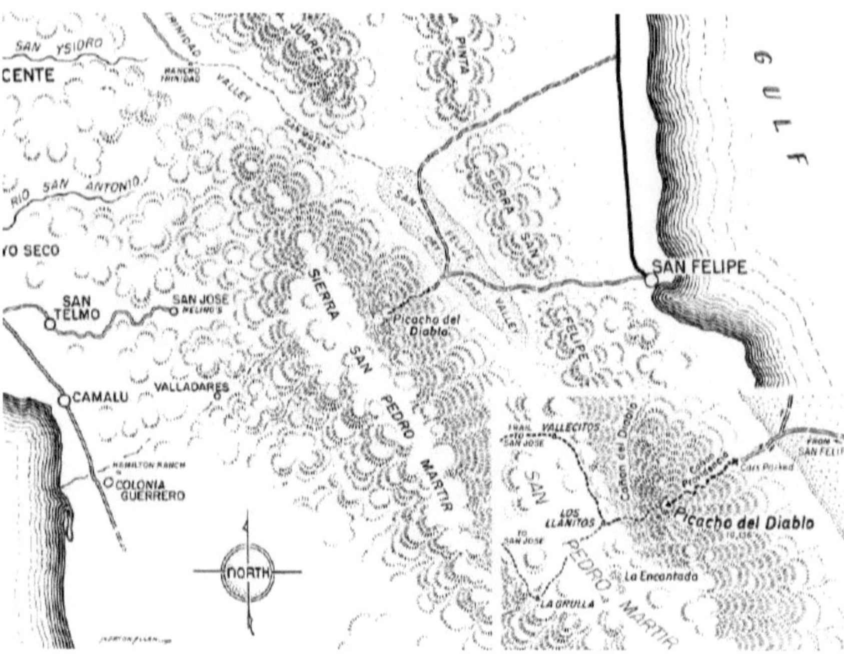

Eastern Routes 1934–37

ing down Providencia Canyon. In a cairn at the summit they found records of the two previous ascents, and confirmed theirs was the first from the desert.

A challenging climb

While today it is summited by numerous climbers, generally from the west, it is considered a highly challenging climb and should only be attempted by experienced climbers.

One such adventurer was John W. Robinson, (1930-2018), author of Camping and Climbing in Baja, La Siesta Press, 1975. A Sierra Club leader himself, the former Costa Mesa school teacher climbed Picacho de Diablo numerous times, making his first ascent in 1958. He once also led a large group to the summit.

Robinson also wrote the introduction to *El Picacho del Diablo: The Conquest of Lower California's Highest Peak, 1932 and 1937* by Norman Clyde, Los Angeles: Dawson's Book Shop, 1975.

Another book to consider is Jerry Schad's *Parque Nacional San Pedro Martir-Topographic Map and Visitor's Guide to Baja's Highest Mountains.*

According to a climber Michael Slezak, who attests online to having scaled the mountain dozens of times, "This is truly one of the finest and most challenging mountains on the North American continent (south of Canada). A very unique mountaineering experience."

Baja's highest peak has attracted some of the best mountaineers around, and still does. While most prevailed, they all admitted that the challenge of ascending to the top of Baja "was not as easy as it seems."

Narratives from Baja Norte

Cantamar Sunset from Deck

A Cantamar Haven "Song of the Sea" (1971–2023)

As a kid in the 1940s, I'd spent carefree summer days on beaches south of Ensenada. Then in early adulthood I also enjoyed a number of Baja visits, but it wasn't until 1971 that I'd sought a place of my own there.

In 1969 a friend had bought a trailer located in a small beach-side trailer park called Cantamar, about 11 miles south of Rosarito Beach. We visited a few times and soon my ex-wife and I began to look around for our own "Piece of Paradise" in Mexico.

We found a little fixer-upper trailer with cabana on the next street over and the elderly owners accepted our modest offer. Thus, ever since February 1971, I have had a refuge in Baja California. I was able to keep it in the 1974 divorce proceedings and, for me, it became a great escape place.

I remarried five years later and my bride shared my enthusiasm but immediately set about making changes. We remodeled, eventually tearing out the trailer to replace it with a cute little 2-bedroom house. By this time more and more of the original Cantamar trailers were being replaced and home construction in the former trailer park was booming.

The metamorphism was another stage in the development of Cantamar that began in 1960 with the purchase of the land by Alejandro Borja. He named the place Cantamar, or "Song of the Sea."

Borjas pioneer Baja coast

"Borja" is the Spanish spelling of the notable Italian family, "Borgia" which had a branch in Spain. Señora Maria de Borja, the General Duchess of Gandia, had heard about the difficulties endured by the Spanish missionaries in developing the rugged Baja peninsula, and donated a sizable sum of money for the establishment of three missions.

Soldiers from the Borja household also helped settle the peninsula for Spain. Many of those early Spanish families, including the Borjas, are still in evidence throughout Baja California.

The Borja pioneering spirit survived and Alejandro had been successful with several Pemex gasoline station franchises in Tijuana before he looked south about 30 miles (K-46) for a summer home.

Cantamar was developed because of the can-do spirit of Señor Don Alejandro Borja. His first well there was salty. Not dismayed, he sunk four more wells. All were salty. Rather than quit, he tried one more time. Agua Dulce. Sweet water. The sixth well, and $15,000, brought results.

Someone suggested that Borja turn his summer home into a tourist community. "Some Americans came to me and asked if they could park their trailers, so I said to my wife, 'Maybe it's a good business,'" the hard-working far-sighted businessman recalled.

By August 1960 three trailer spaces were leased. During the sixties, Borja built a 24-unit motel on the beach, a nearby swimming pool in which a waterfall cascading over lava stones actually cooled the generator that provided power to the whole place.

Borja got grandiose ideas and just went ahead with them. His early Pemex station at Cantamar became the only gas station between Rosarito and the outskirts of Ensenada and would be for over 30 years. The restaurant/bar he built at the entrance to the trailer park could not be complete without a large lighthouse, so he had one built, visible from miles away.

He wanted to light it, but was told by the government that once lit, it would have to be registered and maintained as a working lighthouse. Better to keep it unlit. Still standing in 2023, it has fallen into disrepair over the years. We used to ascend the circular stairwell and in 1971 I took a panorama photo from the top that shows a much different neighboring landscape than today.

Original trailer spaces were cement slabs set at a diagonal off of four dirt roads sandwiched between the old (libre) road and the ocean. Alongside each slab was a dirt space to park one's car.

The park was mostly full by the time I had arrived on the scene and many of the residents had added small rooms or cabanas in the adjacent parking spaces.

Rowdy camp to nicer homes

Early on it was a rowdy camp, with lots of alcohol consumed and a prevailing party atmosphere. Dune buggies and ATVs roared down the dusty streets, fireworks exploded all summer long, and folks would holler at you to come in for a drink as you walked by.

Slowly the image changed. Through the years, people started jettisoning trailers and constructing as nice a home as would fit on those unorthodox lots.

Some residents just built a house around their trailer. Others built elaborate homes with a second, and even third floor.

The hotel was divided into 13 condos. The streets were cobbled, power and telephone service arrived, and hookups for television (and later wi-fi) became available.

The palm trees planted by Alejandro Borja and his son Carlos began to grow, creating an overall tropical impression. To this day, houses have to be built around the sacrosanct palms. For many years, developments up and down the coast acquired their palms from the grove planted by Borja.

By the 1990s, encouraged by Cantamar management, the change was mostly complete and the trailers either had to be gone or covered. More recently, the once tropical entry way and what was Rubens restaurant were razed to support an ugly mini-strip mall and gas station.

We were fairly active Cantamar residents by then, having acquired a trailer and a small cabana on a total of three double-trailer spaces on the next street over from our original place in two separate purchases. Through the years, building in several stages, we built a large 3-bedroom, 3-bath home with a second-floor den and topside deck on that oversized lot.

We created short-term rentals out of the original place and another house we had built. It was very difficult running two vacation rentals when you don't live in the area full-time, so by the late 1990s we had sold both of them. It was quite a relief when they sold, and thereafter our Cantamar weekends were finally ours again to enjoy instead of work.

The Borja family

We got to know Alejandro's son Carlos and his wife Linda socially and Linda kept the books for a long time. Carlos had two children (Carlito and Bruni) from a prior marriage and both of them had also helped manage Cantamar at various times.

Carlos and Linda had two children we enjoyed watching grow up, Antanasio (Tacho) and Stina Borja. Stina mostly eschewed Cantamar involvement, but Tacho, who also liked to be called Mark, got involved as a teenager and supervised many improvements in the area.

Carlos and Linda got divorced and he went to live at his ranch in the valley east of Cantamar, while Linda stayed at their beachfront Cantamar home.

Then in 2007, in his late 60s, Carlos Borja suddenly passed away. Many of us who knew him were shocked and missed his larger-than-life personality. But his death created unforeseen circumstances that lingered for years. I had heard he had remarried but most of us had never met his new wife. But now, with four adult children and a relatively new wife, the battle for control of Cantamar had begun.

We residents were pawns in the long and exhausting see-sawing of events. Fortunately, I had purchased my home outright from Carlos and was able to prove it later, but others were understandably antsy. For years, we got conflicting information and what appeared to be official results from battlers on all sides, and of course, their respective lawyers.

The missives were relentless:

"I'm the owner and I can prove it. Send your rent to me."

"No, I'm the owner and here's my proof."

"The court ruled for me,"

"That's wrong. This more senior court ruled for me."

"Send your rent to the court and they will pay the eventual winner."

"If you don't pay me instead of the court, you'll be delinquent."

And so on...

Finally, in 2013 the verdict was rendered with Carlos' widow, Ivonne Cortez Avedano Borja assuming ownership. Even so, bad blood among residents who took sides continued and took time to temper. The indecision and conflicting outcomes took their toll on many.

Despite the years of turmoil, we still enjoyed our home-away-from-home at Cantamar. Being retired we were not limited to the busier weekends and headed down from Southern California as our schedules permitted.

I loved my deck. I liked to watch the waves crashing, sometimes with surfers riding them, and the occasional pod of dolphins just offshore. The brilliant tangerine sunsets provide a warm glow over the broad Descanso Bay. Looking about, the entire coastal area has been greatly developed since that 1971 photo from the lighthouse.

Homes are sprouting on the hillsides faster than I can notice them. And now there are well over a dozen restaurants on the road just from the Calafia point to Cantamar, In the 1970s there were just two along the highway.

There are a lot more options than before. That's good and very handy, but I miss the simpler times. We had to go to Rosarito Beach almost every visit for most groceries, any hardware items, water, butane, for almost everything including a handful of restaurants.

But today, a mile up the road Puerto Nuevo has expanded to a real tourist attraction with a plethora of restaurants from which to choose. Yep, I may lament the changes, but I like today's wealth of options.

(2024 Update: After 52 years, we finally decided our senior lifestyle and more extensive travel made it harder to get down there. In a bittersweet decision, in early 2023 we sold our Cantamar getaway.)

New Calimax for Puerto Nuevo (2019)

Beginning in the late-1960s, I've watched the lobster village of Puerto Nuevo grow from a few small dwellings on a dusty bluff to a vibrant tourist destination with about 35 restaurants, paved streets, shops, and curio stands.

In the past decade alone, we've experienced the explosive growth (hillside homes, high-rise condos, and restaurants, etc.). along the entire northern Baja coast. Yet I was still unprepared for Puerto Nuevo's newest addition – a huge modern supermarket! Yes, a new Calimax market now creates an in-your-face first impression as it faces the highway from the town's first street.

Calimax, the large supermarket chain which serves 50 million customers annually from 117 locations throughout Baja California and Sonora, opened its 98th Calimax store in Puerto Nuevo on February 21, 2019. The chain also includes one wholesale store, three distribution centers, and 15 stores called Aprecio.

Puerto Nuevo arch with Calimex sign in background

According to operations director Sergio Borrayo, the company, which was founded in Tijuana in 1939, provides employment for 6,000 directly and another 15,000 indirectly. Calimax is partnered with Smart and Final and Angus Beef and maintains its own distribution with thousands of suppliers in Mexico and the U.S. with a fleet of 200 trucks.

The new Puerto Nuevo Calimax employs about 50 local people from Primo Tapia and surrounding areas. Along with traditional Mexican foodstuffs the store offers about 30 percent imported foods, mostly from the U.S.

Besides offering employment, the large market is already a shopping boon to area residents, many of whom had been taking the bus to Rosarito (10 miles north) for similar shopping.

However, some restaurant owners expressed concern over the development. They said that the new store would just exacerbate the ongoing parking problem.

Casting a futile negative vote during the proposal stages, restaurant owner Rosa Marias Plascencia said, "We are not opposing the economic development of Puerto Nuevo, we just want them to do it in another area, because it's going to change the essence of the historic and gastronomic center of Puerto Nuevo."

For sure, the large market is an incongruous fit in a quaint village.

Named for Newport Cigarettes

Puerto Nuevo wasn't even a village when I first discovered it. I used to stay at a friend's place in Cantamar (before I bought my own place there in 1971) and neighbors told us where we could get very fresh and very inexpensive lobster meals:

"About a quarter mile south of El Pescador restaurant, you'll see an old white building with a 7-Up bottle painted on the side. It's right next to a huge Newport cigarette sign. Turn down the dirt road next to that building. Stop at the first house on the left and knock on the door; it's really a restaurant. If they're out of lobster or busy, go to the second house."

Thus, the catch phrase around Cantamar that year often became "Let's go to Newport." Some of us, practicing our Spanish, started calling the place by the Spanish name for "Newport," or "Puerto Nuevo."

The town got its start in the early 1950s when several families relocated there from mainland Mexico. From their homes on the bluff a trail dropped down to a tiny cove. This cove allowed fishermen to breach the surf with shallow pangas and fish the area.

They discovered that succulent California spiny lobster were plentiful there and began to set traps. Aside from supplying local restaurants and markets with their catch, the fishermen started selling fresh lobster and fish directly to tourists and locals alike.

It wasn't long before the first two restaurants opened in the fishermen's homes. Several of the families had set up tables in their living rooms. "Papa" literally passed the freshly severed lobster halves through the kitchen window to be cooked while guests gathered round to watch and choose their dinner.

The parents of Rosa Maria Plasencia opened the first one, and she and her husband Enrique Murillo are still active owners. Those first two in-home restaurants, now enlarged, are called Puerto Nuevo I and Puerto Nuevo II.

We grabbed our own sodas

In those early days, the customers actually felt like members of an extended family. We would just go in the kitchen and grab our own sodas or beers out of the family refrigerator. Before we left, the owners would just tally up the number of empty bottles on the table, a practice many restaurants still employ.

Even today the basic meal is almost the same in each restaurant: two halves of *"Langosta"* fried in lard (now if preferred, also steamed or grilled), mouth-watering hot, home-made flour tortillas, beans, rice, salsa, chips and limes, all served family style, and the term "Puerto Nuevo Style" was born. Much of the basic meal evolved due to lack of reliable refrigeration in the early days. Beans, rice, and freshly cooked lobster and tortillas hardly needed to be refrigerated.

Most of the village is related. Brothers, sisters, cousins and in-laws may all own restaurants. The Ortega family (Juan and Petra and their 10 children) arrived by the 1970s and immediately opened four restaurants. They now have five Puerto Nuevo restaurants and two in Rosarito Beach, further spreading the "Puerto Nuevo Style" fame.

A big demand for lobster

By the late '70s demand outpaced the supply. Long lines formed at restaurants not "sold out." Many people were turned away, no lobster to be had. Now the village imports much of its lobster from farther south in Baja and a good many restaurants eschew offering live lobster for frozen ones.

Today the restaurants run the gamut from a few tables in a modest house to beautiful marble and tile three story extravaganzas with dramatic ocean views. The meals are fairly consistent, with most places offering mixed drinks in addition to beer and sodas, and broader menus which now even include steak. These days, some restaurants include a tortilla soup or salad, others a guacamole dip, and others a margarita included in the package lobster dinner price. Most of the places take credit cards too, but some do not. Best to check.

Puerto Nuevo shops and restaurants attract tourists.

Most of us who have homes in the area have our

favorite restaurants even though the offered fare is similar. I've eaten in probably 80 percent of the places and keep gravitating back to one where I've gotten to know the family and watched the younger ones grow up, get married and have children of their own.

The busloads and carloads of tourists that make for busy weekends at Puerto Nuevo now call for a different strategy. Do like a lot of the Mexicans and eat your main meal earlier in the day. Go during the week. Go only before Memorial Day and after Labor Day.

Puerto Nuevo is more than eating a dinner out. It can be a complete Baja experience: a bustling village, succulent food, strolling mariachis, vendors and purveyors of trinkets and freshly cut flowers, along with killer sunsets over the sparkling blue Pacific.

Mariachi music wafts through the busy streets as musicians stroll from restaurant to restaurant and eager employees hastily point you to their family enterprise.

Today, finding Puerto Nuevo is not so cryptic. It is well identified with a toll road turn-off, a stop sign on the old road, and a welcoming arch.

And the most prominent landmark from the highway today is no longer a Newport sign. It is that bright, large, modern Calimax supermarket.

The Village of Puerto Popotla (2013)

Fishing villages are scattered throughout Mexico, dotting the coastlines of Baja California as well as mainland Mexico. Hardy pescadores (fishermen) set up bases in sheltered little coves and inlets close to where the fish are. Some camps are isolated and very crude, just temporary mesquite shelters in remote areas housing a few men whose catch is periodically sold to traveling seafood vendors. Others are larger, more permanent, and the fishermen sell directly to area restaurants and residents of nearby towns.

Some, especially those close to an expanding tourist population (like Puerto Nuevo), outgrow their original purpose and charm as they morph into something larger and offer the fancier restaurants and curio shops many stateside visitors expect. It's a challenge to even find a boat at Puerto Nuevo these days, but in the 1970s we used to watch the fishermen return and beach their lobster-laden pangas in the small ravine.

Just a few miles up the road, still in the heart of a tourist area – it's a different story.

Still a simple fishing village

I was delightfully surprised this past October to visit Puerto Popotla for the first time in many years. The fishing village is about four miles south of Rosarito Beach, behind the aging white arch and the wall on the south side of Fox Baja Studios. Back in 1996, as the studio next door was filming its first motion picture, "Titanic," I wrote, "What will the future bring to Puerto Popotla? With the area's mushrooming growth, what is the destiny of this authentic settlement and the fishermen who make their livings here? Who knows? But for now it is the most charming of the accessible fishing villages—if you don't mind sitting on a beat-up old car seat while pigging out on fresh fish tacos."

Well, instead of an old car seat from 17 years ago, this time I found a small restaurant with plastic Tecate chairs right on the sand. And the rest of the village? It is virtually the same as 1996, just a little larger and still with the lone dirt road, a few smaller trails and paths, and haphazard clapboard buildings perched precariously on the rocky promontory surrounding the cove.

And there's all that seafood being unloaded from the pangas about midday as the fishermen return. Talk about fresh—the beach is full of vendors selling local species of fish: grouper, snapper, all types of bass, cod, corbina, halibut, yellowtail, and more—along with fresh lobsters, crabs, clams, mussels, and oysters. If it comes from the ocean, they've got it. And you can buy straight from the boat, or any of the numerous stalls on the beach or on the road.

Restaurants on the sand at Puerto Popotla

I had watched the fishing village grow with trepidation. It was kind of my secret place in the early 1990s. I often arranged for an inexpensive fishing day with a couple of the local guys who would take me out to work the kelp beds alongside the pangeros. Loaded with mostly bottom fish, we'd return, round the point and ride the swell into the beach. It was fun and productive, and I'm sure even today if you ask around somebody will be happy to take you out fishing. Some fishermen also make the one hour run out to the Islas Los Coronados for pelagic species.

I noticed more restaurants and, as mentioned, found a few right on the sand next to the boats. Others on the rocky promontory are still rustic, and you still might find an old car seat for seating and perhaps a large wooden wire spool for a table. Many of the floors are dirt or sand. Many are open-sided with tremendous views. You can watch pelicans diving into the ocean to feed and waves crashing on the rocks all the way south to Calafia on the point. The Calafia high rises about a kilometer to the south seem incongruous and far removed from such a rustic location.

The two dozen restaurants range from fish taco stands to a couple of sit-down tiled floor restaurants. There's even one designed like the bow of the Titanic, a tribute to the famous movie made next door. There's also Mariscos Miramar, Mariscos Juquila, Brisa del Mar, Pelicanos, Mariscos Rincon, and the one I enjoyed, Agua Brava Nayarit.

A meal on the sand

There are several small places on the sand and I selected the Agua Brava at random. It is run by Manuel Valdez and his wife Legui, who both hail from the mainland state of Nayarit, just inland from San Blas. I ordered the Pescado Zarandeado and we first selected the fresh fish, a good-sized corbina. While Manuel cleaned it and butterflied it for the grill, Legui made superb accompaniments.

I sat and enjoyed the activity around me, boats being unloaded, fish being carted off, small stands readying their catch, pelicans and sea gulls fighting for fish scraps, locals and a few tourists wandering about looking for fresh seafood to take home, and a couple of trinket vendors.

Buying fresh lobster from fisherman

The big fish was served was served on a large tray with the rice and beans on a separate plate. The delectable grilled fish was basted golden brown and topped with onions, peppers, and tomatoes.

I was there midweek, and one reason I hadn't been there in a while is that the place really comes alive on weekends, especially Sundays. The locals are quite aware of Puerto Popotla and as Mexican families like to enjoy Sundays out, many of them crowd into the village. Their cars are lined up all along the 300-yard-long dirt road out to the big arch and beyond, many walking from the highway (old road) in search of fresh mariscos (seafood) to feed their families.

The party atmosphere often prevails on weekends, and there's plenty of music with amped up loudspeakers in some restaurants often overpowering the various strolling mariachis.

Before I left, I walked around and saw some tourists buying fish and some of the biggest lobsters I'd seen in years. A few local women were haggling with a vendor over some very attractive scallops. Other local Mexicans came with ice chests which they filled with several species of fresh fish.

You can only see a corner of the village from the highway and you won't find big tour buses wending their way down that dirt road. But if you like fresh seafood and a slice of rural Mexico, I'm pleased to report that Puerto Popotla might be for you.

"Seat Your Beautiful Selves" (La Fonda – 2016)

I heard through the Baja grapevine that Orest Dmytriw (Who answers to either "Joe" or "Dimitri") had reopened the *original* La Fonda restaurant. It had been a long time (like 12 years) since his iconic restaurant on that Baja bluff 19 miles south of Rosarito Beach was shuttered in 2002 due to striking waiters.

Wanting to verify that Baja grapevine rumor I returned. Years earlier before the old La Fonda closed, I had interviewed Dimitri and had written about the place.

For years, weekend homeowners in the area—as well as those seeking a discreet hideaway, had been flocking to La Fonda, which billed itself as "The Most Beautiful Place on the Coast."

It was certainly one of the most memorable and romantic settings, an old Mexican inn perched on a verdant brush-covered cliff overlooking a broad, sandy beach where dolphins frolic offshore and whales can be seen in winter. The tile patio had tables half-hidden behind dense potted palms, thick banana trees and magenta bougainvillea. They were shaded with thatch umbrellas to provide framing for dynamite views of dramatic sunsets.

That outside patio was the crowning glory of La Fonda, which is why we sometimes went there for breakfast or lunch. The restaurant inside is perfect for cooler evenings. A rip-roaring fire in the fireplace and dancing to the live music made it a fun place to be.

From the mid-1970s through the 1990s, I went there a lot and got to know many of the staff at La Fonda. Early on, the live combo played more for listening enjoyment rather than dancing and people used to crowd the old piano bar to hear Salvador on the ivories, Carlos on the drums, and Alfonso with the conga drum. They all sang along too and Alfonso had a marvelous rich, tenor voice. About two or three times each night one of us would cajole them into doing "Granada" just to marvel at Alfonso's wonderful range.

Sara and Orest Dmytriw

The La Fonda was built and developed in 1962 by Eve Stocker on a beachfront bluff 37 miles south of the border.

Orest "Joe" Dmytriw, a Ukrainian/Canadian/American and his wife Sara bought the place in 1975 and through their improvements and guidance created the popular retreat. It was a small restaurant with a few rooms and 16 employees when they took over. By 2002, the La Fonda provided employment to almost 100 local people and featured 26 guest rooms.

The old hotel was a real hideaway with the cliff-side rooms reached by stairs meandering down the bluff. The rustic old rooms are whimsical and fun, and even have funky names; no two rooms are alike. There are suites and rooms with private balconies and kitchens, and/or sunken fireplaces and big tubs. The rooms all peek out of the foliage for dramatic views of the ocean.

The Old Mexico feeling is everywhere, from the cobblestone parking out front, to the tile throughout, to the broad sweeping window views, to the tropical plants and thatched patio.

I know several people from Southern California who used to stay occasionally at La Fonda. Many from Hollywood had discovered the charm of Old Mexico. Eva Gabor spent her honeymoon at La Fonda, in #14, the Gold Room. Frank Sinatra, Phil Harris and Bob Crosby have also all reputedly been among the legions of customers to the romantic inn on the bluff.

Dimitri's Greeting

Loyal Customers

Local expatriates along the Gold Coast were loyal La Fonda customers. And with reason. Gregarious owner/host Dimitri has a knack for making his customers feel special. He has a warm, "Hey, good to see you again. How have you been?" greeting to friends old and new. He makes a first-time guest think that the two of you go way back, even if he can't quite recall your name. His welcoming "Please seat your beautiful selves" became a memorable catchphrase.

I'd marveled at Dimitri's graciousness and his and Sara's dedication to preserving the charm that meant La Fonda. I'd watched waiters mature and age and even noted the retirement of the elderly Lupe Fuentes, who often bungled my order, but did it with a smile.

I was thus doubly surprised back in 2002 when striking waiters forced the place to close.

An uneasy labor situation would not allow the restaurant to reopen. Under Mexican law, the hotel was unable to replace the 92 striking restaurant staff as long as its original kitchen and restaurant remained open for business. No problem for the creative Dimitri. He boarded the place up and moved. Not far though.

He and his wife Sara vacated their living quarters on the north end of the property and reestablished La Fonda Restaurant there, just yards from the original place. The "new" La Fonda offered similar wave-smashing views and the quality good value food that made it beautiful destination hideaway.

The Rettigs take over

For some time however, Dimitri had been wanting to sell and slow down, and in 2004 he sold the whole restaurant/hotel complex to Dr. Gary (Doc) Rettig, a retired Newport Beach chiropractor and his wife Shawnie. The "new" La Fonda continued to attract the area's expats and visitors, and the Rettigs added a spa and 10 more hotel rooms, all offering front row seats to the white-water below.

Then things changed. The devastating 2008-2009 recession was especially hard on Mexico. On top of the dwindling U.S. economy, tourists had to acquire passports, but most devastating was the pervasive negative publicity. Americans were constantly being admonished by the sensationalist media that the country was not safe. Tourism in Mexico at the time slowed to a trickle.

The Rettigs had difficulty meeting their financial obligation and in 2009 went back to the table with the Dmytriws. Amicable negotiations soon deteriorated with neither side being totally satisfied with the outcome.

A Tijuana judge finally divided up the property. He awarded the Dmytriws the hotel, banquet room, spa, original restaurant, and the La Fonda name, but it seems negotiations are still pending.

Gary's La Fonda

The Rettigs continue to run what some refer to as La Fonda #2, now changed to Gary's La Fonda.

Dimitri decided he didn't really want to retire and after the 2014 court order he reopened and re-established his original La Fonda (#1). So now there are two!

I had heard correctly about Dimitri's reopening, and I was startled to walk in after almost a decade and a half. It was the same – exactly the same! It was hard to believe. The tables and umbrellas on the patio looked to have emerged from a time warp; the bar was identical, the dance area the same – even the fireplace was lit. I was amazed. It did not even appear to have undergone a partial remodel. I guess why screw with what was once a very successful restaurant.

The Dmytriws hired Francisco Naranjo Cruz as general manager. While he doesn't have Dimitri's flashy charm (who does?), he seemed very helpful and capable running the place -- except on weekends when Dimitri shows up to hold court.

On the north side of the hotel is Gary's La Fonda (#2), still a wonderful restaurant which offers great food, the same broad ocean views, and entertainment. Also, just next to that is yet another restaurant/B&B called Poco Cielo, so it's a busy area and always packed with cars.

But I came for Dimitri's. Sitting on the #1 patio for an early fish dinner was an exercise in nostalgia. Even the large blackboard menus were set tableside just like before. The menu was broad and the prices still reasonable. I didn't see any dolphins that day but as I sat my beautiful self down I realized La Fonda might not get much argument using the designation "The Most Beautiful Place on the Coast."

(2024 update: Orest "Joe/Dimitri" Dmytriw died on November 11, 2021 at the age of 87. He is survived by his wife Sara.)

Wyatt Earp in Baja

Wyatt Earp at age 21

Legendary frontiersman Wyatt Earp is best known for the infamous 1881 gunfight at the O.K. Corral in Tombstone, Arizona, but the part-time lawman actually traveled all over the west – including a little-known trip to Baja California.

Earp even had a run-in with officials in Mexico when he and another wild west legend, Bat Masterson, went to Ensenada to pick up a prisoner.

Wyatt, the fourth of eight children, grew up in Illinois but in 1864, his family moved to Colton, California. In 1868 most of the Earps returned to Illinois. However, Wyatt and his brother Virgil began their wanderlust by working on the railroad in what is now Wyoming.

Throughout his years Wyatt traveled the west working alternately as a teamster, buffalo hunter, professional gambler, confidence man, owner of several saloons and brothels, silver and gold miner, boxing referee, gunslinger, bounty hunter, shotgun guard, and lawman.

In the wide-open town of Dodge City, Kansas, Wyatt Earp became an assistant marshal working on the Dodge City Peace Commission. Another commission member was deputy marshal William Barclay "Bat" Masterson, who had a considerable background as a lawman and gunfighter.

They often hunted outlaws which took Earp to Texas in 1878 where he met

John "Doc" Holliday, a dentist with whom he would also share later adventures.

Earp moved constantly from one boomtown to another. He left Dodge City in 1879 and moved with brothers James, Morgan, and Virgil to Tombstone, Arizona where a silver boom was underway.

Josephine (Josie/Sadie) Marcus

In Tombstone he met his third common-law wife, Josephine (Josie) Sarah Marcus, and they were together for 46 years, until Wyatt died in 1929. (Josie, a former entertainer who was also called "Sadie," died in 1944).

In the weeks following the historic OK Corral gunfight, Morgan Earp was fatally shot and his brother Virgil injured by remaining members of the Clanton gang. Looking for revenge, Wyatt, his brother Warren, and some friends went in search of the assailants and subsequently killed at least two suspects.

Accused of murder Wyatt Earp fled, moving first to Colorado, then to several boomtowns in the West, and eventually to California.

He and Josie first went to San Francisco. Then they joined a gold rush to Eagle City, Idaho where they owned mining interests and a saloon.

They headed for San Diego in 1887 to take advantage of the real estate boom there. In the next decade Earp bought four saloons and gambling halls in San Diego, offering various games of chance. At the height of the boom, he made up to $1,000 a night in profit. He also owned the Oyster Bar located in the four-story Louis Bank Building. The popularity of the bar was aided by the Golden Poppy brothel upstairs.

Bat looks up his fellow lawman

Not long after moving to San Diego, Earp was contacted by old friend Bat Masterson. Masterson and Earp both frequently worked as private investigators for various express companies or as U.S. deputy marshals. Thus, their paths crossed frequently during the 1880s.

Wyatt Earp (seated) and Bat Masterson

Masterson was serving as a deputy U.S. Marshal when he came to San Diego and looked up Earp. Masterson told Earp he was going to Ensenada, Mexico, in the morning to pick up an army deserter who had been jailed there, adding, "They tell me he's a pretty tough bird."

He asked Earp to accompany him to Ensenada and back to San Diego. "...just to make sure this hombre doesn't get any ideas."

In her book, *I Married Wyatt Earp,* Josie explained, "That made sense to Wyatt. There was no thought in his mind that Bat had any real fears about his ability to take care of himself, I'm sure. But this careful approach, so characteristic of both these men, may account to their survival to a ripe old age despite years in a dangerous business that claimed the lives of many. Neither of them took unnecessary chances."

Earp agreed, but when he told Josie about the trip, she was disappointed and complained. She had been visiting family and just arrived back in San Diego after being separated for several weeks. She wasn't eager to be apart from him again so soon and said so.

According to Josie, Masterson intervened on her behalf. "'Why not, Wyatt?' Bat added: 'I don't really expect any trouble. She might as well have an outing too.'

'Suits me,' my husband agreed. 'Pack your grip.'"

A steamship to Ensenada

In 1887, The International Company of Mexico operated two steamships from San Diego to Ensenada, and on to San Quintin, where colonists were in the process of settling there. The steamships, which made three runs a week, were generally busy and later during the ensuing Baja gol rush of 1889, were full every trip.

They were able to get tickets, and the next morning the three of them left the long wooden steamship wharf at the foot of Fifth Avenue.

"I was a little nervous," admitted Josie decades later. "The Ensenada of that day was a far cry from the tourist town it later became. I was pleasantly surprised when we found a clean little hotel operated by a 'Norte Americano.'"

After securing rooms, Bat visited the justice court and made arrangements to pick up his prisoner the next day. With a day to kill before night sailing time, the three enjoyed Ensenada. Josie said that best of all they found a little posada that served delicious Mexican food which they had become fond of living so close to the border.

Just before the steamer left, Masterson and Earp went to get the prisoner. They were gone a long time, worrying Josie. Returning, Earp said that they had to wait for some big wig to show up.

Bat brought his prisoner aboard and shackled him to a steel berth in one of the cabins. Josie and Wyatt retired to a larger cabin, and Josie was nearly asleep when there was a loud knock on the door. It was the ship's purser, informing the Earps that they'd have to vacate and move to another cabin, at once.

Defying the pompous captain

"¿Por que?" challenged Wyatt in his rudimentary Spanish, still not opening the door. But then the purser told him that an important Mexican general had come aboard and had been promised the Earp's cabin.

"The hell you say!" he responded. "We paid for this cabin, and we're staying right here!"

Josie, being in a foreign country, admits she was scared out of her wits at the thought of defiance, and whispered to Wyatt to just let them have the cabin.

But Wyatt was firm. After they argued through the locked cabin door for a few minutes, the purser left.

He returned a few minutes later with the captain, who was a rather short man with a belligerent attitude. The captain demanded that the Earps move out of their cabin; Wyatt refused and told him to put the general in the other cabin.

But the captain kept on shouting until Wyatt felt he had heard enough. Josie described what followed in her memoirs:

"Wyatt's reply was quiet and controlled, but his voice had a quality to it I had never heard before and would only hear a few times after.

"'If you don't go away and leave us alone,' he said in slow, measured words, 'I'll throw you overboard.'"

The captain stalked off muttering in defeat. When they touched ground in San Diego the next morning Josie admitted breathing a tremendous sigh of relief.

A tall tale about Tombstone

It wasn't until later they learned of the sequel of the cabin showdown from Pedro Manriquez, the steamship company's agent and a friend of Wyatt's.

It appears the captain had stormed into the steamship office and informed Manriquez that he demanded the arrest of a passenger who had threatened and defied him.

When he learned who the passenger was, Manriquez said, "Wyatt Earp? Then you're lucky to be here. Do you know who Wyatt Earp is?"

Pedro Manriquez decided to lay it on thick since he had never liked the pompous little pipsqueak. He told the captain that Wyatt Earp had killed at least half the population of Tombstone, Arizona there in a single afternoon.

"Madre de Dios," the captain uttered, trembling and crossing himself in relief.

Later Josie asked Wyatt why he had been so sure the captain would back down and he said "The little such and so wasn't a big enough man for his job – it stuck out all over him."

After their San Diego years, the couple followed boom towns from Alaska to Tonopah, Nevada, to Vidal, California, before settling in Los Angeles.

Earp has been the subject of numerous films, television shows, biographies, and works of fiction which have increased both his fame and his notoriety. Wyatt Berry Stapp Earp died in Los Angeles on January 13, 1929.

Josie always remembered how her husband Wyatt Earp defied a pompous captain and a Mexican general in Ensenada. Along with that memorable Baja meal, of course.

Steve McQueen Races Baja

The SCORE Baja 1000, the "Grandaddy of Off-road Races," celebrated its 50th anniversary in November 2017. Through the years many well-known participants helped popularize the grueling event, including top off-roaders, world renowned race car drivers and motorcyclists, and also a few celebrities.

Getting "down and dirty" in the Baja 1000 have been actors Paul Newman, James Garner and Steve McQueen, as well as a few Hollywood offspring, including McQueen's son Chad, Clark Gable's son John Clark Gable, and Bobby Darin's son Dodd Darin. For the elder McQueen it was a natural extension of his love for racing.

Millennials likely have barely heard of him. Even to Generation Xers he was a name from the past. But to us older folk, actor Steve McQueen was "macho personified" often referred to as "The King of Cool." He starred in numerous movies in the 1960s and '70s becoming the world's highest paid and most popular actor at the time.

Born in Indiana in 1930, the morose icon with boyish good looks was one of the original "The Magnificent Seven" (An incredibly popular tough guy movie -- remade for Fall 2016 release).

Among his many movies, McQueen starred in "Bullitt," "The Getaway" (Where he met his second wife, co-star Ali McGraw), "The Thomas Crown Affair," "Papillon," (which earned him a Golden Globe award nomination), "The Great Escape," and "The Towering Inferno." He received an Academy Award nomination for his starring role in "The Sand Pebbles."

A Baja Connection

Many of his long-time fans may not have known about the adventurous McQueen's relationship with Baja California. He spent a lot of time on motorcycles and off-road vehicles there and raced in the 1969 Baja 1000, only the third running of the off-road classic.

Then sadly, he returned to Baja on his deathbed in an attempt to fight off the cancer that had invaded his body.

Son of a stunt pilot father, he was raised by his grandparents and then sent to be reunited with his mother and her new husband. It was a difficult time and McQueen got into lots of teenage trouble, eventually being sent to Boys Republic reform school in Chino, California. (In later years he made numerous visits and donations of cash and supplies to Boys Republic.)

He left Boys Republic at age 16 and drifted around the country the following year, working as a roughneck, lumberjack, and even a towel boy in a brothel. He joined the U.S. Marines at age 17. Still averse to discipline, he got demoted a few times and spent 41 days in the brig before he "turned it around" and went on to get an honorable discharge. Using the G.I. Bill to study acting after his release in 1950, the former "bad boy" soon got bigger and bigger roles.

Wanted to be a race car driver

McQueen always enjoyed living life to the fullest and was an avid motorcycle and race car enthusiast. He performed many of his own movie stunts, including the famous car chase in "Bullitt" and the exciting motorcycle chase in "The Great Escape."

Steve McQueen

McQueen had a remote cabin in the desert near Palm Springs (before he built a home there) where he'd go to let off steam and race his numerous vehicles. For a screening on "The Ed Sullivan Show," McQueen drove the famous host around a desert area in a dune buggy at high speed. Sullivan later said, "That was a 'helluva' ride!"

McQueen considered being a professional race car driver. He came third in a British Touring Car Championship outing. In 1970 at Sebring, he and co-driver Peter Revson won their class and missed winning overall by only 23 seconds.

Later that same year McQueen was scheduled to drive a Porsche 917 with the inimitable Jackie Stewart at LeMans, but film backers threatened to pull their support if he did.

But there was still off-road racing in which McQueen loved to compete, on either a motorcycle (a BSA Hornet or a Triumph 500 cc, and later a Husqvarna) or four wheels. He raced in many top off-road races, including the Mint 400 in Nevada before he tackled the SCORE Baja 1000.

The 1969 Baja 1000

He entered the Baja 1000 adventure accompanied by co-driver Harold Daigh, riding a custom off-road vehicle called the "Baja Boot." The Boot had been specifically designed for the Baja event by leading off-road vehicle designer Vic Hickey.

Prior to the race Hickey gave McQueen some specific pointers on driving the Baja

Boot. Journalist Tom Madigan's *Motor Trend* magazine article mentioned the lessons:

> *"Without showing the slightest fear, McQueen slid behind the wheel of the powerful machine and took to the dirt with a vengeance. It was not McQueen's driving that impressed me, but the fact that whenever he screwed-up or abused the race car, Hickey would jump in his face and chew his tail up one side and down the other. McQueen did not react like a prima donna movie star, but would stand quiet like a child getting instructions from a parent."*

Co-driver Harold Daigh, later technical director for both SCORE International and the Baja 1000, said about the movie star, "We spent about six weeks prerunning, and we covered about 4,000 miles. He was just a really regular guy and a fierce competitor. He just wanted to be known just as a real race driver, trying to do the best he could." Daigh admitted the pair got lost while prerunning and camped out in various places on the peninsula.

Once the race got underway McQueen and Daigh were holding a solid overall position, but, with just 237 of the 1,000 miles completed, a broken transmission put them out of the event. They made their way to Rancho Santa Ynez in the Cataviña area where they secured one of the rustic sleeping rooms while awaiting help.

"On Any Sunday" – 50th Anniversary!

It was over 50 years ago, 1971, when McQueen's Solar Productions funded the classic motorcycle documentary "On Any Sunday," in which the movie star is featured, along with racing legends Mert Lawwill and Malcom Smith. The same year, McQueen also appeared on the cover of *Sports Illustrated* magazine riding a Husqvarna dirt bike. Steve McQueen was inducted into the Off-Road Motorsports Hall of Fame in 1978.

He was a serious collector of cars, trucks and motorcycles, and reportedly owned more than 60 rare vehicles, as well as a few airplanes. While some were top-of-the-line performance cars, others were more utilitarian in nature, such as the 1952 Chevrolet pickup truck and custom camper. The green Chevy pickup, which was the last of the star's vehicles he rode in, sold at auction in 2016 for just short of $100,000.

Fighting cancer

McQueen's experiences in Baja did not end with his racing and he became a brief resident of Plaza del Mar on the Baja coast in 1980.

The Plaza del Mar and Pyramid Resort, now a housing development on a bluff at K58 (about a mile north of La Fonda), was for a long time a clinic, more specifically a laetrile clinic, where cancer patients could make one final attempt to find a cure after all other avenues had been exhausted. Not legal in the States, the controversial treatment still attracted those with but a few strands of hope remaining.

One early patient was Steve McQueen.

By 1980, McQueen had contracted mesothelioma, a rare and painful form of lung cancer. One of the main causes is asbestos, a substance the actor had been around much of his life.

In fact, while in the Aleutian Islands with the Marine Corps, McQueen had been sentenced to six weeks in the brig where he was assigned a work detail in the engine room of a ship. He had to rip out and replace the asbestos linings on the pipes. He later mentioned that the air was so thick with asbestos particles that the men could hardly breathe.

By the time the cancer is detectable, the patient usually has just months to live.

After being told his condition was inoperable, he went to Baja and underwent a three-month crash program at what was then called the American Biologics-Mexico SA Medical Center. At Plaza Del Mar, McQueen was housed in a double wide trailer near the bluff top. Before the area was developed for homes, some of us in the area would show visitors the exact trailer.

His treatment included the powerful B17 laetrile, animal cell injections, over 100 vitamin pills a day, diet and exercise. Unfortunately, it did him little good. While laetrile clinics did have some anecdotal successes reported, there has been little documented evidence to those claims.

McQueen's condition deteriorated and he left the Plaza Del Mar and shortly went to another clinic in Ciudad Juarez, Mexico. There he died on November 7, 1980 at age 50 after undergoing surgery to remove a tumor. He was cremated and his ashes were scattered in the Pacific Ocean.

The Plaza Del Mar has been a hotel with tennis courts, swimming pool, restaurant and bar. Twice it had been a clinic. While Steve McQueen loved Baja's dirt road challenges, it was the Plaza Del Mar on the coast where the popular actor met a challenge he could not conquer.

The Twin Towers of Tijuana (2017)

Tijuanenses call them "Las Torres," the twin, 28-floor, 295-foot skyscrapers that in 1982 became Baja California's tallest buildings. The west tower is the 400-room Grand Hotel Tijuana, and it shares a symbiotic relationship with its partner tower, the Plaza Aquacaliente.

The office tower houses facilities that cater to long-term medical care and depend upon the hotel next door for out-of-town patient lodging. Along with medical tourism, the east tower includes various businesses, including the home offices for some maquiladoras, attracting business people from around the world.

Completing the symbiotic relationship between the towers, the hotel depends upon the medical and office complex for its core clientele.

Medical patients are allotted a designated hotel floor to cross between towers, completely bypassing the lobby. In addition, the 5-star Grand Hotel has a special floor for patients, many of whom are there for weight reduction surgery. Called Grand Care, the 11th floor offers medical and/or reinforced beds, wide doorways, a private lounge and special menus.

Along with weight reduction (A Lighter Me), the medical offices include body contouring, post bariatric plastic surgery, rejuvenating facial surgery, hyperbaric oxygen therapy, a spa, dental and vision services, and more. Weight reduction surgery, for example, requires several days on premises, and follow-ups.

We met an older couple from Florida who were staying at the hotel for nine weeks while the wife endured continuous treatments for a form of cancer. They admitted to us that they were paying a fraction of U.S. prices.

While medical tourism is important to the Grand Hotel, they offer lodging to the flight crews of three airlines (Aeromexico, Interjet, and Volaris), and 12 teams of the Mexican Baseball League. During my visit, I saw several flight crews and the León Bravos baseball team.

Along with a business center and meeting rooms, there is a swimming pool, Jacuzzi, and gym. The Plaza Café has daily buffets, including a Friday Seafood Buffet with a great paella that left me waddling out of there. There is subterranean parking and the rooms have incredible city views.

Officially called the Grand Hotel Tijuana Casino and Resort, the adjacent Arena Casino is completed and now awaiting final permit approval to open. It will boast 550 slots, 6 tables, poker, and roulette. It has an agreement with Harrah's to honor their 40,000 card members. There is also a Caliente Sports Book in the hotel.

The twin towers are located in the Rio Zona section of the central business district. Within a short walk are malls, upscale restaurants (The Fonda Argentina is across the street), American style fast food (Carl's Jr., McDonalds, Burger King), and a Smart & Final and Sam's Club. There are also a Marriott, Hyatt, and Holiday Inn in the area.

Campestre de Golf

Perhaps most intriguing is the fact that the towers are immediately adjacent to the oldest golf course in Baja. The 18-hole, par 72, Tijuana Country Club (Campestre de Golf) was built in 1927, way before high rises began to dot the landscape. Initially designed by William P. Bell, the course was redesigned by the famous Alister MacKensie (who also designed Cypress Point and Augusta).

The course hosted two former PGA Tour events, the Agua Caliente Open and the Tijuana Open Invitational. The semi-private course has greens fees of $44.00 during the week and $79.00 on weekends and also offers golf clinics. Guillermo López Mendoza, Director of Golf, was eager to share the storied course's history.

The hotel's Plaza Café features a panoramic view of the verdant course. Many of the lower windows of the complex have been screened to ward off errant golf balls. Stateside golfers often stay at the hotel.

The Agua Caliente Casino Resort

The golf course opened when an entire resort complex was being designed to draw Americans to Tijuana. In 1928 the Agua Caliente resort, covering 655 acres and costing $10 million at the time, opened nearby. It included a 500-room hotel, health spa, hot springs, Olympic size swimming pool, dog-track, private airport, railroad link, bungalows, and casino. Everything was first class, and it became the most lavish and popular resort in the western hemisphere. A year later, the Agua Caliente Racetrack joined the complex adding horse racing to the attractions.

With Prohibition in the states, Americans flocked to the Agua Caliente hotel casino and spa to gamble and imbibe spirits. They were joined by Hollywood stars and celebrities. Rita Hayworth was discovered there while doing a nightclub act. Musical nightclub productions from Caliente were even broadcast over the radio.

It was heady times in Baja and other casinos opened or were planned. Then came the death knell in several forms over a four-year period. In 1931 Nevada legalized casino gambling. Then in 1933 Prohibition was repealed in the U.S. Also in 1933 California legalized pari-mutuel racetrack wagering; and the Santa Anita Racetrack opened in 1934.

But most damaging, in 1935 Mexican President Lâzaro Cárdenas decreed an end to gambling and casinos throughout Mexico, hitting Baja California hard. The lavish Agua Caliente complex faltered, then closed.

In 1939, it was reopened as a junior high school (now Lázaro Cárdenas High School). Most of the buildings were torn down in the 1970s and replaced by modern scholastic architecture.

Agua Caliente today

While the Campestre de Golf and the hills beyond dominate the south view from the Grand Hotel, from my hotel window we saw an intriguing tower that looked like a Muslim minaret. We learned that the minaret is actually a decorated former incinerator chimney that was part of the Aqua Caliente resort.

Remnants of the Agua Caliente casino including the minaret, Olympic size pool, and a few buildings, now anchor the west end of the 5,000 student Lázaro

Cárdenas Preparatory School on Avenida Sanchez Taboada just off Agua Caliente Blvd. The proud principal of the college prep facility allowed us to enter and roam the historic site.

Up the hill a couple of blocks is the famed Agua Caliente Racetrack. While the large Casino Caliente today occupies most of the interior, out back is the Carrera de Galgos (Hipodromo), a greyhound dog racetrack which still offers racing nightly.

Beyond the track a large orange building looms large. It is the Estadio Caliente, the city's main soccer venue. In and among the 655 original Agua Caliente acres are businesses, restaurants, the golf course, and of course, the Grand Hotel Tijuana.

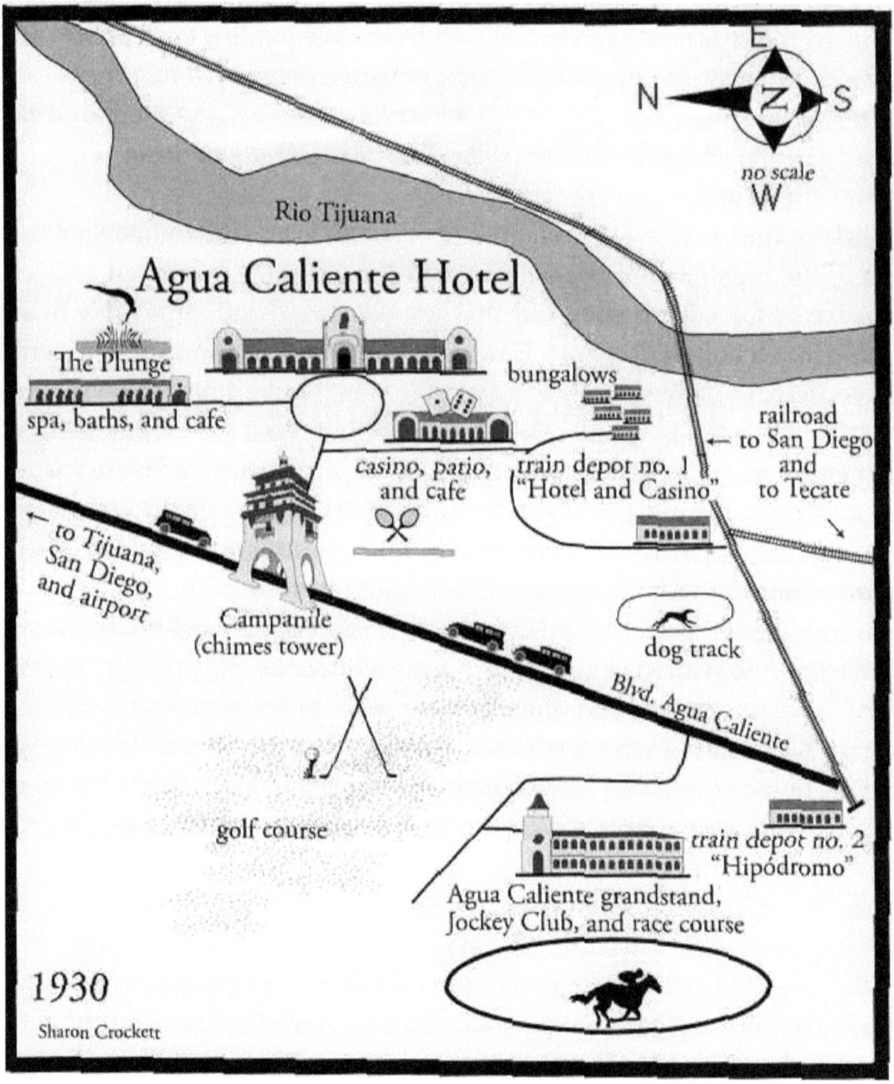

1930s Map of Aqua Caliente

The Bustamante Family

While their business roots do not go back to the 1920s, the developers of the Grand Hotel are among Tijuana's most influential families. Family patriarch Alfonso Bustamante Sr. was a bank teller in the 1940s who had vision and dedication. He began by establishing a heating and cooking gas (propane and butane) company which grew to the largest gas monopoly in Baja California, earning him a fortune.

He invested in real estate, construction and development and by the mid-1960s was one of the originators of Playas de Tijuana. He had gained international influence rubbing shoulders with politicians from both side of the border. By 1979 the *New York Times* estimated his wealth to exceed $200 million. That year he started construction on the twin towers next to the historic golf course.

Alfonso Bustamante's four children and grandchildren have taken over the running of the hotel complex since he passed away in 2011 at age 95. His children are still prominent in Tijuana and throughout Baja California. Son Carlos Bustamante Anchondo was elected Tijuana Mayor in 2010 in a huge upset, serving until 2013. Son Alfonso Jr. was director of binational affairs for the city.

In addition to the Grand Hotel Tijuana, Grupo Bustamante today encompasses a wide range of industries, including land development, industrial parks, and Offshore Promotion, a subsidiary that facilitates investments in Tijuana's maquiladoras. The family continues to support Project Concern and other charitable endeavors.

Tijuana's future growth

While the twin towers of the Grand Hotel Tijuana complex were the first high rises in Tijuana, they certainly are not the last. Towers are going up all over the place, some of which have already exceeded 30 stories. Over the next two years over 2,000 condos will be completed, many in the Tijuana Country Club neighborhood.

Horizante Luxury Condos overlooking the golf course are now being sold at prices mostly between $200,000 and $300,000. The Bajalta development is also going up on 63 downtown Tijuana acres. Bajalta will feature 400 condos in four residential towers, and include one office tower, a hotel, and mall.

The Tijuana condo phenomenon is currently geared for Mexican clientele. About half of the buyers work in the San Diego area and about half work in Tijuana. Fewer than two percent are Americans. Those demographics could change with more Americans visiting Tijuana.

But regardless, the skyline of Tijuana is changing, and it's going up, up, up. A principal of Probien Business Development said in 2017, "Give us five years – the whole city is going to be vertical." He was prophetic. Today (2024), the once distinctive Twin Towers are hard to spot among the city's other hi-rises

The Rio Zona area has led the way in Tijuana for decades. And it was Alfonso

Bustamante with the Plaza Aquacaliente and the Grand Hotel Tijuana that started the city's high-rise boom!

The Mysterious Islas Los Coronados (2012)

The intriguing Islas Los Coronados, being only 18 miles out of San Diego, are Baja California's most accessible islands for southern Californians. The four largely barren and craggy islands have long been an attraction, today drawing snorkelers, scuba divers, fishermen, nature lovers, and adventurers.

Only about seven miles straight off the northern Baja shore, the islands catch your eye from the toll road between the border and Rosarito Beach. Their hues and shapes change with the variable daylight. Sometimes they resemble a supine pregnant woman. Sometimes they are just grey outlines, almost lost in the maritime mist. And other times, when they glisten and shimmer in the morning sun they seem to be just offshore, taunting your imagination as they beckon to reveal their mysterious and fascinating past.

History indicates that due to lack of fresh water, no Indians ever lived permanently there. Only one Indian shell midden was discovered, probably left by visitors seeking fish or lobster.

When the Portola-Serra land expedition saw them in 1769, the trailblazers recognized them from earlier records by Juan Rodriguez Cabrillo (1542) and Sebastian Vizcaino (1602) and figured correctly that they were just eight leagues from their destination of San Diego. It was Vizcaino who named them, calling them Los Cuatro Coronados—the Four Crowns, shortened to The Crowns.

South Coronado Island from Mexico 1-D north of Rosarito

The North and South islands are the largest and highest. North Coronado has no bay but boats can anchor on the eastern side. The two middle islands, Pilón de Azúcar (Pile of Sugar) and Central Coronado are just rocky peaks that rise to about 100 feet. A cove below a lighthouse on South Coronado forms the only bay on the islands.

Pirates did stop by, and one old legend has it that a pirate named Jose Arvaez used the bay, later called Pirates Cove or Smugglers Cove, as a base of operations. Allegedly he killed the crew of a British ship, the "Chelsea," but he and his men were caught when they returned to their cove and were hung from the yardarm of their own schooner.

In 1911, a group of 10 Chinese nationals were left stranded there by two San Diego smugglers who never returned to pick them up. They were starving and delirious when spotted. They had food and water thrown to them, but due to political implications were not picked up for some time. After the ordeal they ended up back in Ensenada where they started.

With prohibition in the U.S. in the 1920s, Mexico's bars and casinos were flourishing in Rosarito Beach and Ensenada, and rum-runners often stopped at the islands. Gambling speculators even developed an elaborate two-story gambling casino and hotel on the rocky cliffs of the South Coronado Island. The timing couldn't have been worse, however, because before it got up and running, Mexico clamped down on casino style gambling.

Abandoned and forlorn, it later housed soldiers based on the rocky island who had their water and provisions shipped out to them.

L. Ron Hubbard shelled Mexican islands

An interesting chapter of the islands' history occurred during World War II and involved an American Lt. Commander who would later become the founding father of Scientology. In May 1943 the U. S. Navy's USS PC-815, commanded by L. Ron Hubbard, conducted unauthorized gunnery exercises and shelled the Coronado Islands. He claims he thought they were uninhabited and belonged to the United States. Being that the islands were occupied by the Mexican Coast Guard at the time, the Mexican government complained and Hubbard was relieved of command.

Various people tried to make a go of living on the Coronados. A robust woman called "Crawfish Jake" ran a small eating house at Smugglers Cove, catching, cooking and serving lobster to boaters who went ashore.

Battered by the wind and waves, only the stone foundation of the original casino remains though the name Smugglers Cove can be seen on some maps.

One Manuel Aguilar lived alone on the North Coronado catching lobsters. A small boat from Ensenada picked up his lobsters and brought him water and other supplies. Then one time they didn't show for two weeks so he had to row his small boat all the way to San Diego. That dependency almost cost him his life. He never went back.

Today, along with fishermen, the islands are visited regularly by divers and snorkelers who consider them among the best dive locations on the west coast with conditions similar to the Caribbean. The nearby deep ocean currents regularly wash the islands with clear blue water creating visibility often exceeding 80 feet.

Pukey Point on the north end of North Coronado has rough currents and is for more experienced divers. Easier are the Lobster Shack on the east side, and McDonalds, an arch at the south end of North Coronado.

Currently, the islands are again used by human traffickers who occasionally hide people there when worried about getting caught by the Coast Guard or when the weather is too bad to continue. Similar to the Chinese situation of a century ago, the would-be illegal aliens are sometimes left on the island for days.

A wildlife refuge

The Coronado Islands are actually a Mexican wildlife refuge and humans are not allowed to go ashore. Animals thrive there. There are colonies of gulls, pelicans, petrels and sea ducks, and the largest known colony of the rare Xantus's Murrelet.

Ten species of reptiles and amphibians are also found on the islands, as well as two types of land mammals—rabbits and mice. Sea mammals are plentiful, and it is not uncommon to see groups of sea lions, seals, sea otters and elephant seals.

Today nature tours have taken their place alongside the fishermen and divers and snorkelers in being attracted to the Coronados. One outfitter, Flagship Cruises of San Diego, offers a six-hour guided nature tour of Islas Los Coronados and participants have a chance to spot whales, dolphins, harbor seals, sea lions and kelp forests, including a visit to one of only two elephant seal rookeries within 300 miles. The tour also teaches about life on the islands, including the infamous "rum running" days.

One nature tour guest summed up her experience, "We saw whales galore. We were seeing them in groups of 4, 6 and 8. Pretty amazing! What's nice is that these islands are relatively untouched and the wildlife there is in its own ecosystem and it works to keep the animals alive and well."

In addition to Americans visiting the islands, Rosarito Beach officials have in recent years been speculating on ways to somehow use the island as a tourist attraction. That would be nice, as long as they remember to take water out to them.

Street Bargains – Baja Style (2018)

Many Americans have a hard time passing up outdoor markets and garage sales. On Saturday mornings they are out among a veritable army of bargain-hunters following brightly colored neighborhood signs that indicate someone's once proud possessions might end up in their homes.

Sometimes a bunch of neighbors dedicate the same day for their garage and yard sales, thus increasing the number of prospective customers and allowing the buyers a more concentrated experience.

Not strictly a local U.S. phenomenon, urban areas worldwide have large outdoor markets. I've been to big swap meets in cities around the world. Closer to home there are several well-established markets, like Pasadena's monthly Rose Bowl flea market or San Diego's Kobey's Swap Meet at the Sports Arena.

There are also those swap meets, street fairs, flea markets, and farmers markets that sprout up in many communities, usually on a designated day. However, many smaller outdoor markets are relatively narrow in scope: perhaps offering only produce, or handicraft items, or fine art, or antiques, or are geared around a specific seasonal or gastronomical event. A multi-purpose swap meet therefore offers the most diversity.

Mexico is no exception, and Baja has numerous options for outdoor and street markets with most conveniently set up in residential neighborhoods.

Expats and tourists alike are welcome to join the hordes of locals in Baja hitting the streets for the best deals. And you can find virtually anything at a Baja street market: new and used clothing, household items and supplies, tools, hardware, packaged groceries, sundries, school supplies, fishing tackle, toys, exercise equipment, and fresh meat, produce, and seafood. In addition to take-home food, there are lots of stalls offering on-site meals for the shoppers.

For many Mexicans a street market is much more convenient than taking a bus to various stores, or a city's central Mercado, and is a major way to trade and buy necessities. Neighborhoods wait for the stores to come to them.

Like in the U.S., these Mexican street markets have several names: for example "Tianguis" is defined as an open-air market or bazaar traditionally held on certain market days in a town or city neighborhood. This tianguis bazaar tradition in Mexico has its roots well into the pre-Hispanic period and continues in many cases essentially unchanged into the present day.

The word "tianguis" comes from tianquiztli in Nahuatl, the language of the Aztec Empire. Here again, there are also specialty tianguis events for holidays such as Christmas as well as for particular types of items such as cars or art.

In Baja, the markets are often called Mercado Sobre Ruedas (market over wheels). In the Rosarito Beach area, there is a market almost every day in different parts of town. They range from very small (just a block or two) to so large they encompass an entire neighborhood.

Saturdays at Primo Tapia

From my Cantamar house it's just about a half mile walk up the hill to Primo Tapia and that's where we often head on weekends in Baja. The Saturday market there covers about 6-8 blocks, and surrounds the civic plaza, the library, and the primary school.

There are three or four fruit and vegetable stands and numerous new and used clothing stands, including many by locals who just lay their treasures out on a tarp in the street, augmenting their family's source of income.

This Primo Tapia market has many food stalls and several specialize in pizza, probably the biggest food draw there. Families crowd covered picnic benches under bright blue tarps sharing pizzas. It seems take-home pizza is just as coveted as you see the familiar squared flat boxes carried everywhere.

Every type of food for sale

I have a favorite bolillo (roll with a thick crust and hot and chewy inside) stand and I will munch on one while I wander about. There are taco stands specializing in the various popular types: carne asada, carnitas, barbacoa, shrimp, fish, whatever you want. The birria taco stand near the end of the first street on the left always has a long line attesting to its popularity.

After wandering the entire place, we always grab any produce and fruit just before we head back down the hill, stopping at our favorite stalls for mangoes, papayas, cantaloupe (melón), and watermelon (sandia).

What makes it even more fun for us is running into people from long ago and meeting their families. Long-time area shop owners and/or workers we've hired in decades past (electricians, plumbers, and construction people) have mostly stayed in the area and it's kind of fun seeing their children grow up and have families of their own. To us, the Primo Tapia Swap Meet is a home away from home.

Rosarito's Big Sunday Market

We'd heard about the big Sunday Los Panchos Street Market in Rosarito and finally made it there early this year. Of course, we've been back more than once.

It's easy to find, just off the free (Libre) road to Tijuana on the north end of town. We immediately saw booths and stalls, parked a couple of blocks away, and started hoofing it.

We walked on the street parallel to the highway for a couple of blocks thinking the market was not as big as we were led to believe. Then we came to the outdoor mart's main street which takes off east up the hill with stalls on either side and down the middle.

You can find anything in those few blocks, from bicycle helmets, to infant seats, to freshly hewn furniture, to live goldfish. And there's lots of food, fresh fruit, ice cream, pastries, peanuts in the shell, and the inevitable tacos. On our second visit we discovered some outstanding tamales. The proprietor Francisco even had some Oaxacan style (our favorite – wrapped in banana leaves versus corn husks). Thus, we stood in the street, munching moist *tamales de pollo estilo Oaxaca.*

Most of the larger food stands offer covered seating, but walking and eating is part of the Mexican street experience. I also found a place that sells a sweetened bolillo, and another with small waffles.

The market extends up to the crest of the hill, and a block or two in either direction from the main street. Used goods abound on many of the side streets as here too women just lay out personal items for sale to help feed and clothe their families.

Sunday markets are also good because in Mexico that's family day and you'll see just as many fathers holding kids on their shoulders as you do mothers pushing strollers.

These markets might not be for everyone. We see very few gringos and you should have at least a smattering of Spanish. Many tourists might be more comfortable at the handicraft market downtown Rosarito or other places that cater to tourists and where almost all the sales people speak English.

I just described two street markets, but there are similar outdoor markets every day of the week in the Rosarito/Tijuana area.

Most markets start in the morning and end in early to mid-afternoon, generally from about 7 a.m. until 2 p.m. Not only are they an enriching experience, but you might have a lot of fun – and possibly come home with a treasure or two.

Cows with an Ocean View (2020)

Americans have been flocking to the Baja California coastline seeking ocean view properties for years. To about 7,000 cows on a bluff at Descanso (south of Primo Tapia) however, it's no big deal. For years the Jersey Dairy cattle have been chewing their cuds on that hillside above the sea, oblivious to the coveted ocean vista below.

It had been about 25 years since I'd last visited the Jersey Dairy stables, even though it is just to the south of our place in Cantamar. Recently I noticed the on-ramp to the toll road across from the popular Splash restaurant, and remembered that to get to the dairy, you just continued up that hill.

Curious and nostalgic, I turned and drove up past the on-ramp where a narrow pot-holed road continued. As I could see it was still well used by trucks going and coming with supplies and milk, I realized the dairy was still there. Farther up the hill, however, there is now a guard gate to restrict access.

I was seeking what was formerly a very pretty and well-maintained Parque del Niño behind the Jersey Dairy. The hidden park is actually part of the dairy and nestled snugly against the bluffs behind it. Few even know there's a large dairy between the toll road and the hills, especially with the prevailing breezes blowing the dairy scent away from the beach communities.

Fewer still knew about the "childrens' park," a wonderful garden of swings, teeter-totters, slides and much more. Back in the 1980s several of us from Cantamar used to take grandchildren and other Baja guests who had young ones.

Gaining entrance, I found the Parque del Niño still there, still maintained and as inviting as ever. But it was vacant, locked, and appeared to have been closed for some time.

The Jersey dairy operation there is officially called Establo (Stable) No.2 de la Cuenca Lechera El Descanso. The Parque del Niño was built for the children of the employees, many of whom live in company housing on site. It was opened to the public and became popular with families from around the area.

Wanting to know more, I found the dairy operation offices just down from the park. There the affable 83-year-old manager Rogelio Reynoso and his son confirmed that the childrens' park was closed and had been for three years; reopening it was still uncertain. Yet they provided gardeners and maintenance people to continue keeping it in very tidy operating condition.

Jersey Leche is everywhere

Jersey, officially Pasteurizadora Jersey del Noroeste, S.A. is a large regional dairy serving the northwest Mexican states of Baja California, BCS, Sonora, and Sinaloa. Based in Tijuana, it has been a familiar Baja mainstay for decades, providing pasteurized whole milk, 2 and 1%, non-fat, and chocolate milk, creams, yogurts, butter, and assorted juices.

Originally called Lecheria La Suiza, the Jersey Dairy was founded in 1926 by Don Cesareo Jimenez Perez. His son Don Ernesto Jimenez Orozco took over and, along with many innovations to the entire dairy industry, he became a major Baja California benefactor.

For example, Don Ernesto Jimenez donated his company's products to orphanages, asylums, rehabilitation centers, convents and religious orders that fulfill community work. He also offered scholarships and donated books and school supplies to children in need. He financed the construction and equipment of the building that houses the Tijuana Historical Society and created the Tijuana History Museum.

Tradition of Parks

Wanting to do more to thank the communities served, early on the company began building parks for children and families. There are similar parks to the one at Descanso in Tijuana and Ensenada. Some are still in operation, but the jewel in the Jersey crown is the Valle de Guadalupe Zoo.

What was originally slated as a kiddy park like the others but larger with more entities, Don Ernesto's Valle de Guadalupe project morphed into a full-fledged zoo, becoming the state's second largest zoo. Now 11 years old, Zoológico Parque del Niño Jersey has become a hit.

Along with camels, monkeys, baboons, hippos, emus, guinea pigs and other animals, the 30-plus acres in Guadalupe Valley features swimming pools, paddle boats, playground equipment, palapas and picnic tables. There's a petting zoo and even a little train for rides around the park.

The zoo, not that far from Ensenada, has become a welcome addition to the flourishing Guadalupe Valley. I'm glad that Jersey has expanded its efforts in providing community recreation, but still saddened that that original Parque del Niño at Descanso has not yet been re-opened.

Don Ernesto Jimenez Orozco passed away in 2014 at the age of 89. Jersey is now being run by his sons, Horacio Jimenez Berumen and Ernesto de Jesús Jimenez Berumen.

A Case for Gerontology

With Jimenez actively running the company at age 89, the company culture has set a good example for employing the older set and there are numerous long-time employees.

For many years a very old man named Daniel Flores tended the flowers at the Descanso Parque del Niño. The aged, yet friendly dairy worker took noticeable pride in the park's gardens.

Talking to him in 1993 I asked how old he was. Daniel Flores, whose appropriate surname means "flowers," answered with a proud smile. At first I thought I misinterpreted the Spanish and made him repeat his answer. He was over 100 years old! Yet he was still quite mobile and agile. Not only that, his mind was active too.

One day in 1995 I saw him walking briskly up the street at the Primo Tapia Saturday market and introduced him to a visiting friend. According to what he had told me, he was then 108 years old!

Six months later I noticed an article about him in the Mexican newspaper Ecos de Rosarito. The article confirmed, "...Daniel Flores Maldonado, de 109 años de edad, nacio en Patzcuaro, Michoacán, el 27 de Julio de 1887..." Born in 1887! 109 years old!

Flores had an interesting life before he was employed by Jersey Dairy and loved to talk about it. He was an early political leader, helping to found the PAN party. As a young man he had known Francisco I. Madero, President of Mexico (1911-1913).

In my researching birth dates of mostly rural-born Mexicans, I have found poorly-kept or non-existent records. But even if off by a couple of years, based on his life experiences he was still well over 100!

Two years later I found the centenarian sitting peacefully in a wheelchair in the backyard of the modest home of his caretakers on the Jersey property. He tilted back his "Jersey Dairy" baseball cap to show a full head of hair and he smiled when he saw me.

Caretaker Agripina Arias Castillas commented admiringly, "He's only been in the chair this last year. He doesn't move around too well now, but then again he's pushing 112 years old." She added, "And he loves to eat and still enjoys ranchero music."

But his favorite pastime was sitting outside in the backyard overlooking the broad, sweeping Descanso Bay just like the cattle across the road.

His life had been full; it has transcended over a century in which he's seen his country in revolution, wars, peace, and growth. It was a tribute to his employer that he was able to spend his declining years with Jersey Dairy where he finally passed away.

Upon revisiting last month I asked Rogelio Reynoso if he remembered Flores. His eyes lit up as he recalled Daniel Flores. "Si, El Viejo." As I looked out past the cattle and the superb ocean view, I thought it interesting for an 83-year-old man to call someone else "The Old One."

Ready to leave, reminiscing about Daniel and admiring the company policies on keeping and respecting older employees, I noticed a couple of high-rise buildings on Highway 1 fronting the sparkling blue ocean. Called Palacio del Mar it seemed obvious that tenants in upper floors would have a commanding view of the dairy – and the 7,000 cows looking back at them!

Mr. Smith Goes to Baja (2015)

He was once again in my mind as I bounded down the dusty Baja dirt road from Santo Tomás to La Bocana.

"He" was Jack Smith (1916-1996) and I idolized the guy. Besides his largesse as a journalist, he was a fellow southern Californian and also a veteran. Although I served in the detente of the Cold War, Smith survived the bloody WWII landing at Iwo Jima.

Jack Smith

His columns in the west's largest newspaper, the *Los Angeles Times,* were so popular for over 37 years they were syndicated to over 600 newspapers. He wrote about a neighborhood in which we both lived, the Mt. Washington area of Los Angeles. And, more importantly, he also wrote about Baja.

In 1973 I had invited the crusty old curmudgeon (as he was referred to me) to be one of the judges of the former Miss United Way Contest of which I was the Los Angeles Chairman. While I found him to be opinionated and stubborn, I was delighted by his wry sense of humor. That day we also shared some of our Baja experiences.

In 1970, Smith and his wife Denny had built a two-bedroom, one-bath home on a Baja bluff south of Ensenada at La Bocana, the mouth of the Santo Tomás River. His columns featuring stories on the travails of the construction delighted his many readers and resulted in the classic 1974 book, *God and Mr. Gomez.*

His earlier *Times* columns where he introduced Mr. Romulo Gomez and the construction project helped convince me to make my first Baja purchase, which I did in 1971. I felt a little kinship to Smith in my original little trailer and told him so. We shared Baja fever.

Smith's endearing book

I had moved to Orange County and never saw Jack Smith again, but it wasn't for lack of some half-hearted attempts. On a spontaneous whim in 1976 a buddy and I had driven down the 17-mile dirt road of the Santo Tomás Valley to La Bocana. The Smith house was pointed out by a neighbor, but they were not in residence that week. We enjoyed chatting with the neighbor, Hal Schmidt, a banker Smith had mentioned in his book.

The homes sit on a chaparral-covered bluff facing the frothing sea. Kelp beds undulate with the constantly pulsing tides just offshore. You can see the small fishing village of Puerto Santo Tomás a couple miles north. It's a beautiful, wild, mesmerizing and captivating location.

We met Mr. Gomez

On another excursion in 1983 several of us, my wife and another couple, drove down to La Bocana again. We enjoyed the scenery on the narrow road along the valley floor, past small farms and ranches, stopping to picnic and splash our feet in the several stream-bed pools of the not-so-mighty river.

Again the Smiths were not there, but we met Mr. Gomez at his house and took photos with the local builder/grocer/character who had been immortalized by Jack Smith. We found him more of a delight than Jack's enigma, but then again he was not building a house for us.

Jack Smith's House

I had been along the highway through Santo Tomás numerous times since, but never down to La Bocana. I knew the Smiths had sold their house in 1990 and that Jack had passed away some years later. I'd heard that the house was owned by two Santa Barbara couples and then sold again in 1997.

But the little settlement down at the end of the Santo Tomás Valley was still a draw for me, and in May 2015 I decided to take a solitary day trip from Cantamar. I wondered what might have changed since Jack romanticized the area.

For starters the urban sprawl of Ensenada now extends almost all the way to the once-small village of Maneadero. And it's no longer all Mexican tiendas or loncherias you drive past. Oh no. Today, it's Walmart, Office Depot, Costco, McDonald's and other Yankee icons that extend "vanilla" merchandising to foreign countries. While an economic boon for the locals, this type of Americana elsewhere still seems like pollution to me. I don't think Jack would have felt that he was in his beloved Mexico.

And former sleepy Maneadero, which in his day had one stop sign for the La Bufadora cutoff, now has over a dozen stops and a few traffic lights to boot. And most of the road south to Santo Tomás has been widened; even the old "s" curve dropping you into the Santo Tomás Valley has been bypassed.

The El Palomar of Santo Tomás

Mr. Smith would have been pleased to note that Santo Tomás is much the same as it was, even to the old El Palomar Store/Restaurant/Motel, hardly changed since the Smiths spent a night in the motel upstairs. In my book *Baja Legends*, I mention Jack Smith's comments about his El Palomar experience. He also introduced the proprietors, the Villareal family, who are still there. Over the years the Villareals have occasionally sold my Baja books and Emma Villareal was most gracious on this current visit. I enjoyed lunch there before I headed off the pavement.

The valley was lush with olive groves, and with fat grapes on bright green vines, but the huge new winery by the cutoff from the highway would have seemed alien to Jack. I turned down the dirt road toward the ocean, through a little community amid the broad valley boasting corn, chiles, and melons along with the grapes.

I was surprised and a little confused when the road left the valley floor to climb up and hug the hillside. It seems that heavy rains and flooding five years ago wiped out much of the valley floor taking the old road with it. This new all-weather, well-graded dirt road is mostly cut into the hillside. Jack may have preferred it to fording the stream on several occasions and opening and closing gates when the old road went through private property.

As I neared the ocean the valley opened out and fields of chard and calabasa (pumpkin) were being worked by locals. A road to the small community of Punta China took off to the south just before the intermittent river opened to a broad and beautiful reed-lined lagoon – la bocana (the little mouth). Sandbars enclose the lagoon from the pounding ocean.

Next to some broad and shady casuarina (pine-like) trees on the lip of the lagoon is Gomez's La Bocana store, now sadly shuttered. The house where I had met Gomez looked different too, the vestiges of a happy family life obviously gone. Romulo Gomez was gone too, succumbing to cancer in 1994 at age 83. His wife Delia preceded him in death, and they left two sons, Sergio and Pepe; a daughter, Marisa, and several grandchildren.

I realized with sadness that it was all a chapter of the past. Things change, just like the valley's Misión Santo Tomás. Founded back in 1791, high water forced the mission to change valley locations three different times. A Dominican padre said the last Mass in the final adobe mission in 1849. The diminishing number of Indians in the area and the government's interest in secularization sealed its doom. Santo Tomás became a military base and territory capital.

Things usually change slowly in Baja, often reflecting the pace of its inhabitants. But they change. The Indians had their era, the padres, theirs, and the soldiers, theirs. The Smiths had their getaway home for two decades and now they too are gone.

Jack Smith's columns energized many thousands of followers. He went on to author a total of ten books, bringing many of his columns to life for an even broader readership.

A lot of Baja buffs were inspired by the writings of Jack Smith, including Rosarito area resident and Baja Nomad board member Gypsy Jan, who once commented, "The stories in his *LA Times* column and the resulting book about Baja helped create and nurture my love affair with this strange and mystical place."

Smith's last column appeared on December 25, 1995. He died on January 9,

1996, aged 79. His papers were donated to the Huntington Library in 2005 and he and Denny established the Jack and Denny Smith Memorial Fund for Literacy.

While Jack Smith is gone, his legacy lives on.

Children of the Streets (2004)

One long-time Baja visitor who has made numerous donations to the orphanages of Baja California and even adopted four Mexican children, commented, "It was something like going to the dog pound in the States. Have you ever gone to the dog pound and not wanted to take half of them home?"

Only a few people who devote their time, energy, money, goods, and dedication to the children housed in Baja orphanages actually go so far as to adopt some of the children. But caring individuals cross the border regularly in efforts to improve the lives of those homeless youths, known as the children of the streets.

There are about 50 orphanages in Baja California and no two are alike. They range from housing a handful of children to approximately 120. Some are in rural ranchos, others in the cities, some are close to the border, others harder to reach; some are gender specific (only boys or only girls), and others provide care for children with special needs, or are specifically for toddlers and infants; some are *alberque temporals* (temporary shelters), and others are affiliated with schools or churches. Some are well-run and well-organized; others are so slip-shod and/or dreadful that they are ultimately shut down.

Regardless, they all must feed, clothe, shelter, and provide physical, emotional, and other support for their charges. To meet all these needs, it takes about $2,000 per child per year. All of the orphanages (Casas-Hogar) are overseen by the Social and Family Services department of the Mexican Government. They help regulate the quality, and place children, but do not provide for them financially. That is up to each individual Casa Hogar. In essence, they are wholly dependent upon private individuals, organizations, and churches.

Children from the streets

The great influx of migrants from all over Mexico to the border area has abetted the problem. Children are left at orphanages by parents who simply cannot feed them, or they are taken from abusive situations, or they are abandoned. With little or no family support or influence, they are, in short, children of the streets.

Ideally, these children will grow up in a stable environment that will allow them to complete some sort of schooling, either trade schools, technical institutions or high school and/or college that will allow them to enjoy as normal a life as possible.

There are numerous southern California church groups as well as non-religious, non-denominational organizations, such as Rotary Clubs, that provide support for one or more of these orphanages.

Genesis Expeditions of Mission Viejo is a non-denominational, non-profit group that encourages people to become involved with the Casa Hogar and help in any way they can. They can assist a private donor by helping them select a specific orphanage, and they also lead regular trips to the Baja Orphanages.

The Corazon de Vida (Heart of Life) Foundation helps raise contributions in the form of food, money, materials and volunteer work to benefit and empower the children of all of the 50 Baja orphanages. Corazon de Vida (CDV) was founded in 1994 and is supported by Orange County Congresswoman Loretta Sanchez. CDV currently makes regular monthly one-day trips, which leave from Orange County and San Diego.

CDV also encourages corporate sponsors to lend support and inspires companies to enroll employees in matching donation programs, holiday drives and company trips to visit the sponsored orphanage. Individuals or groups can also "sponsor" a child through Corazon de Vida. CDV currently feeds more than 350 children every day through these programs.

Volunteers welcome

Anyone can go to a Baja orphanage with Corazon de Vida by either calling to reserve a space on the van or driving down on their own. A different orphanage is visited each month, all within a one-day round trip from Irvine in Orange County. Volunteers might help with a building project, or bond with and support the emotional needs of the children.

The philanthropic International Community Foundation, founded in 1990, supports numerous charitable causes in Baja California, including the orphanages.

Baja Christian Ministries works specifically with one orphanage, City of Angels, in La Gloria, a southern suburb of Tijuana. It is currently home to 27 children but is being expanded and hopefully will house 125 children. Building work is being done by Team Casa de Dios in association with the Baja Christian Ministries.

One of the largest Baja orphanages is the Door of Faith in La Miśion (between Rosarito and Ensenada) which the founders, Curtis and Sylvia Freeze, started in 1959 with a vision and $35.00. It has been considered a model orphanage, and the "grads" have nothing but praise for the Freezes.

Door of Faith is now run by DJ and Lynette Schuetze who have been on site for 10 years. They care for 117 children, including 30 in diapers, one of whom, just weeks old, arrived the night before my visit. They have a staff of seven Americans and about 25 Mexicans to care for their charges. The DOF stresses family, education, and community service. All of the children go to public schools and there is a study hall on premises for homework and special education. They all are taught Spanish, English and computers and many graduate into careers once deemed unlikely for a Baja orphan.

The dorms, segregated by age and sex, are spotlessly clean. Young children bustle about either doing assigned chores or playing on the colorful playground equipment. It appears to be a well-organized and model orphanage.

Check things out first

It is recommended that people wanting to help donate to an orphanage do some homework. Sometimes orphanages are poorly run, administrators have been known to pocket money, and counselors have been negligent or abusive. Not only that, but there are always supporting American organizations that get so mired in red tape and overhead that very little assistance actually trickles down to those who need it.

If possible, physically check things out, and follow up. I visited one high in the barren hills above Rosarito Beach that housed about 20 boys in less than ideal circumstances. The pastor in charge was not in attendance that day but a young toddler who kept clinging to my leg was. I was saddened that the child and his mates were in desperate need of affection. However, those in charge couldn't even keep clean toilets for them.

Sometimes a well-run place can go downhill with a change in administration. This happens, and organizers of those who provide aid should stay on top of changes.

That Baja orphanage supporter who adopted four children has visited over 30 orphanages over the years. He says he can spot a bad one in about 10 seconds. Recognized as an expert, he has helped the Mexican government close two of them in the past, and has also encouraged people to discontinue supporting a couple of others. The *L.A. Times* has used him as a resource person. He advises, "When you walk into a place and it reeks of pee, and puke, and lice abound, then it is time to pull the plug, even if it means back to the streets. Sorry, tough talk, that is the reality. Otherwise, you condemn generations of kids to pee and puke, and that is just not where I want my support to go. It costs so little to be clean."

Find out what's needed

Another caveat is that many people don't know what to donate to the orphanages. About ninety percent of the clothing, for example, is for adults.

Administrator DJ Schuetze at the Door of Faith told me that most people donate the obvious clothing and toys, so their needs are beyond that. "We could use household goods, like pine cleaner, bleach, shampoo, toilet paper, brooms, mops, and always canned food and diapers. We do our major shopping at Costco, so a check or Costco gift card would be especially helpful," he added.

One orphanage that is visited by Corazon de Vida, as well as other groups, is a current success story. El Faro (The Lighthouse) is in the Tijuana suburb of Villa Fontana near the Otay Mesa border crossing. Founded in 1998 by Pastor Jorge and his wife Carmen, it started as a beaten-down two-bedroom house which served as church, living quarters for the pastor's family, and dormitory for about 13 kids.

An early visitor said, "The children were all clean and happy....I was impressed and burdened that the pastor's wife would still cross the border three times a week to clean houses after working who knows how many hours feeding and cleaning all those kids."

In short time El Faro moved to newly purchased land in Villa Fontana with a single building on it and soon increased to over 90 children. They began a separate school and a church. There are now nine buildings housing 120 children at El Faro. The fruit of their success is that most of the staff of this growing orphanage are graduates who have been helped by the pastor and his wife.

A volunteer or donor need not be affiliated with a specific church, nor a specific denomination, nor any church at all. Those without a religion conviction can just as readily recognize a need to help their fellow man, or in this case their fellow child.

By supporting the orphanages that deserve to be helped, the children are being fed and clothed. They are provided a bed and a pair of shoes. Most importantly, they sleep safely. They are no longer children of the streets.

Cruz Roja – Baja's Red Cross (2021)

Most people appreciate a comfort zone, even when they travel. They want to feel safe and protected. That's why they buy automobile insurance when going to Mexico. Many Baja California visitors, however, do not give much thought to a possible physical emergency such as a life-threatening heart attack.

That's when the familiar Red Cross (Cruz Roja) can be a big help, and many expat volunteers in Baja California work side by side with the locals to assure that assistance is always there.

The Cruz Roja Mexicana functions 24 hours a day, 365 days a year. Like the American and Canadian Red Cross, it assists at disasters, but additionally acts as an Emergency Medical Service. authorized to render first aid to anyone injured in an auto accident.

The Red Cross is recognized around the world and known as **the** organization that helps those in need. It began in Switzerland in 1863 when businessman Jean-Henri Dunant inspired a few others and they formed what became the International Committee of the Red Cross. The familiar symbol of a red cross on a white background is the opposite colors of the Swiss flag. It was an easy way to identify medical workers who were on battlefields.

The Red Cross began in the U.S. when former Civil War nurse Clara Barton and a few friends founded the American Red Cross in Washington, D.C. on May 21, 1881.

The humanitarian idea spread around the world and most European countries quickly formed organizations. Spain's was so successful, they convinced Mexico that they too should have a "Cruz Roja" which Mexico did establish in 1898.

Throughout Mexico the needs of less affluent members of the community who have non-emergency medical problems are generally handled in free clinics, mostly supported by Cruz Roja. The local Cruz Roja Delegations usually request a donation, but what is received seldom cover costs.

Most Cruz Roja Mexicana Delegations are fortunate to have auxiliary volunteer groups generally comprised of locals. However, in many areas that have large expat populations, there is often a group made up of American and Canadian volunteers. They are aware that Cruz Roja provides a safety net for all who live or visit Baja. The quality of life in Mexico, particularly in rural areas, depends on the ability of the Cruz Roja to collect enough money to keep solvent.

The Cruz Roja expat volunteer groups, through various fund-raising activities and membership fees, provide localized assistance and help fulfill the mission of providing humanitarian aid. One such group is the **Cruz Roja Voluntarios Americanos de Primo Tapia.** The Cruz Roja Primo Tapia operates a thrift store just up the road from our Baja retreat. As members of that volunteer organization, we've been dropping off donated items there to be resold to locals and thrifty tourists alike. The donations through membership fees and donated items helps insure greater emergency medical aid in our area.

We've known of the Cruz Roja Mexicana for years. Before our 1979 wedding at the old city hall in Rosarito we had to have the Rosarito Cruz Roja draw blood and give us physicals. Over the years in various cities around Mexico we've had occasion to seek their assistance for minor maladies and/or tests and checkups.

Cruz Roja Voluntarios de Rosarito

In the northern Baja area, some Rosarito expats got together in 2009 and formed Cruz Roja Voluntarios Americanos de Rosarito to assist that long established delegation.

That Rosarito Cruz Roja volunteer group, with over 550 active members today, is an larger and older chapter than ours in Primo Tapia. The Rosarito group operates a huge thrift store (behind Waldo's. on Ave. Lazaro Cardenas). If you're a reader like I am, you'll spend some time browsing through the huge paperback collection there.

That thrift store operation, along with other special events, also enables them to support the local Cruz Roja Hospital Rosarito.

Cruz Roja Primo Tapia

Even with the assistance from the Rosarito expats, a shortage of funds forced the Cruz Roja Mexicana to cut back its ambulance service in the Primo Tapia area (12 miles south of Rosarito) to part-time. Thus motivated, a group of Americans living in the Primo Tapia area decided to act. One such resident and Rosarito Chapter volunteer, Lana Jordan, emailed friends and neighbors to possibly form a Cruz Roja Primo Tapia.

An initial meeting in November 2014 attracted over 100 people, giving birth to the Primo Tapia chapter. Founding officers elected were Lana Jordan, President, Drew Juvinall, Kathy Schy, Treasurer, Pam Saltzman Membership Chair, and Val Valle, Thrift Store Director.

Over 60 people became members of Cruz Roja Primo Tapia that day, and more joined as their memberships to Cruz Roja Voluntarios de Rosarito expired. There continues to be a close relationship between Cruz Roja Rosarito and Cruz Roja Primo Tapia.

At that first General Meeting, donations generated enough money to get an ambulance on call the other 12 hours each day and set up the local Cruz Roja Primo Tapia Thrift Store. The store is a success, netting enough each month to pay for all of its expenses and also address Cruz Roja objectives. In fact, 2021 President Paul S. Ross noted that they are now looking for a larger location for the thrift store.

Thrift Store about to open

The income from memberships and special events (which include Oktoberfest activities, St. Patrick's Day parties, and Bingo nights) provides invaluable support to Cruz Roja Mexicana.

Cruz Roja Voluntarios Americanos de Primo Tapia continues to work raising funds to support the overall mission of Cruz Roja Mexicana, and specifically to extend its services to maintain an ambulance in Primo Tapia 24/7.

As an example of the services offered to members, the Cruz Roja Primo Tapia Administration provides a Membership Card and an important 9-1-1 Alert Form.

9-1-1 Alert Forms

The 9-1-1 form provides individual medical information to Cruz Roja in case of an emergency. Members list all medications, address and location of house, emergency contacts, etc. Cruz Roja suggests that it be kept in a safe place in case of a medical emergency, as well as copies made for designated others.

Cruz Roja Membership Card

The Cruz Roja Primo Tapia Membership Card could be needed in case of an emergency. The Administration stressed the importance of members to always carry their cards with them.

Regardless of whether one is a member of a Cruz Roja Voluntary Organization or not, all expats living in Baja California should have a list of documents to have on hand in case of a medical emergency. These should include:

- 9-1-1- Alert Form (your personal medical information),
- Cruz Roja Membership Card (if you're a member),
- Copy of Covid Vaccination Card,
- DNR (Do Not Resuscitate), if you so desire,
- SENTRI Card (if you have one),
- Passport (if you don't have SENTRI),
- Credit Card or $100.00 cash in case of transport to border.

Along with the financial support to Cruz Roja Mexicana and the possibly life-saving advice for expats, the advantages of becoming a Cruz Roja Voluntarios member are well worth the minimal annual dues.

If you're not a member of one of these groups, you can still help. In urban areas throughout Baja California, you will often see volunteers standing at stop lights with white cans and a red cross. Give a few pesos.

Those who live full time in Baja California, or visit seasonally as snowbirds, and even weekenders or vacationers, should recognize that when they help support the Cruz Roja Mexicana, the life they help save may be their own.

Searching for Baja's Perfect Wave (2010)

The proximity of Baja California has long attracted California surfers. The more isolated breaks and vast stretches of lonely beaches have proven irresistible to many.

While pioneer surfers began tackling California waves with their heavy monster boards in the 1940s and 50s, some of the more adventurous crossed the border to check out the surf in Baja. Back in 1963, surfers Mike Hynson and Bill Fury documented the wave action somewhere just south of Ensenada.

Then the Windansea Surf Club, which was established in San Diego in 1962, began making trips to surf Baja the following year.

Baja's first surf contest, the Baja Surf Club International, was held at San Miguel, just north of Ensenada, from 1966-1969 and was attended by most of the leading California surfers.

After the Transpeninsular Highway opened in 1973, many hardcore surfers who had honed their skills in California and northern Baja, began heading farther south in search of that "perfect wave," often negotiating rutted dirt roads to camp on lonely, windswept bluffs in their quest. They discovered and popularized the surf at places like Scorpion Bay and Abreojos.

For all the fine wave action way down south, the proximity to the border and consistent surf insured that Northern Baja would never be an overlooked destination. And sometimes the waves got huge.

Surfer Catching a Wave

When K2 Surf promoted its $50,000 Big Wave Challenge back in winter 1998, everyone expected the winning "biggest wave" ride to take place along the North Shore of Hawaii, or maybe even at Maverick's in Northern California, both areas known for huge surf. The world's best big-wave surfers tried their favorite spots only to see the biggest wave prize won in Baja.

World pro surfer Taylor Knox, of Carlsbad, CA, won the contest by successfully riding an amazing 50-foot wave at Todos Santos Island, out in Ensenada's Bay. The 50-foot wave ride could be compared to falling off a five-story building. The world's biggest ride that year in Baja may have surprised a lot of people, but locals have known of giant, gnarly surf off the island for years.

Besides Todos Santos Island, Baja has some legendary surf spots along the Gold Coast between Tijuana and Ensenada, like Baja Malibu, Power Plant, Mushrooms, Calafia, K-38, La Fonda, Salsipuedes and San Miguel.

These days southern Californians can follow the surf-seeking trail blazed by those before them. And rather than asking a local rancher in Spanglish if there are big waves ahead, there is a lot of information out there—from fine magazines, like *Surfer, Surfing, The Surfers Journal,* to a few top-notch websites—and several books.

There are several websites for surfing Baja: some not only offer destinations, but surf maps, Mexico insurance information, photos, charts, seasons, water temperatures, and more. You can find site details for all of the surf breaks along the Pacific coast, from Playas de Tijuana to Punta Rosalillita, including such legendary breaks as Renes, K-38, Rauls, K-55, San Miguel, Quatro Casas, Shipwrecks, and the Seven Sisters.

Surfline editors report: "This is not—nor is it intended to be—a comprehensive surf guide for every surf spot in Northern Baja. The reason is partly philosophical and partly practical: surf spots are sacred places and deserve more than just a sentence and directions. They're the closest thing to shrines we've got, and are worthy of a little examination, if only to give travelers a sense that they're not the first ones there. It comes down to respect, really—the more you understand about a particular place, the more you'll respect it. And that's a good thing. Northern Baja's cheap, close, interesting, and has some damn fine surf—go have a look around."

Baja Surfing Books

Surfer's Guide to Baja by Mike Parise. This 128-page gem (SurfPress Publishing) is already in its third edition and has been updated regularly. A 30+ year surfer, L.A. account executive (when not surfing) Parise shares his knowledge with this detailed and current guide for surfers heading to the Baja peninsula.

This fine book features over 120 breaks, including the legendary points, reefs, beach breaks and islands from Tijuana to Cabo and around to the East Cape, with maps, travel tips, wave height chart, tips on when to go where, accommodations and more.

Surfers voiced their approval online. One said, "This is the one truly invaluable tool I took with me to Baja. It was detailed and precise, and really took a lot of the work out of the planning. Basically, it's the bible when it comes to surfing through Baja."

Another added, "It led us to many spots that there would be no other way to find. Odometer setting gets you through a vast network of obscure, unmarked dirt roads and magically to the camp/surf spot of your dreams."

Parise also penned the *Surfer's Guide To Costa Rica,* which has sold over 25,000 copies.

Wave-Finder Surf Guide Mexico by David Small. This is a pocket surf guide for all of Mexico, Baja included. This 2006 book has been criticized by some as being too small. Yet others really like the book. One said, "When was the last time you saw a surfer carrying War & Peace or the Encyclopedia Britannica to the beach? It is small for functionality, and the writing is great. Very informative...."

Small is a surf journalist, writing for *Transworld Surf,* and *Surfer,* among other publications.

Morning Glass by Mike Doyle. For a nostalgic peek into the Golden Age of Surfing, this book covers the beginnings of surfing in California and Baja. Doyle was there in the sport's early years, sharing the waves with some of surfing's biggest names, including Phil Edwards, Mickey Dora, Ricky Grigg, Pat Curren, and Corky Carroll.

Doyle was a classic waterman (surfer, paddler, lifeguard, rower, and skier) who grew up on the beaches of Southern California and lived in the Cabo San Lucas area. Published by Manzanita Press, this 256-page treasure is a must-read for those interested in the origins of the sport in Southern California.

(2024 note: Mike Doyle passed away in 2019 at the age of 78 and was mourned by surfers everywhere).

California's First Winemaker

Despite the hype and popularity, the fine wine and vineyards of Baja California did not begin in the famous Valle de Guadalupe. It was an unlikely mission outpost far to the south that is credited as the birthplace of the Baja California's wine industry. In fact, all California wine, even that of the world-renowned Napa Valley, can trace its roots to Mexico's missional system.

The first recorded planting of a vineyard in the Californias was by the Spanish Jesuit Padre Eusebio Kino at the short-lived San Bruno mission near Loreto in 1683. The vines did not survive. Jesuit Padre Juan de Ugarte in 1701, while making Baja California's second mission of San Javier a model outpost, cultivated California's first grapevines and wine press there.

Among Ugarte's many accomplishments he established schools, brought sheep and goats from the Mexican mainland, cleared land for orchards, and imported olives, pomegranates, figs, citrus, and grapevines. He learned that the most valuable crops were figs and grapes because they yielded dried fruit and wine which could be pressed and handily stored or transported.

Baja wines were made from the mission grape, a common red vinifera variety from Europe, presumably from Spain, with a somewhat fruity taste. That variety dominated California wine production until about 1880. The early peninsula Jesuits, like Ugarte, had been making sacramental wine at a few other missions, some of it quite good and used for trade.

Cuttings were then transferred from established missions to the newer ones. San Ignacio mission (1728) for example, with its secure water supply, became the most prolific supplier of mission wine for many years. While Ugarte was the first to plant grapes, it was Padre Jorge Retz, a robust German Jesuit priest, who is credited with being the first master winemaker.

Mission Santa Gertrudis

Retz' wine experimentation began to produce quality wine in 1752 at what is now considered the birthplace of the California wine industry, the remote Baja California Mission of Santa Gertrudis la Magna.

Santa Gertrudis is unique for several other reasons as well; it was the first mission established in the present state of Baja California (Norte); for 10 years it served as headquarters and outpost for exploration to the north; and the graceful stone church in a peaceful setting makes it one of the most attractive Baja missions even today.

Located 23 miles east into the desert from El Arco, Santa Gertrudis is just north of the 28th parallel which separates Mexico's two peninsular states.

The site was discovered in 1751 by Jesuit Padre Fernando Consag who did preliminary work on what was originally called Dolores del Norte before the name was changed to honor St. Gertrudis. He placed the construction of simple buildings under the guidance of a blind Cochimi Indian, Andres Comanaji Sistiaga (or Sestiaga), who achieved amazing accomplishments in spite of his handicap.

The walls of mud and small stones supported a roof constructed of timbers across which were laid reeds or rules. As it rarely rained and the Indians preferred to sleep outside, these rough buildings sufficed in the beginning.

The mission was dedicated in 1752, but Padre Consag soon died and Padre Retz was sent there after spending a year in San Ignacio to learn the Cochimi language.

According to custom, the other missions contributed whatever could be spared of provisions, cattle, horses, mules, sheep and goats for the new mission. Padre Retz, also ably assisted by the blind Indian, built a substantial building of stone and lime mortar.

Padre Retz soon found himself in charge of 1,400 Indians who had agreed to be baptized in this strange European religion. Some estimates indicate there were as many as 3,000 Indians living in the mission area during its heyday.

Creating fine wine

Retz discovered a reliable spring and cut a canal from solid rock 1½ miles to a small field that could be farmed after hauling in topsoil.

This small aqueduct is still in evidence today. Padre Retz and his charges grew and harvested wheat and corn. They planted date palms, olive trees, fig trees, peaches, and pomegranates, along with the significant grapevines.

According to Arthur Walbridge North in his 1908 book *The Mother of California,* "Padre Retz, an industrious German Jesuit, planted grapevines in this garden, after having enriched its soil with fine loam brought from distant arroyos. Later, he made from the grapes of Santa Gertrudis such excellent wine that he ranks as the first California winemaker."

The manufacture and storage of fine wine called for great ingenuity on his part in addition to his enriched soil and care of his vines.

Casks being unknown there, Padre Retz designed containers hewn from blocks of stone. He filled them with the juice of the grapes, then covered them with boards and sealed them with a gum from the pitahaya plant. This ingenuity and care resulted in California's finest wine at the time.

Mission Vineyards

Decades later, in 1791, Baja wine production increased when Mission Santo Tomás was established in a fertile valley 26 miles south of Ensenada. That region, including Guadalupe Valley to the north, afforded the perfect vineyard climate, and by 1800 there were 5,000 vines there, eventually giving birth to Mexico's oldest commercial winery, the Bodegas de Santo Tomás (1888).

The over 30 wineries that have developed in the region since the 1970s have found that numerous varieties do well there, including some fine merlots and syrahs. However, some of those original mission grapes are still in existence, even producing wine today in the Valle de Guadalupe.

Franciscan Padre Junipero Serra, who established nine California missions, planted the first sustained vineyard in the U.S. state of California at Mission San Diego in 1779. For that he has sometimes been called the "Father of California Wine."

Center for Exploration

Perched on a ledge in a small arroyo, Santa Gertrudis became the center of the frontier region and base for further exploration until San Borja was founded 10 years later.

Life at Santa Gertrudis apparently agreed with Padre Retz because it is said that he was a rather corpulent man. He was also somewhat infirm and, at best, had difficulty traveling. When the Jesuits were expelled from Baja California in 1768 by an order from the King of Spain, Retz had a severely injured foot. So he had teams of his mission Indians hand-carry him 200 miles to the ship at Loreto.

That year the Dominicans arrived, completing the present stone church at

Santa Gertrudis in 1796. They also built a campanile or bell tower separate from the church.

Date palms are in evidence near the mission, and you can see portions of the over 270-year-old aqueduct. Cattle and horses bask around the small pond near its terminus. While the earlier adobe buildings have been reduced to crumbling walls, the mission chapel and bell tower are in splendid condition. Thick stone walls render a cool interior which still has one room used as a chapel, and another set aside as a crude museum, complete with an original tabernacle in a glass case, an old crucifix, and simple models of the church made by local children. There is a small container for donations.

The Santa Gertrudis Indian population suffered greatly from diseases. By 1785 there were only 300 Indians. By 1822, the mission was finally abandoned due to a dwindling indigenous population of fewer than 100. The mission was extensively remodeled in 1997.

Today the quiet arroyo is home to a few hardy families who still use a portion of the two-century-old irrigation system. They tend the dwindling historic grapevines, olive trees, and date palms, along with their own crops.

The birthplace of California's world-class wine industry is a picturesque gem: a palm oasis surrounded by desert chaparral, cacti, and the indigenous cirio (boojum) tree. Colorful mountain cliffs stand guard over one of the better preserved and more attractive of Baja California's missions. It was so idyllic, even the little old winemaker Padre Jorge Retz had to be carried out of there.

The Wineries of Guadalupe Valley (2012)

In October 2011, I participated in a Baja Book Festival held in the lovely Valle de Guadalupe 15 miles north of Ensenada. The eight-mile-long valley along Highway 3 is a picturesque, undulating landscape blanketed by lush vineyards and upbeat wineries.

I'd been to Guadalupe years before, having written about the area's history of padres, settlers, miners, and the original wine industry. In recent years many more wineries have been established, resulting in the area becoming a major tourist destination.

The rich, fertile land is home to orchards with straight rows of peach, apricot and olive trees, bright multi-hued flower fields, and the main lifeblood of the valley—the vineyards—whose gnarled stumps come alive with bright green leaves and clumps of fat, juicy grapes in summer.

Currently over 90 percent of Mexico's wines come from vineyards in the Ensenada region of Baja California. This includes the Santo Tomás and San Vicente Valleys to

Santo Tomas Winery

the south, and the popular Guadalupe Valley. The region provides the ideal vineyard climate: warm summers and mild winters, bright sunny days and cool nights with frequent marine moisture. The Guadalupe mission (Baja's last) was established in 1834, and later (in the 1870s and 1880s) American gold miners passed through the area.

A curious Russian settlement started there when a religious group of about 500 settlers split from the official church of Russia and fled their mother country. In 1905 they made their way into Baja and the Guadalupe Valley with the blessing and help of Mexican President Porfirio Diaz.

Later, in 1938, the populist Mexican President Lazaro Cardenas designated lands for the peasants of Mexico. Guadalupe was engulfed by 3,000 Mexicans and the main town was renamed Francisco Zarco. Many Russians left at that time. Others stayed, most assimilating into the culture.

By that time the fledgling viniculture originally brought by the padres had sprouted. The settlers realized the warm valley area, at just over 1,000 feet elevation, was perfect for grapes.

I had known that Baja's main wineries, including L.A. Cetto, Domencq, and Monte Xanic, were there, but was totally unprepared for the proliferation of smaller wineries of the past decade.

I discovered that the old graded dirt road from the Tijuana-Ensenada (libre) Highway had now been paved to the Guadalupe Valley. I have known Baja long enough to realize that pavement meant people.

The Book Festival with over 20 authors, music, food and art, was held in and around shady olive trees and rusting winery equipment of historic La Casa Vieja in the heart of a small village called San Antonio de las Minas. There's a working winery, a deli, and an arts and crafts store which hosts an art show there on the first Sunday of each month.

Fellow author/writer and the foremost American expert on Baja wines Steve Dryden told me that in 2004 there were only seven wineries in the Guadalupe Valley and that by 2011 there were over forty-five!

Several of the valley wineries have won international awards for excellence and have been producing world-class quality wines. One international wine expert and judge said, "This (Barolo) is the best Nebbiolo wine in the world outside of Italy." Along with several more popular varietals, that slow-budding Italian grape does well in the region.

The greater involvement of more capable Baja vintners has resulted in tougher competition, enhanced quality, and a more viable industry. Some oenologists have even purchased selected blocks of grapes from the Baja region and are making high quality wine from that in their US wineries.

Fiestas de la Vendimía

Each August, the Valle de Guadalupe wineries host a wine festival to herald the annual harvest. The Fiestas de la Vendimia takes place in nearby Ensenada and among the valley's wineries during the first ten days in August.

But if you miss early August, don't despair, as the party generally continues until the end of the month with events, tastings, food/wine pairings, vineyard tours, art, and the requisite music and dancing.

La Ruta de Vinas

Along with nearby Ensenada, the Guadalupe Valley has become a tourist destination. For example, it's a popular shore excursion for cruise ship passengers that disembark in Ensenada.

There are also several different companies that offer day winery tours into the area from San Diego.

For those driving, attractive wooden signs distinctively marked "Ruta del Vino" (The Wine Route) direct tourists from one tasting room to another throughout the valley. Most wineries are open on weekends with about half of them open during the week; tasting fees range from free to $7 per person.

In San Antonio de las Minas, along with La Casa Vieja, are Vinisterra which offers a cabernet sauvignon-merlot blend and other award-winning wines, as well as Hacienda La Lomita which produces merlot, tempranillo, shiraz, and chardonnay.

The valley is home to wineries large and small, established and fledgling, with several in and around the villages of El Porvenir and Francisco Zarco.

The Italian-owned L.A. Cetto winery is the largest not only in the area—but in all of Latin America. There are no fees for tasting or tours at this popular winery which offers tranquil gardens and a picnic area.

Baja's most acclaimed winery, Monte Xanic produces 50,000 cases of wine per year, and many of its varietals have won international awards.

There are so many other smaller wineries that a person could make several trips to the area and visit different ones each time. For example, check out Casa de Piedra or the award-winning merlot at family-owned Viña de Liceaga. Family-run JC Bravo produces 800 cases a year and also offers cheeses and olive oil.

How about a wine-making class? In the community of El Porvenir, a former olive oil factory has been converted into the Estación de Oficios El Porvenir, known locally as La Escuelita. This wine school runs a popular four-week class each summer for aspiring winemakers.

Chateau Camou features Bordeaux-style reds, and then there's the Italian-run Villa Montefiori. Another boutique winery making 10,000 cases of wine a year from their adobe brick building is Baron Balch'é.

I was pleased to see a bit of the Russian heritage remaining. The Museo Comunitario de Valle de Guadalupe is still there crammed with old Russian photos and artifacts. Run by the Samarin family (From 1905), they now have a little shop next door selling fresh preserves, jams, and Russian foodstuffs including a Pan Russo (Russian Bread) so heavy you do not want to drop a loaf on your toe.

Russian family operates small Guadalupe business

The Eastern Orthodox inspired onion-shaped-domes on the logo of the Bibayoff Winery logo also reflects the Russian influence in the valley.

Where to stay

One of the biggest changes I noted was the current availability of lodging, from small motels to world-class retreats.

Ranked Number 1 on Tripadvisor is the Adobe Guadalupe Vineyards & Inn, a B&B and winery that puts you right there among the vineyards. Also popular were the Hacienda Guadalupe Hotel, Vinedos Malagon, and La Villa del Valle.

A new hotel in the valley (late 2011) featured in *Conde Nast Traveler* magazine is the Hotel Endemico, a luxury eco-hotel perched on the hillside of a 40-acre winery overlooking the Valle de Guadalupe. Its modern design features 20 free-standing units, each with terrace and outdoor clay chiminea. Also on site is a dramatic pool cut into the hillside and a restaurant overseen by the Culinary Arts School of Tijuana.

The Valle de Guadalupe can be a regular day trip from the San Diego area, but visitors might find they experience a more relaxed visit by spending the night right in the vineyards.

Beyond Guadalupe's Wineries (2021)

What else can one do in a famous wine valley besides partake in winery tours and enjoy samples from the eclectic palette of culinary offerings? Perhaps you want to see what else is in the area? Maybe some people in your group want to do something else? Or do you want to entertain children?

Yet people sometimes ask me, "What's there besides the wineries?" As it had been several years since I had visited the valley, I decided to check it out. I learned that today the valley also offers several museums, the Jersey Dairy Zoo for children, an old western town, and some interesting and historical hiking trails.

Visit Mission History at Guadalupe Museum

Back in the 1980s, I visited the Guadalupe Valley seeking the ruins of the Misión Nuestra Señora de Guadalupe, Baja's last mission (Est. 1834). It was abandoned in 1840 following attacks from local Indians. The ruins were hard for me to find back then but today a historical park has been established with a small museum at the site overlooking the river valley. *(Town of Francisco Zarco: On Calle Tercera, 2 blocks east of Calle Principal).*

Museum of the Russian Settlers

In 1905 Mexican President Porfirio Diaz provided 13,000 acres of fertile land in the Guadalupe Valley to a religious Russian Sect of about 500 people who had split from the Eastern Orthodox church, settling in the town of Guadalupe (later renamed Francisco Zarco).

Museum of Russian Heritage

Along with ranching and farming, the settlers realized the warm valley area to be perfect for grapes and they started making wine. In fact, the Russian family-owned vineyard Vinedos Bibayoff (The valley's oldest, established in 1906), is still around and still open to the public.

In researching my book *Baja Legends* in the late 1990s, I was pleased to see a bit of the Russian heritage remaining near the Bibayoff winery when I discovered the Museo Comunitario de Valle de Guadalupe. It was crammed with old Russian photos and artifacts and I met several members of the Samarin family who ran it. On my 2021 visit I noticed that is still there *(On Calle Principal, just west of central Francisco Zarco).* Today there is an adjacent restaurant Familia Samarin and the tasting room of the Bibayoff Winery. (Vinedos Bibayoff). The museum is worth a visit and is a good representation of the Russian sect that settled the Guadalupe Valley.

Museo del Vino

There is also the comprehensive Museo del Vino (Wine Museum) across the road (Highway 3, at K-81.3) from the Finca el Mirador and the sprawling Hacienda Guadalupe Hotel. The modern-looking two-story museum is divided into several sections and also hosts four temporary exhibitions each year.

Wine Museum

One room is dedicated to the worldwide history of wine and the specific viniculture industry in Mexico. Other rooms explain the production process as well as the promotion of wine, festivals, and the wine culture in Baja California.

The museum is open from Tuesday to Sunday from 9 a.m. to 5 p.m. There is a small fee. Some of the Wine Tour groups do stop at the museum.

Other Museums

Along with the large Museo del Vino, many of the larger and more established wineries also have exhibits, primarily centered on their vineyards and particular viticulture. These include the small handful of large wineries that were established before the 1990s, including L.A. Cetto (1928), Domencq (1972), Mogor-Baden (1980) and Monte Xanic (1987).

Jersey Dairy Children's Zoo

I learned about the Zoologico Parque del Nino Jersey when researching Baja's Jersey Dairy. The Dairy-sponsored kiddy park has morphed into a full-fledged zoo, becoming the state's second largest zoo. Now 13-years-old, Zoologico Parque del Niño Jersey is very popular with local families. *(On Calle Principal about a mile west of Francisco Zarco).*

I arrived one morning just after it opened and excited kids were heading for all the attractions as their parents set up picnic tables. There is much more than just the zoo. Along with camels, jaguars, monkeys, baboons, hippos, emus, guinea pigs and other animals, the 30-plus acres features 3 swimming pools, ponds, paddle boats, lots of playground equipment, and covered palapas and picnic tables. There's a petting zoo and even a little train for rides around the park.

It appeared to be mostly local Mexican families and almost all of the signs are in Spanish, but kids on playground equipment for sure don't care. It can be a good outing for the family, and a memorable day for children. Entry is 80 pesos for children, and 85 for adults (About $4.00), (Also small fees for the tram, bicycles, paddle boats, etc.).

Rancho Las Delicias – A Touch of the Old West

Entrance to Delicias

I was surprised to see a Western Village on the side of the road leading from the old Tijuana-Ensenada Libre (Mex-1, free) road to the Guadalupe Valley.

Ecoturistica Rancho Las Delicias, just to the west of the valley's first wineries on the main road is not a bone-fide old western town, it just was built to look like one. A touristy stop primarily for Mexicans, there were three busloads of them wandering the grounds and taking photos like mad when I was there.

It is picturesque with old storefronts, western wagons, and assorted rusting detritus. There's a pond, several shops with souvenirs and western clothing, and guests can also purchase a Mexican buffet meal. For small fees there's also horse and pony rides, and miniature golf. Tours are available. Worth a brief visit.

Hiking in Baja

For people who like to keep active and get out and discover nature, there are several hiking trails available in or near the Valle de Guadalupe. They range from easy, to moderate, to hard. Here are a few for your consideration:

Valle de Guadalupe Hot Springs and Ruins

Moderate, 3.6 miles out/back to hot springs, 5.4 miles to ruins, 50 peso fee. Turn east off Highway 3 at Domenq Winery on paved road. Pass El Cetto Winery, continue on dirt to rancho at far end of valley. Pay people at rancho, and park there or continue driving up to rustic camping area and walk from there. Follow the trail by the stream up.

There's a beautiful waterfall on the way (mostly dry in summer), and two hot springs up the trail from the waterfall. The springs make a good destination or you may continue to the old way-station ruins (once used by miners). The trail is easy except for few boulders.

When I went in May 2021, I noticed several people in a large group even had toddlers and babies. (The trail is little changed from when I hiked it in March 1997 except with a wet winter that year the waterfalls were superb. (My hike that year became a chapter "Taco and the Mountain Man" in my *Baja Fever* book.).

Guadalupe Canyon Hikers

Dona Petra Canyon

Moderate 13.3 mile out/back hike with scenic views (elevation gain 2,244 ft.) From 3-D to Ojos Negros on Lib. Ensenada. Take Prolongacion Avenida Ruiz north off 3-D to end of pavement and trailhead. Trail ends up on the eastern reaches of San Antonio de las Las Minas/Villa de Juarez.

This hikes gets 4.5 stars on online reviews, which include these comments: "Nice views," and "Excellent trail."

Santa Cruz Trail

Moderate. 5.1 mile loop in the heart of Guadalupe Valley. Offers great scenic views and mountain biking. San Antonio de las Minas/or Villa de Juarez, just north of Plaza Fatima and El Porvenir cutoff off of Highway 3, on west side. Turn off at sign for "aerodromo" and park near a couple of old Airstream trailers. Take your mountain bike or hike.

El Salto Trail

Popular 2.1 mile out/back (Easy) or 3.7-mile loop (Moderate). Elevation gain 728 feet. Near community of El Salto north of Guadalupe cutoff, off Highway 1. The trailhead is off a short dirt road and leads east to a trail that features a pretty waterfall (salto). Good trail for all levels with a little bit of rock scrambling. El Salto Trail also offers opportunities for rock-climbing enthusiasts.

Cerveza Tecate – Pride of Baja (2020)

The most ubiquitous symbol in Baja California is undoubtedly that of Tecate Beer, the "cerveza" that is a source of pride to Baja Californios. The familiar red and gold symbol is seemingly everywhere, huge signs above every bar, restaurant, and market where the product is sold.

Card tables, umbrellas and white plastic chairs are emblazoned with the logo and provide an odd backdrop for many functions, even weddings, graduations and quinceñeras (a girl's 15th birthday and coming-out celebration). The Tecate logo is almost always visible whenever you rent party equipment.

But most party attendees could care less, in fact many love it. They grew up with Baja California's most popular product and consider Tecate to be Mexico's best beer, if not the world's best.

Tecate Brewery

It started in 1944 when Alberto Aldrete took over an old brick building in the Baja border town of Tecate that had been producing vegetable oil. Aldrete was operating a small malt factory in town and had been brewing beer as a sideline for over a year. He named his new brew after the town and it became one of the first maquiladoras (factories) in Baja California.

In 1954 the Tecate Brewery was sold to Cervecería Cuauhtémoc Moctezuma, a major brewery based in Monterrey, Mexico. Founded in 1890, Cerveceria Cuauhetemoc had been producing Bohemia and Carta Blanca beers.

In 2010 the entire Cuauhetemoc operation, including Tecate, was acquired by the estimable Dutch conglomerate Heineken International. The Cuauhetemoc brewery continues to produce Bohemia, Carta Blanca, Superior, Sol and Dos Equis in several different locations.

Today Tecate, Tecate Light, Tecate Titanium, and Tecate Michelada Cocktail are produced in the Tecate Brewery. Tecate is sold in both distinctive red and blue aluminum cans and in twist-top bottles. Tecate Light came out in 1992, and in 2013

Tecate Titanium, which contains a greater amount of alcohol, was launched.

Tecate Light has just 110 calories, 3.9 percent ABV, and 7 IBU (compared to Tecate Original's 141 calories, 4.5 percent ABV, and 13.5 IBU). The company states that the Michelada Cocktail is made with Tecate beer, tomato juice, salt, lime, and "a little extra spice."

The Tecate beer that is exported is of a slightly lesser alcohol content, but that doesn't make it any less popular north of the border. Tecate has the highest canned beverage sales of any import to the U.S. While available in the U.S. for years, in 2017 Heineken announced that Tecate would be exported worldwide.

Tecate's international acceptance goes beyond North America. It has garnered prizes in competitions in Madrid, Rome and Paris. The mother brewery Cuauhetemoc is the only Mexican company to earn the distinguished ISO 9002 international designation based on the consistent high quality at its seven production plants.

Tecate beer is one of the major sponsors of the SCORE Tecate Baja 1,000 off-road race and the Rosarito-Ensenada 50-Mile Bike Ride, and many other promotions throughout Baja California. It's also sold at Padres games in San Diego and has become a tradition at many other Southern California sporting events.

Tecate is "the official beer of boxing." It has financially supported the sport since 2007, when it sponsored the Oscar De La Hoya-Floyd Mayweather fight. It also endorses individual fighters.

Marketing the Tecate Brand

For years, Tecate's advertising was aimed at men. For example, note this ad: "Unmistakably bold, Tecate is the #1 preferred beer in Mexico and is now enjoyed in 16 markets across the globe. A true champion of men, Tecate encourages fans to always be bold. How bold? You take it from here."

To help broaden the appeal, in 2017 Heineken USA promoted Esther Garcia Martín to Tecate Vice President of Marketing. Garcia said. "Joining a brand that stands for masculinity both in Mexico and the U.S. — it was cool, it was a challenge."

Originally at Heineken Spain, Garcia was later the Innovation team leader at Heineken USA where, among other projects she helped introduce the new Amstel XLight. She is known for partnering Heineken with the Champions League, a soccer league that counts more than 4.2 billion fans globally.

As Tecate VP, she touted the Tecate brand across genders and cultures, including emphasizing its versatility at family meals and its low-calorie appeal. She solidified Tecate's reign in the world of boxing, and increased market share in soccer. Garcia has a history of affinity for boxing and soccer, and that personal passion increased Tecate's presence in major sporting events.

Her involvement in boxing and soccer on both sides of the border made her, as

AdWeek announced, "One of the most powerful women in sports."

After over six years with Heineken/Tecate, Martin returned to Spain to oversee communications at L'Oréal, a European company specializing in beauty products around the world.

Visit the Brewery

In 1994, to celebrate its 50th anniversary, Tecate Brewery opened a small beer garden on the premises. I stopped for a visit back then and noted bright white chairs and tables with the familiar Tecate logo scattered about in a pleasant garden setting where a bartender poured samples.

In December 2018 the current Tecate Beer Garden (Jardin Cerveza) opened to the public. The new modern Beer Garden offered an inside bar area, ample seating, an outdoor patio on the main floor and an upstairs balcony terrace with tables. There is a gift shop to purchase caps, shirts, and anything else you might want with the Tecate logo.

The brewery tours

The brewery, only seven blocks from the International border crossing in Tecate, offers guided tours. Most tours are on Saturdays but groups can make arrangements for tours during the week.

The brewery tours feature 24 large 250,000-gallon tanks which produce 5 million gallons of beer each month. The product takes 25 days from start to final packaging. Once in the canning facility, 4,000 cans per minute can be processed. The cans themselves are manufactured by a subsidiary company, Ensenada's Fabrica Famosa, and shipped the 70 miles to Tecate. Every effort is made to recycle (cardboard boxes, etc.) or reuse (bottles are sterilized and reprocessed) materials generated by the company.

Note: The brewery suspended tours during the COVID pandemic, and as of June 2024 have not resumed tours. Please check before going.

From San Diego you can get to Tecate via public transportation and walk across the border. The bus from the El Cajon Trolley Station goes to the Tecate border eight times a day.

One used to be able to arrive by train. Unfortunately, due to a collapsed tunnel, the nostalgic 15-mile train ride from Campo, CA through hills and wooded valleys direct to Tecate has been suspended. According to the Pacific Southwest Railway Museum Association, there are no immediate plans to resume that service.

Brewery tour notwithstanding, Tecate, one of Mexico's charming Pueblos Mágicos, is a great place to visit. At 1,770 feet elevation, Tecate is in a picturesque valley near the base of Mount Tecate (Mount Kuchumaa to the indigenous locals) which straddles the international border. You can hike to the summit up a nine-mile dirt road gaining 2,000 feet more elevation and a magnificent vista.

Tecate is also home to the world-class spa Rancho La Puerta, a relaxing retreat nestled among the oaks on the slopes of Mount Tecate.

For a more in-depth knowledge of local history, a visit to the Museo Comunitario Kumiai in Tecate is worthwhile.

Many head to Tecate just for the food. The highly regarded (5 Star) Restaurante Amores offers contemporary dishes with a varied menu. And then there's El Mejor Pan de Tecate, one of Baja's better bakeries.

Or you can just join the locals relaxing in the inviting Parque Miguel Hidalgo, a tree-shrouded plaza in the heart of town.

The city of about 120,000 also hosts the annual Tecate-to-Ensenada bicycle ride, with thousands of cyclists from both sides of the border participating. The city also hosts a two-week celebration in July that features dance groups, crafts, food concessions, and exhibits (Los Encinos Park).

Tecate Can

However, the name Tecate is most often identified worldwide with that ubiquitous Tecate beer, whose distinctive logo is a cultural icon.

Those cans often get a second life too. It seems that whenever you drive the Transpeninsular highway and come across a stalled truck, or an accident, or construction, that the shiny bright red and glimmering gold Tecate can is often used as a highway flare.

(For a couple of great books set in Tecate I recommend any of Daniel Reveles' books, including *Tequila, Lemon and Salt*, or *Enchiladas, Rice, and Beans*. While Reveles passed away in December 2019, his insightful glimpses of life in Tecate live on.)

Trout Streams in Baja (2023)

While the piscatory stars that put the Baja California fishery on the map are saltwater species, there are freshwater fish in Baja. They're in the Sierra San Pedro Martír and the surviving native trout there can thank a dedicated businessman from Orange County for their continued survival.

Back in 1905 a native species of rainbow trout was discovered in the San Antonio Creek and a few streams of the San Pedro Martír by Edward W. Nelson and was subsequently called the Nelson Rainbow Trout *(salmo nelsoni)*. Nelson was a biologist who later published *Lower California and Its Natural Resources* for the National Academy of Sciences in Washington D.C.

Later, in 1925, the University of California Museum of Vertebrate Zoology sent an expedition to Baja to study the rare new species.

Expedition member Chester C. Lamb, Assistant Curator of Mammals for the museum, said, "So far as known, only one stream in Lower California is inhabited by trout, namely the Santo Domingo River. This stream heads on the west slope of the San Pedro Martír Mountains, and the trout exist chiefly in one of its branches, San Antonio Creek, and in that branch almost altogether above Rancho San Antonio.

"At the time our fish were collected, it is believed that the species existed in only about five miles of the course of the stream, for the reason that at least 15 miles of the lower course was, at that season, dry. About five miles above Rancho San Antonio are waterfalls above which no trout are known to occur."

A 1926 University of California Press booklet *The Trout of the Sierra San Pedro Martir, Lower California* by John Otterbein Snyder detailed the findings of the expedition. Snyder wrote, "The cañon of the river in which these trout live is narrow and deep, and the water, according to Mr. Lamb, at times becomes warm. Insect life, too, is plentiful. The trout were found to be extremely abundant and easily caught. About 150 were taken on two fly hooks, one a brown hackle and the other a royal coachman."

While the scientists offered pages of measurements and comparisons, in layman's language they concluded that the new trout is most closely related to the Kern River trout and various species of the golden trout of the Kern River region. The similarities are the position of the dorsal, and the bright tips of the dorsal, anal, and ventral fins.

It is a wonder that the fish survived and proliferated given their limited habitat. Responsible for resurrecting the Baja fishery was Charles E. Utt, (1866-1950) a self-driving person who was in the habit of making things happen.

Based in Orange County, California, he owned the Utt Pioneer Store in Tustin. In 1896 he established the Tustin Water Works and later became president of the First National Bank of Tustin. He played a prominent role in establishing the Tustin Union High School District and what became the C.E. Utt Middle School.

In 1906 he leased 1,000 acres from James Irvine and became one of Orange County's most progressive agriculturists. He was president of the San Joaquin Fruit Company and the Utt Juice Company,

Utt's interests and enthusiasm knew no bounds. In 1924 he read the "fairly lengthy report of Mr. Nelson" and had to check out Baja's trout for himself. With a couple of companions he drove down to Hamilton Ranch and secured a guide, Claro Martorel, who lived near the ruins of the Santo Domingo Mission. "At San Antonio," Utt later wrote, "About 40 miles out by pack train we found trout in the river and in a branch commonly called La Zanja, which enters it at San Antonio."

After a little trout fishing, they went duck hunting and then bivouacked one day "beside a beautiful babbling brook near the old mission (San Pedro Martir) and mourned the absence of trout where there was such a beautiful home for them."

Over the next several years Utt was haunted by those several streams barren of trout. His solution: Do it yourself!

"It was in the summer of 1929 that with a companion I went again to San Antonio armed with a quantity of five-gallon cans for transporting the fish. As this was my first experience of the kind I did not know how many fish to put in a can nor how long they would live between changes of water. To be on the safe side I put five fingerlings (taken with ordinary fly hook) in each can....I loaded one mule with fish and another with four cans of water for change as I did not know how long it would be to water or how long the fish would live without change."

Utt flyfishing newly stocked stream

It was a difficult and challenging several days fine-tuning the process, including dumping fish in streams in the middle of the night, before they had stocked fish "both above and below the gorge."

"I did not again visit the newly stocked stream until 1934 (five years later) at which time I found it teeming with trout. The experiment had been so successful that I determined to extend my fish farms each summer."

Over the next few summers, when Utt did revisit and restock the streams he usually took family members, including his son-in-law Tomás Robertson. He often took two school-age grandsons (In 1938: Alan Robertson and Jack Deaver; in 1939: Leigh Robertson and Ted Deaver).

According to Leigh Robertson, "Grampa had developed cataracts in both eyes, and this was to be his last trip before having surgery. He really did not see very well, so he had Ted and me do most of the driving, even though we were not licensed.

"In those days the pavement ended about two blocks south of Hussong's, so it was a long day to the Hamilton Ranch, near present day Colonia Guerrero, about one hundred and ten miles.

"He had me stop and he took over the driving, as he alone knew the way. So, off we roared in the way Grampa did most things – impulsively, and at full speed. He said, "Boys, you know my eyes aren't too good, so you watch for boulders, cactus, or anything else that gets in the way." So, we frantically yelled warnings to him as we raced through sandy washes, over sagebrush, and around numerous large objects. It was an exciting ride to say the least.

"The next day, Grampa had Ted and me hike upstream, fishing along the way, to get some idea of how the fish were growing, in size and number....My brother, Alan, and cousin, Jack Deaver, had helped Grampa release fish several miles upstream the previous year. As a result of these efforts there are several miles of productive trout stream today."

In the 1940s Utt continued his project, getting help from the Meling brothers, Phil and Tom, from the area's Meling Ranch. Together, they had transported Nelson Rainbow Trout fingerlings to eight permanent streams including the San Jose, San Pedro and San Rafael streams (Mike's Sky Ranch). They did it by mule-back, pumping air into the cans every 30 minutes, day and night. The San Jose later dried up and the fish in that stream were lost. Trout in the other locations have survived.

Not content with all of his life's successes, Utt went on to establish the Utt Development Company in Oxnard and established ranches in the Simi Valley and Point Magu areas (Ventura County).

Utt's daughter and son-in-law Dorothy and Tomás Robertson had a farm near San Telmo and lived in San Miguel (near) Ensenada. Author Tomás wrote *Historical Notes on Baja California,* 1972, and *Baja California and Its Missions,* La Siesta Press, (1978). Their son Leigh Robertson (1923-2010) was born in Sinaloa, Mexico; he enjoyed his Baja trips and wrote me about some of his adventures.

C.E. Utt's son James B. Utt went on to become a U.S. Representative in Congress, serving all of Orange County (1953-1970).

Continuing the trout project implemented by Utt, in the early 1980s a group of Mexico City naturalists also transported trout to area streams.

In 2004 California outdoors writer Jim Niemiec joined Andrew Meling of Meling Ranch near San Telmo to fly fish for the trout of the San Pedro Martír. Their trout camp was located at the confluence of La Zanja and Santa Domingo creeks and was reachable only by way of a "narrow trail that zigzagged down a mountainside, taking about an hour from the end of the two-hour dirt road from Meling Ranch."

Niemiec happily reported then that the creeks were loaded with trout and the trek was worth it.

C.E. Utt modestly recapped his epic stocking undertaking: "I have added some 50 miles to the trout streams of this grand mountain but posterity owes me nothing, for I have had double pay in the satisfaction of work successfully accomplished. This exploit has given me more satisfactions than any or all of the numerous business enterprises I have helped develop—because it is more permanent.

"As long as water in sufficient quantities to sustain trout runs off the slopes of San Pedro Martir the disciples of Izaak Walton will be taking trout from its streams."

Memos from Mexicali and San Felipe

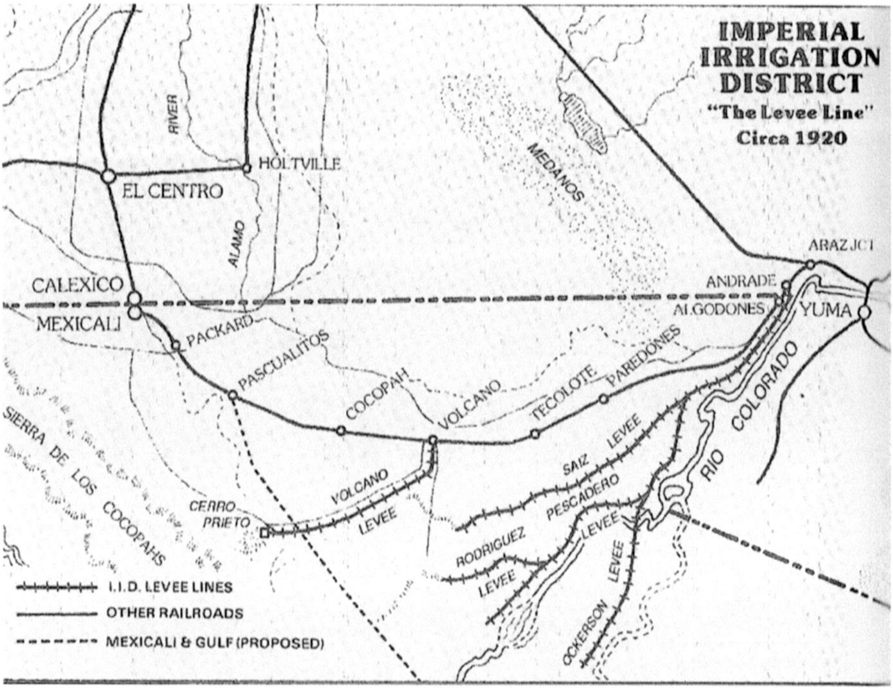

Mexicali Imperial Irrigation District circa 1930

Mexicali – Baja's Diverse Capital (2015)

Early in the 20th century American developers found what is today's Mexicali (Baja California's state capital and second largest city) in a hot barren desert of dust storms and desolation. Not far away was the Colorado River so they began building canals to divert water west, creating the vast Imperial Valley. The whole area on both sides of the international border became a fertile agricultural center.

Mexicali, earlier called La Laguna del Alamo, was first settled in 1898 by former miners who left the dwindling pickings at El Alamo near Ensenada to try their luck in the desert.

Going further back, it is known that Juan Bautista de Anza camped near the site in December 1775 on his way north. The desert was forbidding, however, and for well over 100 years the border area in what is now the Imperial Valley was claimed by no one.

One of the American agricultural pioneers, C. M. "Limpy" Holt, was the first to coin California's "Imperial Valley" name, thinking it projected a more positive image for a difficult and desolate area. But Holt did not stop there. He tinkered with the words California/Mexico, switched some syllables around and came up with names for the towns on opposite sides of the border (Cal-exico and Mexi-cali), and the names stuck, La Laguna del Alamo to be forever called Mexicali.

Water tamed the desert

After the Imperial Canal was finished in 1902, Mexicali began to grow as water became available for irrigation. Many of the earliest settlers came to work on the irrigation projects for the Colorado River Land Company, an American company which owned practically all of the land in the valley. The company then leased land for cotton and the workers stayed to cultivate their ensuing crops.

The founding date of Mexicali is March 14, 1903 and Manuel Vizcarra was elected the town's first Civil Authority. In 1904 Mexican President Porfirio Diaz authorized Mexican canals to divert more water to the Mexican side of the border.

A big flood occurred in 1906 as the waters of the Colorado River went over their banks. Levees and dikes were painstakingly reinforced and the planting of cotton, cantaloupes, alfalfa and corn resumed.

The Inter-California Railroad, a branch of the Southern Pacific, was built and went south from Calexico, through Mexicali, continued east through Baja California farmland and reentered the United States at Yuma. Not only was it a shorter route from the Imperial Valley to eastern markets but was able to tap the rich cotton and agricultural areas south of the border.

During the Mexican Revolution of 1911, soldiers of fortune came into Mexicali. Under the banner of an American labor movement, the IWW (Wobblies) tried to make Mexicali a Socialist enclave. They were driven off by the Mexican army but not before lives were lost and numerous wounded. Once the Wobbly leader was shot, the remaining anarchists gave up.

Stability was restored in 1915 by Colonel Esteban Cantu who served as Baja California Norte Governor in 1915-1920. He moved the Baja California territorial capital to Mexicali and was responsible for much of the infrastructure around the entire state.

In 1922, *Los Angeles Times* owner Harry Chandler, president of the Colorado River Land Company, was approached by Governor Canu's brother Jose Cantu to build and operate a railroad to San Felipe. That project, as well as later attempts, never got off the ground.

However, the railroad was doing well in the Mexicali area, and by 1928 an average three train loads a week of cotton (with up to 98 cars) were delivered from farms to Mexicali cotton gins.

Then, in 1936, the Colorado River Land Company was ordered by the Mexican government under President Lazaro Cardenas to sell most of its holdings to Mexican farmers and farm communities known as ejidos.

An exemplar of diversity

During the early years of Mexicali's history, the town was an exemplar of diversity with one report listing among the laborers approximately 5,000 Mexicans, 3,500 Chinese, 300 Japanese and 200 Hindus. But it doesn't mean they got along. For example, many Mexicans blamed the Chinese for taking 'their' jobs. Sound familiar?

There is still a large Chinese population, one of the largest concentrations per capita outside Asia. You can find excellent Chinese food among the reported 200 Chinese restaurants in the capital city. Recently the government began offering tours of La Chinesca (old Chinatown), including underground tunnels and hideaways.

Today's Mexicali covers 5,254 acres and is home to about 700,000 inhabitants, or right at 1,000,000 people if you count the surrounding area. The city maintains a highly educated and skilled population, having modernized to become an important population center.

While historically an agricultural economy, today Mexicali has gradually embraced other industries. Mexicali pioneered the aerospace industry in Mexico, when Rockwell Collins, (formerly Hughes Tool Company) decided to establish an operation there in 1966, becoming the oldest company under the maquiladora program nationwide.

Since then, many other companies, such as Honeywell, Gulfstream, SunPower, Mitsubishi, Autolite, Nestlé, Coca Cola, and Goodrich Corporation have built maquiladora plants in the city.

In 1986 Mexicali achieved international recognition with a meeting between then Mexican President Miguel de le Madrid and U.S. President Ronald Reagan.

The huge sand dunes to the east of the city have become an attraction unto themselves. Sandboarding has become big in the Algodones dunes. In fact, the 2016 Continental Sandboarding Cup was held there and attracted the sport's best athletes from countries like Peru, Switzerland, and Brazil as they tackled the massive mountains of sand.

Earlier this year I crossed the border at Mexicali and noticed a large construction project underway just south of the border on the right, confirming continuation of an expanding economy.

Gringos most often just drive through Mexicali on their way to San Felipe or other points south along the newly completed Highway 5, and that's a shame. Along with great Chinese food, there are a number of good inexpensive hotels to choose from, including those of the Fiesta Inn and Real Inn Mexican chains. Even the popular five-star Hotel Lucerna is still less than $100 a night. That iconic hotel with a cascade falling into the pool has been there a long time too, as we stayed there once back in the 1980s.

Mexicali is an interesting city, hugging the international border on the north, and continuing to sprawl in the other directions. On my last visit I made a wrong turn and found myself in a suburban area I never knew existed. But we found a great restaurant on our impromptu detour.

Mexicali is unique: farmers, ranchers, factory workers, merchants and politicos work side by side to keep it a viable city. It still seems a little weird, though, to cross the border into Mexico and order dim sum instead of tacos.

A Root Canal Holiday (2016)

When asked recently about dental care in Baja, I had to admit I was stumped. I had not been to a Mexican dentist in over 20 years, and back then that Rosarito area dentist did not do that great a job. Thereafter I got my "ivories" checked stateside, paying ever-increasing prices. But even in California I've had some hit and miss experiences too: having to redo a root canal, having a crown break within weeks, etc.

So I was ready to try Baja again, especially after learning more about Los Algodones. Following a personal recommendation, we were able to go online and set up appointments with a dentist in that border town dedicated to medical tourism.

Los Algodones (population 5,474 in the 2010 census) is unlike any Mexican destination you'll encounter. Almost everyone in town seems to speak English; and they use the U.S. Dollar way more than the Peso. In fact, most prices are posted and/or quoted in dollars. But most striking – the small town is home to over 40 dental offices, over 900 total doctors, 50 dental laboratories, and a goodly number of pharmacies.

Much lower dental costs

For roughly one-third to one-half of the price you would pay in the U.S. you can get everything in the way of dentistry procedures, prescription glasses, prescription drugs and other types of medical procedures and supplies. As Medicare and many private health plans do not include dental care, seeking lower costs is especially important to many seniors.

Near the extreme southeast corner of California, Los Algodones is less than 8 miles west of Yuma, AZ. And it is only a half-day drive from either San Diego (165 miles) or Palm Springs (162 miles). Part of the municipality of Mexicali, B.C., Los Algodones is the northernmost town in Mexico, and all of Latin America for that matter. An obelisk by the boundary fence that runs along the north end of town commemorates that fact.

I was surprised to see only one Los Algodones hotel listed on the internet. The Hacienda does have several on-line recommendations. They have a swimming pool, an improved newer section, and it looks private and inviting. It's on the east edge of town but still a short walk to everything.

Hotels are not that in demand as most people stay in the U.S. where a large, fenced parking lot (inexpensive) is designed for day-tourists. They simply walk across the border from California.

Some visitors opt for the closest stateside hotel, the Quechan Casino Resort, Winterhaven, California. It has a restaurant, pool, and of course the casino. Prices are decent and some of the dental clinics offer discounts at the Quechan Resort.

Nearby Yuma has about every type and price range of accommodation and we had made reservations there. So following our initial mid-day dental appointments we crossed back to the U.S. and headed for Yuma.

An easy border crossing

It was a pretty simple process driving across the border as most people walk across. Once in the little Mexican town you can park on the streets everywhere. There are also a couple of parking lots if you're antsy about leaving your car on the street.

Los Algodones

As Los Algodones relies on the Yankee dollar and Canadian Loon, there are hawkers everywhere, leading you to a medical service if you have not lined one up. Billboards, for example, advertise $20.00 teeth cleaning and all types of prescription drugs.

Stores and shops are full of typical Mexican souvenirs: serapes, sombreros, carved items, ceramic art, papier-mâché flowers and birds, t-shirts, and more. Those items did not entice us as we see that stuff all too often in our Mexican travels. But some of the day-crossers enchanted by the novelty items were dragging lots of them back to California.

We found a couple of great little open-air restaurants where fish and shrimp tacos came with all the trimmings. We especially liked Taqueria Molcas where you could almost fill up on the chips and appetizer platters. Mariscos El Paisa also looked appealing.

The town is so small (just several blocks in each direction), it is easy to find your doctor or dentist. We had been referred to Dr. Jorge Jimenez DDS, of Circle Dental Group. We made a right on the first street after crossing into Mexico and it was on the next corner. My wife got her teeth cleaned, but I had some major work done that afternoon. We returned the next morning for the impressions and crowns.

No waiting for crowns

One thing that I found commendatory is the promptness of the labs. Where stateside dentists take a couple of weeks to get a crown made, the dental demand in Los Algodones propagates numerous labs which all create crowns in less than an hour.

Along with Dr. Jimenez, I was attended to by a seemingly very young dentist, Dra. Ana Fajardo. She had a very gentle touch and friendly no-nonsense mannerisms.

I was impressed with the workmanship, and even more impressed with the price, about a third of what I was quoted in Palm Springs for a simpler process. To give you an idea, Circle Dental charges $30.00 for teeth cleaning, $50.00 for a filling, $190.00 for a porcelain crown, $70.00 for a tooth extraction, $220.00 for a root canal, and $800.00 for an implant (2016 prices).

There are larger and smaller clinics and every type of dental specialty is offered including teeth whitening, orthodontics and endodontics. The doctors and dentists are for the most part highly trained and have completed their studies at major universities and medical schools in both the U.S. and Mexico.

What border wait?

I'm always apprehensive about the long lines often encountered driving from Mexico back to the U.S.. Thus, we have Sentri cards which simplify and speed up the process. We didn't even need the Sentri leaving Los Algodones! The first time we crossed there were about six cars ahead of us, and the second time, only three. Sometimes you're the only one in line. I really like that border crossing!

Border Crossing Algodones

As mentioned most people don't even take their cars across. For that matter, many people don't even bother to drive to that remote part of California. There are organized day trips from the Coachella Valley and San Diego areas that are very popular with seniors.

Los Algodones doesn't have a lock on Medical Tourism. There are numerous pharmacies and dentists in Tijuana, Rosarito and Ensenada. One, called My Baja Dental offers free transportation across the San Ysidro border. Their listed prices appeared just a little higher than Los Algodones, but still way less than the U.S.

There's also Pacific Dental and the large Washington Dental Clinic in Tijuana, Baja Dental and the Avila Dental Group in Rosarito, and Clinica Dental del Puerto in Ensenada.

We figured that the money saved on just two teeth cleanings alone would pretty much pay for the fuel and night in a hotel. Plus, not only do they have great tacos at Taqueria Molcas, but I love that simple border crossing.

Into the San Felipe Desert (1999)

Way up the canyon Bruce waved his arm that all was clear. I turned to the next dune buggy in line and gave it the go-ahead signal. It slowly climbed up over the rocks, negotiated the tight canyon curve and plopped back onto the sandy arroyo to rejoin the others.

It was the tightest part of this off-road adventure and we wanted to negotiate the narrow space one at a time, as incredibly fast on-coming traffic had already come roaring down the canyon. While my group of 10 San Felipe-based dune buggies was out pre-running new desert tours, those heading in our direction were out pre-running the Tecate/SCORE San Felipe 250 off-road race, a shorter version of the Baja 1000.

Our objective was to learn a new tour route to take prospective dune buggy enthusiasts. It differed quite markedly from the objective of those coming directly at us – they wanted to see how fast they could drive over the same terrain.

Fortunately, only a short section of our opposing routes overlapped, and most of that was in a broad, sandy arroyo some 20 or so miles into the desert southwest of San Felipe.

It was back in March 1999 and it was the San Felipe 250 that lured me to town to help on a pit crew. While the racers were out pre-running, I looked up fellow writer Bruce Barber who covered San Felipe and the northern Sea of Cortez area for the old *Baja Times.*

My timing was perfect

My timing was perfect as Bruce, then President of the San Felipe Association of Retired Persons (SFARP), was leading a team of buggies out in the desert the next day and invited me along. Bruce, then 69-years old, had produced a very fine *San Felipe Magazine* and since my visit, has penned the book "*...of Sea and Sand*" (2003)

Bruce is a leader and knows and loves the San Felipe desert like no other. "I think he knows every single cactus by name," admired Irene Smith, owner of Baja Creations, a boutique and craft shop in town.

I had respected his desert knowledge from those earlier columns of a decade previous and this day I was in for a first-hand lesson. As he led the procession of buggies out of town he regaled me with facts. He reminded me of the way James Michener began one of his epic novels. He started his one-on-one class on the area's history by pointing to the barren and colorful hills and saying, "It started with the ice age." No lie!

He pointed to various colorations in the strata of the hillsides, naming the types of rock. He explained the forces of the area's infrequent water, how it gouged the depth of the gullies and created temporary reservoirs. "I call that depression Cardon Lake," he said, gesturing to delineate the depression, making it obvious even to the uneducated that water had at one time been backed up there.

As he and his buggy cut new trails up the arroyo, his whole presence was one of enthusiasm. "Oh, I love it out here; it's so beautiful. It's incredibly interesting, and so vastly different each day," he exclaimed exuberantly.

We stopped for lunch, everyone setting up handy little collapsible tables and chairs. The group relaxed and enjoyed sharing and swapping tall tales and stories along with specialties from various kitchens. Bruce's wife Freda was unable to attend this ride (that's how I gained a seat), but her short-lived chocolate chip cookies quickly gained a new fan.

Later, while drivers, spouses, and the handful of accompanying kids and dogs explored the nearby terrain, a few lead drivers pored over maps and discussed routes. It was obvious they deferred to Bruce's expertise, but he always made it a democratic decision.

Rain was threatening

While the others wrapped up lunch, I accompanied Bruce and Lou Wells in another buggy to explore a nearby arroyo. They wanted to see if it would link up with a road heading north. It didn't, and we returned to report to the others. Bruce laid out the facts and let democracy take over. We were running late and rain was threatening. We could either head back the same way or continue around to the north by first going south.

As five of the buggies were based south of town at Laguna Percebu, those five drivers opted to return. Bruce lives in town and the other four lived north at El Dorado Ranch. They opted to continue. It was a good decision for all.

The other drivers had plenty of experience too. After all, they were the leaders for the organized off-road dune buggy trips then offered in the San Felipe area. They lead enthusiasts who arrive in San Felipe to the Giant Cactus Garden, or Shell Beach, or Indian Caves and Fossil Fields. They also visit any of several waterfalls in what from a distance appear to be dry canyons.

Don Dunn and his Barney Car

One of the drivers, Don Dunn, had become quite an expert in buggy design. He experimented building a different style buggy, a larger one for more passengers and payload. He also wanted larger front wheels. His unorthodox design has become known as a "Barney Car," in reference to the similar looking vehicle driven by the cartoon character Barney Rubble of the Flintstone fame. No one laughs at this car anymore, not after its performance in the desert. Bruce said, "They're great. We were out on the beach the other day and those Barney Cars ran circles around me."

Bundled up for warmth in the cold wind under ominous and threatening clouds, five of us continued on up the canyon. Our eyes strained to see oncoming traffic and a couple of times we moved off the rocky and sandy track to allow a racer to roar past.

It got colder as the wind picked up and finally large rain drops started pounding our open cars, drenching my jacket and setting my teeth to chattering. Hard to believe it could be that cold in a place where summer temperatures rise above 100 degrees almost daily. Some hail even fell before the storm passed on, pelting our exposed bodies with machine-gun staccato.

While uncomfortable, the infrequent rain brought a new dimension to the desert, heightening the senses. The sweetly pungent aroma of damp sagebrush, ocotillo, and mesquite mingled with the odor of fresh wet sand, created an invigorating and bracing fragrance.

The road's previous billowing dust had also dissipated with the rain, rendering a dark, not-quite-muddy, fast dirt road, like that of a hosed down baseball stadium infield.

During the day I'd seen a red hawk, several quail and roadrunners, vultures feasting on a dead cow, three wild horses, numerous cattle, jackrabbits, skinks and lizards. I saw forests of giant Cardon cactus, several the size of the 42-footer that was dug out of the area in 1992 and shipped to Seville for the World's Fair.

I also saw a gritty group of people who appreciate the desert for what it is. Unlike the race cars, the vehicles of these dune buggy enthusiasts take their riders <u>to</u> a place, not <u>through</u> it. Even though it was a nasty day in the desert, I loved it!

(2024 Update: Bruce Barber, retired Naval officer and consummate San Felipe expert, died in November 2018 at age 88. His wife Freda preceded him, passing away in 2015. The well-liked "Baja Lou" Wells died in November 2012.)

The Helping Hands of Baja (1986)

Back in 1986 I set out alone from Cantamar with my Baja-based CJ-5 Jeep loaded with toys (fishing rods and spears, boogie board, inflatable boat, etc.), and emergency-related gear like plenty of water, shovel, and two extra gas cans.

Objective: unwind, surf fish, explore old missions and mines, take notes and photos for a few stories, cross to the gulf and drive up the old road to Puertecitos (today's Highway 5) eventually reaching San Felipe to rejoin my wife and friends.

After camping on a deserted bluff overlooking the pounding waves near Punta Baja (south of El Rosario), I explored the San Fernando mission ruins, lunched at historic Rancho Santa Inez and drove out to the El Marmol onyx mine.

About 10 miles before the Cataviña/Santa Inez area, I stopped to offer assistance to a stranded Mexican couple. I refused his offer to pay for a gallon of my gas we siphoned for him. Little did I realize I would be on the receiving end of such assistance before the day was over. In Baja, help is generally freely offered.

Later I left Highway 1 and set off across Laguna Chapala's dry lakebed to begin my trek on the dreaded dirt roads further up the gulf. The road seemed "a piece of cake" as it crossed the lakebed and entered the foothills near Las Arrastras de Arriola.

The vibrations from the road's washboard effect were soon to take their toll however. Thump! Thump! I pulled over and through the thick, white cloud of dust saw a piece of my tailpipe in the road. I tossed it in the Jeep and continued onward.

The new graded road to Gonzaga Bay was still under construction, and just as the bay loomed into view, I had to rejoin the old road.

Alfonsina's appeared to be a cluster of homes on a sandbar off the bay. Heading for it, I was surprised at the depth of tidal water in the access road. One puddle was so deep, water flowed into the floor of the Jeep!

At the lagoon entrance at the south end of the appealing and inviting sandbar I noticed residents had even lined the road bottom with rocks and boulders for entrance and egress. But it still looked deep, so to check, I waded until my shorts were wet – and it was deeper still ahead! I decided to pass on Alfonsina's! I learned later that the highest tide of the month occurred the very hour I was there.

In hindsight, I should have camped nearby and waited because my troubles were about to begin. In the hills before Papa Fernandez's five miles away, I heard a "Pow" and felt the uneasy sway of a rapidly deflating tire.

Going through a narrow draw I must have hit a protruding rock, sharp enough to puncture both right side tires. And these were big, heavy duty desert tires. I wobbled to the right and parked, and with only one spare tire!

Knowing Papa Fernandez's place had to be about two miles up, I pulled over as far as I could and started walking. I felt a little uneasy leaving all my stuff in the open Jeep but knew that the people who inhabit and visit the wild hinterlands of Baja California are among the most honest on earth.

Just as I hiked up the draw, a stake truck came bouncing up the road behind me. The driver, a good-looking young man, stopped for me. I figured he'd give me a ride to the settlement ahead, but no, he took me back to the Jeep to see if he could get it rolling again. He was immediately willing to help without my asking; it was just the thing to do.

Back at the Jeep, it became apparent that even his innate resources were not enough. As the right rear tire was only three quarters flat, we tried to see if it would hold air. He removed a spark plug from his truck's engine and used the compression of his running engine to inflate the tire. Unfortunately, it would not hold the air long, so we jumped in his truck and set out to find help.

My Samaritan told me his family owned the Las Encantadas camp about seven miles up the gulf. But home could wait; I needed help. He drove directly to a small fisherman's camp of plywood shelters just to the south of Papa Fernandez's.

No, no one had a patch. Yes, one of the fellows would help me change my tires if we could find a patch. With my willing worker also in the truck, we set out to find a patch and drove into "downtown" Papa Fernandez's, where a few cottages surrounded a hard-packed clearing adjacent to a small store and palapa.

An American appeared from one of the cottages. He offered a patch and refused payment saying, "Favors have a way of coming back to you."

My Samaritan and I went to the Jeep but discovered the patch was useless without a tube and the tire was tubeless. Great. We threw the flat in the truck and headed back to Papa Fernandez's to hunt for a tube. Everyone looked around the compound. Soon an excited little kid emerged from a small shed waving a well-used tube that already had about 17 patches on it. Success! Sort of.

My helper added yet another patch but now mounting the ill-fitted tube into the large Jeep tire became a chore even with the engine-compression method of inflating. A bubble developed on one side, we dumped water, then oil on the rim so the tube would seat properly. It never did.

Back at the Jeep we put my spare on the front and the mishappen monstrosity on the rear. I paid my two saviors for their now over four hours of concern, help and time.

I had hired the helper outright and almost forced the driver to accept something for his time. I was then advised that the only place in the vicinity that "might" have some spare tire components would be at Punta Bufeo, a small development up the road.

Not graded yet, it was a brutal road, yet the jarring apparently helped the misshapen tube to seat properly and I arrived at Punta Bufeo as darkness was setting.

I set up camp on the beach and went for a quick dip to wash off the dust and relax off the frustrations of a long day. After breaking camp in the early morning, I sought the proprietor of Campo Bufeo.

After an hour of searching through his accumulated piles of rusting parts and scraps, we found an old Chevy tire mounted on a rim that had the correct number of lug bolt holes, and spaced correctly, but the axle hole would never have fitted over the protruding front axle on the Jeep.

"No problema," he said. "If you get a flat on the front, you take your rear tire and put it there, and put this one on the back." His broad smile and irrefutable logic prevailed, and I bought the tire and rim for an absolute-emergency spare.

It was 40 miles of very difficult road to Puertecitos, often called "Baja's worst." I set out full of anticipation.

The heat bore down on the Jeep. The 20 miles to Nacho's Camp was still bad; rocky ravines had to be traversed and sandy gullies negotiated. On a couple of occasions at rocky hills, I parked and got out to assess the road, to determine which tires I wanted on which rocks.

The volcanic cliffs north of Nacho's, having a history of proving superior to many vehicles, had been my greatest concern. My father even had to get towed out after smashing his oil pan in there in 1977. Others have had to abandon their vehicles there.

But by June 1986, highway crews were busy blasting and widening what would eventually be Mexico Highway 5. I felt exhilarated that the end was in sight.

Puertecitos glistened in its quiet, small bay. It looked as large as Acapulco to me at the time. At the town's sole restaurant, the owner set three different cold sodas on the counter. I chugged them all before she had the cooler door shut. She looked at me quizzically, I paid, smiled, tipped my cap and walked out.

About 20 miles out of San Felipe, my clutch foot went all the way to the floor. No clutch! It turned out to be a screw that had been jostled loose – but I didn't know. I was afraid that if I stopped I might not get going again.

So I limped into San Felipe in high gear, lugging the engine and aimed the chugging Jeep toward the campground, relieved to rejoin my wife and friends.

In many ways it was a good trip. I experienced and photographed a lot of interesting and fascinating sites. But my difficulties became positive too. The way the people of Baja attack adversity with help and kindness almost made the adversity welcome.

Books on the Balcony (2002)

There's a balcony in the heart of San Felipe facing the sun-kissed rocky peaks across the bay. As shrimp boats head off each morning into the rising sun and pelicans begin their pursuit by skimming the placid Sea of Cortez, the balcony comes to life.

It's still dark out when the first of the three gringo-based businesses that share the balcony prepares its day. Lights go on at Baja Java and soon the tantalizing smell of fresh coffee and their signature cinnamon rolls help lure the town's early risers upstairs for their morning caffeine fix.

Then the proprietors of the bookstore called the San Felipe Title Company arrive and begin preparing the outside bargain racks. The third business, the one-man Shadetree Computer Services, depends less on normal pedestrian traffic and more on reputation to help keep the town's gringo community on-line.

The many expatriates and snowbirds who escape colder climes for the winter make a regular pilgrimage of visiting the balcony. They come from their in-town abodes, or from campos and developments from El Dorado up north to Percebu to the south where their homes run the gamut from temporary trailers to beautiful waterfront residences.

Gringos in foreign countries tend to band together, to insulate themselves from the very exotic, foreign culture that attracted them in the first place. This is true too of those in San Felipe, a fishing village turned tourist destination on the Sea of Cortez, some 120 miles south of Mexicali. Some gringos only peripherally enjoy the Mexican culture, while others learn as much as possible about their host countrymen and get involved in local affairs whenever they can.

Regardless of their bent, most Americans and Canadians who spend time in San Felipe enjoy the same habits and the same rituals. For example, a trip to town usually means a stop on the balcony, just left above the stop sign where the Mexicali highway dead-ends at the sea.

Fascinating backgrounds

The balcony businesses have more in common than their location and clientele. I've found that all of the principals share fascinating backgrounds; indeed they have all been successful in other endeavors.

Baja Java was the first on the balcony and an endless parade of gringos meet there for coffee, breakfast or lunch or just to chat. Fruit plates, large waffles, piles of pancakes, thick club sandwiches and typical burgers are served along with more Mexican fare like Huevos Rancheros.

Affable owner Karen Bradley established Baja Java back in 1997. Most of the tables are outside on the balcony where they either overlook the sea or the town's main street. Karen cordially oversees her competent staff and takes time to enjoy small talk with her customers.

As an example of the fascinating backgrounds, in another life Karen is Major Karen Bradley of the United States Air Force Reserve. She often spends time at March Air Force Base in California as a Flight Nurse.

Her husband Vince, who used to work in California and only joined Karen in San Felipe on weekends, now assists at Baja Java full time. Interesting job he left too. He was Dr. Vincent D. Bradley, an internist who is a Diplomate of both the American Board of Gastroenterology and the American Board of Internal Medicine. You never know who's serving your scrambled eggs.

A passion for reading

The bookstore is the result of the reading passion of its founder and owner, Catalina (Cat) Meders. Her husband Ed claims, "She reads all the time; I bet we still have 2,000 personal books at home."

The Meders originally discovered San Felipe after winning a lot at El Dorado through the National Pen giveaway of a few years ago.

Originally the lots there were free, a National Pen promotional giveaway in which a sweepstakes offered deeds on license for property in El Dorado Ranch Estates. Back in the 1980s I had several friends dubiously ask me about the "sweepstakes" they won and I learned that the giveaway was valid and legal, but added to my report that most of the lots were a long way from anything, with no water, no power, and no services.

Ed and Cat of The San Felipe Title Company, 2002

As more and more people claimed their lots and began development, that isolation is no longer the case and El Dorado is now San Felipe's largest residential and retirement community.

Drawn to the area by the lottery, Ed and Cat decided to settle in downtown San Felipe as the charm of the small fishing village had hooked them completely.

Cat started the San Felipe Title Company in early 2000 and expanded into a formerly vacant space next door to Baja Java. Incredibly organized, there is a book section for everyone: Fiction, Mysteries, Computers, Biographies, Inspirational, Children's, Management, Psychology, Cooking, Mysticism, Self Help and much more. There's a large selection of Baja-related books by the front door, and even small sections of books in German and French for European tourists. The books are mostly used, but there are many new ones, especially guidebooks and Baja books.

Cat, originally from Connecticut, attended the New York Institute of Art and is an accomplished artist who has shown at juried exhibits. She has several fine scratchboard art drawings (where black clay is scratched away to reveal wonderful white images) available in the bookstore.

In San Felipe, Cat teaches English to local kids three days a week. That they respect her and cherish their time with her is an understatement as I've seen them come by to visit even on weekends, one little guy even proudly bringing his parents to meet her.

Ed too is not necessarily what he seems. The Oakland native served 20 years in the U.S. Navy, retiring as a 1st Class Petty Officer. Then he spent three years in law enforcement as a sheriff up near the Oregon-California border. Now Ed leaves his wife's bookstore periodically to work trade shows in various major U.S. cities. He's a Trade Show Coordinator responsible for transporting and assembling large trade show booths and equipment for major corporations. He coordinates and dispatches scores of truckloads of equipment for each show. He also admits to being an employee in his wife's bookstore.

Keeping the gringos online

Since the coffee shop patrons are attracted to the books and the browsers need to grab a quick bite, it made sense when a small computer business entered the scene. A Canadian who attended the University of Victoria, owner Randy Kerr is an admitted former air force brat who has been self-employed most of his life. He came to San Felipe 17 years ago, spending eight months a year in Mexico and returning to Vancouver Island, B.C. the other four. In 1991 he moved to San Felipe permanently. He's an accomplished electrician, photographer, carpenter (He built the beautiful new bookshelves for the bookstore) and computer technician.

Among his many skills and interests, Randy is an avowed reader and writer. He has sold about 15 articles to mostly literary magazines and has been working on a novel. He is also currently in the process of compiling his collection of Baja-related writings into book form. Already spending time at the bookstore and helping many in town with their computers, it seemed a logical step to open the one-man shop in the balcony's remaining space. His eclectic and varied background fits right in with his neighbors too.

I could have named this article "Books, Bagels and Bytes on the Balcony." But as the proprietors all interact and relate not only to each other but to a large appreciative community, perhaps "Buddies on the Balcony" might be better.

As I look out over the sea and watch the bright blue waters of the gulf come in with the spectacular tide, I readily feel the warmth of Mexico. It's a multi-faceted warmth: warmth from the sun, warmth from the friendly locals, and the warmth of companionship. It becomes easy to see how successful people have been tempted to slow down, switch direction, and begin a more satisfying life on the balcony.

(2022 Update: The balcony has changed. Ed and Cat Meders initially moved to an enlarged space a few blocks away and have since closed that bookstore. They are now living in Puerto Vallarta and we enjoy seeing them on our annual visits. Karen Bradley had moved Baja Java to a larger location on the highway. And Randy Kerr splits his time between San Felipe and Canada.)

San Felipe Attracts Snowbirds (2005)

It's not the same old San Felipe on the Sea of Cortez, where hot desert sands merge with warm gulf waters. The dusty little fishing village that used to signify the end of the road some 120 miles south of Mexicali has been changing. While

Mexican locals have paved most of the streets in recent years, that's not the biggest change. It's that the gringos have discovered it.

San Felipe Snowbirds

Adventurous gringos, you understand, have been going to San Felipe for years, but it's been primarily off-roaders, fishermen and party-bound college kids.

The new breed of gringo is older, definitely raising the community's average age. Instead of helmet and goggles and a fishing rod, it's silver hair, wrinkles and a walking stick. And these newer "party animals" prefer a night of bingo to an amped-up disco.

No permanent settlement was attempted in San Felipe until a road was put in to a radar station south of town by Abelardo L. Rodriguez, Governor of Baja California from 1923-1929 and later President of Mexico.

The paved highway came in 1951 and hastened the development of San Felipe. Fishing and other limited tourist activities began to attract adventurous gringos to the little village between the mountains and the Sea of Cortez.

San Felipe's population now increases from about 20,000 to almost 30,000 each winter as U.S. and Canadian expatriates, mostly retired snowbirds who flee their northern climates, come to enjoy their second homes in the San Felipe area. In fact, the very active San Felipe Association of Retired Persons has numerous meetings and activities from October through May.

Some of these retirees live in town, but most are in communities, both basic accommodations like trailer parks, and luxurious waterfront homes, strung out along the gulf to the north and south of town.

El Dorado Ranch

The biggest development by far is that of El Dorado Ranch, thanks to the aforementioned National Pen Company lot giveaway. It's about seven miles north of town, and it's got something for almost every budget.

According to Mike Delaney of National Pen, the property was subsequently sold to the current owners and they have been running it ever since. He said, "From what I understand it has expanded quite a bit and has become quite a nice resort."

Today 35,000 acres of the vast 200,000-acre El Dorado Ranch are being developed into about 10,000 homesites, with approximate quarter-acre lots with sea and mountain views priced from $28,500.

The developers are aggressive marketers, primarily targeting "baby boomers" throughout California, Oregon and Washington. They even offer "flyaway weekends" to San Felipe from the Bay area. It's hard to attend a west coast festival, home show or fair without seeing an El Dorado Ranch booth. In fact, they lured 10,000 visitors to San Felipe last year to check out their offerings.

People have been snapping up lots and many homes have been built, some for as little about $50-$60 per square foot. While many sections being developed are across the highway from the sea, some are right near its shores. Regardless, the desert terrain slopes about 3-4 percent toward the sea, so most lots do enjoy sea views.

Over 3,000 El Dorado lots have been sold and 900 home sites leased. In addition there are two RV parks, two restaurants and bars, and casita rentals. One subdivision contains the world's largest solar and straw bale home community. Homes made from straw bales and coated with stucco are extremely energy efficient.

The El Dorado Beach and Tennis Club is the hub of activity and features heated swimming pool, spa, wading pool, La Palapa open air bar and lounge area. Nearby are tennis courts, riding stable, the General Store, Juanito's Cantina, horseshoe and pool tournaments, and yes, weekly bingo games.

If the snowbirds thought that was something to crow about, "they ain't seen nothing yet." A new community called the San Felipe Beach Club is rising along the shorefront adjacent to the El Dorado Beach and Tennis Club.

A Golf Course in San Felipe

Situated on 266 acres, the more upscale San Felipe Beach Club will feature a 240-room all-suite hotel with spa, 160 condos, time-shares, 760 additional home sites and an 18-hole golf course. Lots at the San Felipe Beach Club start at $62,000 and all of the 355 residential lots allocated in Phase One have already been sold.

Phase One includes a nine-hole golf course (construction commenced on March 28, 2003 and is expected to open in Spring, 2004), 355 residential lots (sold out), the hotel with spa, and 160 condos. Phase Two will begin directly upon completion of Phase One and will include nine holes of golf, a practice range, golf clubhouse, and 405 additional homesites.

The La Ventana del Mar Golf Course at the San Felipe Beach Club will be only the second one on Baja's Sea of Cortez (The other is at Loreto some 600 miles south), and one of only a few outside of the Los Cabos area. Bradford Benz, a noted golf-course designer from San Jose, CA, with 31 years' experience and 136 golf courses worldwide to his credit, was called upon to lay out the course in harmony with the natural environment.

Salt-tolerant grass and plants, called halophytes, are being utilized hoping to greatly reduce the need for fresh water in an area where that is a scarce commodity.

The completed 18-hole championship golf course will be 7,152 yards with three lakes and 80 bunkers. It will be open to the public with discounted green fees for San Felipe Beach Club residents.

The fishermen, off-roaders, adventurers, and party animals will still be finding their way to the village of San Felipe to enjoy their pursuits. Old Baja Buffs can still set up camp under the stars on nearby beaches and rise to a glamorous and dramatic sunrise and later munch fish tacos on the streets.

The area has so much to offer, with its 340 days of sunshine each year and with the beautiful sparkling Sea of Cortez, that it was inevitable that communities "just like home" would eventually spring up. "Fore," or should I say, "Bingo, anyone?"

A Big San Felipe Welcome (2009)

San Felipe, that northernmost village on the Baja California peninsula near the broad, sandy mouth of the Colorado River, is unlike many Mexican towns. There is no graceful old cathedral bordering a busy and shady central square where wizened old men, weary vendors, and bony dogs hold court. But it's not quite American either. A visitor might find those missing iconic Mexican hosts hanging out by the beach anyway.

It's a unique sort of place, with incredible tides, lots of sun, and lots of gringos – especially in the winter when the snowbirds come to roost.

It had been seven years since my last visit and San Felipe had grown considerably in that time. After driving down the flat 120-mile road south from Mexicali, I neared town to be greeted by a four-lane highway bordered by a few emerging businesses. And I was still some five plus miles out!

It was November 2009 and I was invited to do a book signing at the downtown bookstore, San Felipe Title Co., which had moved from its earlier balcony home. I was also scheduled to give a slide presentation at the Mexico Living Home Show at the El Dorado Ranch the next day.

The Home Show, with over 65 exhibitors and a dozen speakers, is indicative of the area's growth. Booths ran the gamut from promoting restaurants to realtors, storage facilities, medical, insurance salespeople, contractors, cabinet makers, and landscapers. A lot of service companies I noted. My early journeys there

San Felipe Title Company with Event Announcement

camping on the beach seemed so much simpler.

The show was held at the La Ventana del Mar Golf and Beach Resort, an 18-hole championship golf course managed by the efficient Sharry Appleyard, a transplanted Canadian. Open to the public, it offers discounted green fees for La Ventana and El Dorado Ranch residents.

The La Ventana del Mar development is all part of the huge El Dorado Ranch, which occupies much of the area north of town.

J. Patrick Butler is the developer who bought the vast 200,000-acre El Dorado Ranch from National Pen. He's continued to divide about 35,000 acres into approximate quarter-acre homesites with sea and mountain views.

It turns out Pat Butler's home in Palm Springs is less than two blocks from mine. But Baja is what Butler is all about, and he has definitely put his money where his mouth is.

He mentioned that over 9,000 El Dorado lots have been sold and 2,200 homes have been built, a far cry from the 2005 projections above. They dot the desert on both sides of the highway, from the gulf to the mountains – tile-roofed stucco buildings rising up from the sand here and there to lord over the ocotillos, palo verdes, and cacti.

Butler also waxed enthusiastic about his downtown San Felipe projects. He's building the Light House condominiums with a planned 200 units, restaurant, and pool. The former Los Misiones Hotel is closed and being remodeled by Butler as he transforms the place into the Club Habana Resort and Spa, a modern 120-room hotel, and an additional 201 condominiums next door. Butler's a Hemingway fan, and the name is kind of a tribute to "Papa" and his years in Cuba.

President Rodriguez' family

I was surprised when a young man with a camera approached my Home Show booth and said, "I like what you wrote about my family."

"Well, thank you, and who is your family?"

He gave me his business card, "Victor Rodriguez Ratliff." Turns out the photographer is the grandson of, and raised by, the former Mexican president.

I had written about San Felipe in my book Baja Legends and how Abelardo L. Rodriguez, Governor of Baja California from 1923-1929 and later President of Mexico, was instrumental in paving a road to town.

The Rodriguez family founded and still operates the El Cortez Hotel, where I've stayed several times. The downtown hotel was celebrating its 50th anniversary in 2009.

I enjoyed seeing old friends and making a few new ones. Along with Ed and Cat Meders, Randy Kerr, and Karen Bradley, it was good to see residents Lou Wells, Erv and Sally Hand, and Casey Hamlin (Casey's Vacation Rentals).

A new restaurant, La Vaquita, opened downtown since my last visit. Managed by Sergio Leon Cuevas, it specializes in the area's abundant seafood.

I revisited the brothers who own and run the "Rosita's" and "Rice and Beans" restaurants, both on the malecón. Luis Romo Corta operates Rice and Beans, and brothers Rigoberto and Martín cater to a mixed crowd of locals and tourists at Rositas.

From October to May there is always something going on in San Felipe. I was there a week after the big Shrimp Festival and a week before the SCORE Baja 1000, although a lot of racers were already in town prerunning the nearby course. There's also the Baja 500, Baja 250 (which starts and finishes in town), other off-road races and much more.

There are numerous gringo groups and organizations to keep the "expats" occupied, and the town "parties hearty" during spring break. The mostly older snowbirds rule, but the fishermen, off-roaders, adventurers and party animals still find their way to the village of San Felipe.

It may not be a typical Mexican village, but the area has much to offer, including 340 days of annual sunshine and spectacular sunrises over the beautiful sparkling Sea of Cortez.

(2022 Update; As mentioned earlier, Ed and Cat Meders have relocated to Puerto Vallarta.)

La Unica, a Baja Hideaway (1999)

Imagine being on your own private island with a small staff cooking meals and bringing made-to-order drinks at your command. A place where you can lay on the broad, sandy beach or languish in tepid water all day long. Where you can grab a kayak or snorkel on a reef teeming with tropical fish. A place where your own modest bungalow faces a dramatic sunrise and a night sky so black the Milky Way looks like an artist's creamy brush stroke across a black canvas.

Sounds like an ultra-expensive mid-Pacific hideaway for the mega-rich, doesn't it? But what if I told you it's not really an island but a landlocked cove, and not in the mid-Pacific but only a short two-hour plane trip away, halfway down the Baja California peninsula. And that the price is within reach of most families. Intriguing? Yes. Unique? Yes. In fact, that's what the place is called, La Unica, The Unique.

Baja AirVentures, owned and operated by Kevin Warren, flies its guests 286 air miles south to this rustic wilderness retreat on Baja's Sea of Cortez. A paragon of isolation, La Unica hugs a broad, white sandy beach facing a beautiful, emerald-green bay bordered by its own island.

Last month I visited La Unica, a unique trip for me as well. I've driven all over Baja on my own and this was the first time I sat back and let someone else entertain me.

La Unica has no shops, no town, no television, no electricity even, save that provided by a small generator for the kitchen/palapa/social center. Furthermore, it has no road and no landing strip, rendering it more of an isolated island than most islands really are. In addition to the flight, guests and supplies are shuttled in by a 26-foot panga. While it may lack amenities often taken for granted, it offers some priceless beauty and solitude of a kind impossible to find only a few hours away.

We flew from Brown Field

I joined Kevin, who also serves as chief pilot, activities director, guitar strummer and more, at San Diego's Brown Field where a guest family and I piled into his Cessna 207 for the two-plus hour flight to the small village of Bahia de los Angeles. Another pilot, Baja AirVenture's Tom Wood brought the guests' friends, another family, in a Cherokee Six.

Upon arrival, we buzzed the small town so the taxi van could pick us up. While Kevin and Tom loaded the panga, we guests (two professional couples from San Diego and their total five children between the ages of 9 and 12 plus a 5-year-old girl), visited the small town's wondrous Natural History and Cultural Museum.

As I had driven to the town earlier in the summer, the main adventure for me was the flight itself. A long day's drive was reduced to a couple of hours. Most exciting was seeing the Baja California terrain from only a few thousand feet. I saw canyons I'd hiked and towns I knew and roads I'd driven. I saw enticing places that demand further scrutiny in the future.

One doesn't arrive at La Unica by air or car so we piled into the large panga for the 45-minute boat ride south to the Bahia de Pescadores. As we turned into the inviting bay, the only visible life on the virgin landscape was La Unica itself.

Ten blue and white bungalows lined up like soldiers face the bay. In their center was a larger structure, a 25' high, 40' diameter palm-thatched palapa which would become our social center over the next few days.

We were assigned bungalows, each furnished with two cots, padding and sleeping bags. Hey, it's a wilderness retreat, not a luxury hotel. Most relaxing was the hammock outside.

Small Cabanas at La Unica

Each bungalow has its own bathroom with flush toilet and a big shower stall where solar freshwater shower bags are strung. Each room has a lantern as the only power is the generator for the main palapa; even that is turned off about 9:30 rendering guests time to sit on the beach and sing, time to marvel at the starry night, time for reflection or to go to bed early, tired from the pace of doing nothing but play.

And La Unica has lots of toys. There are several types of kayaks including three with rudders and inside seats. There's snorkeling equipment, fishing poles, windsurfing equipment, a small sailboat, horseshoes, badminton, ping pong and more. We hiked; we snorkeled with sea lions; we saw whales. The panga was in use constantly; a couple of us fished for yellowtail, dorado, bonito, grouper and bass just outside the cove. In the afternoon it was used to pull the boys water-skiing on a surfboard around the bay. By the third day two youngsters had mastered standing up on it.

Catching squid by lantern light

Most exciting was the night we all went calamar (squid) fishing. We boarded with life jackets after dark and took off across the bay. Kevin, Tom and Captain Maleno Leyva Hernandez, who's been with La Unica for three years, then fired up a lantern creating an eerie light across the water, and we dropped our lines. One of the boys asked, "How do we know when a squid bites?"

"You'll know," laughed Kevin, "You'll know."

I realized what he meant as just then my rod doubled over and I was hooked into an 18-inch squid. Before I could land him everyone else had hooked up and it was a riot landing all these heavy squid that were squirting water all over the place. Within minutes we had well over a dozen of them and headed back. We were all drenched, but exuberant from the quick and powerful action.

Chef Dagoberto Camacho Urias outdid himself preparing our fresh calamar the next day. We ate fresh fish, and the other meals and snacks were good and filling. The staff remembered who drank what and constantly offered Cokes, beers, and margaritas. It was a strange blend of rustic opulence.

Kevin, whose Baja AirVentures has been flying surfers to Natividad Island and points south since 1989, opened La Unica in March 1996 with just the palapa and two cabins. He presently can accommodate 16 guests and has two more cabins under construction. He found the pristine bay by flying over it. One day in late 1995 he stopped in Bahia de los Angeles, made some inquiries and secured 228 acres with over a half mile of beachfront on the spot.

He would like to put in an airstrip. There's talk about a road going over the mountains to the bay, but no one really believes that will happen soon. Plus, its isolation is its charm.

This type of unique adventure is not for everyone. But for a quick few days' getaway, it should appeal to couples or families.

(2024 Update: Baja AirVentures is still operating but has moved its operation to Las Animas, a nearby bay. It is now called the Baja Airventure Las Animas Wilderness Ecolodge).

Tales from Baja Sur

Along the Pacific

The Big Tuna and the Storm (1998)

The tuna hit the bait hard, snapping me out of my reverie. It was 1998 and we were fishing out of the La Paz area. Leaving Punta Arena, we were north of Cerralvo Island at a seamount called El Bajo. My fishing buddy Don Lund, the skipper Jesús and I were drifting cut squid from our 23-foot panga, occasionally pulling the lines in to maneuver to another spot.

Most of the other pangas that day were commercial fishermen hand lining for bottom species. A half dozen boats also carried sportsfishers like us and we'd seen several tuna hookups nearby. So we drifted and waited, basking in the hot, humid July sun.

The tuna hit so hard I didn't even have to set the hook. The rod doubled over and my 50-pound line began singing off the reel. I tightened the drag a little lest I get spooled too easily, while Jesús and Don pulled in their lines.

Jesús even helped with the 65-horsepower outboard motor, maneuvering in the same direction as the fish. I cranked the reel, gaining a little line. The big fish pulled the hard-earned line right back out.

It was a stand-off and we'd just have to battle it out. Tuna don't seem to tire like marlin or sailfish, who after a few dramatic leaps in the air seem easier to boat. Pound for pound, tuna are the fightingest fish I've ever caught.

Don's 30-pound yellowfin tuna the day before took him a half hour to bring in. A few years previous, my 100-pound yellowfin tuna with my same equipment took two hours and ten minutes.

Tuna go straight down, deep. They circle. They fight. They don't jump, and they don't give up. I was in for a battle.

The heavy humid air along with the physical exertion had me sweating rivulets. My arms started getting sore.

Black cloud on the horizon

Looking about, I noticed a heavy black cloud above the horizon out over the gulf. The rest of the sky was bright blue with intermittent ivory clouds.

I battled the fish, gaining, then losing, then gaining again for about 40 minutes. That black cloud was coming closer, and as it did the wind picked up. We all noticed the abrupt change in weather. White caps roiling the water were moving closer to us.

I'd heard of chubascos, those often-regionalized, abrupt violent hurricane-like storms that strike almost without warning but had never experienced their fury. I'd been surprised by wind and a quick, choppy sea before, but never a full-blown chubasco – until this day!

Several of the boats took off to escape the approaching weather. Jesús was concerned. He agreed we too should leave as soon as we brought the fish on board. I fought standing up, without a shoulder harness, just a leather rod butt belt for another 10 minutes. The storm got closer, and the remaining boats were hastily beating retreats.

Fighting Tuna on Panga

I handed the rod to the younger, stronger 29-year-old skipper, hoping he could bring the fish in before we had to leave. Jesús knew time was of the essence better than either of us, and he tried to muscle the fish in.

The rod doubled over to where I was sure it would snap. For 15 minutes Jesús fought and fought, niggardly gaining back some of the line. The storm was now almost fully upon us and we all knew a decision had to be made. The last boat had just left and we knew we had to go.

We looked seriously at each other, saying nothing, but our eyes spoke volumes. I knew what I had to do. With Jesús holding the line taut, I grabbed my knife and cut the line, releasing my huge tuna to fight another angler, another day.

Jesús quickly grabbed the tiller and made for Cerralvo, about three miles away.

The sea got violent

The storm hit suddenly and the Sea of Cortez got violent. Not only were white caps all around us, but the ocean swells were huge and powerful.

The rain came in sheets, drenching us completely. With the rain the wind intensified. Don's cap blew off and sailed into the mean sky. The fish tank hatch blew off. I couldn't see. The salt water stung my eyes. My throat got sore from swallowing so much salt water which splashed over us with the wind and rain.

Visibility became minimal for all of us. Occasionally out of the dark cloud I could see the outline of the island which seemed so far away. Then it would disappear. I don't know how Jesús kept the panga in the right direction.

Wind-whipped waves came at us unrelentingly. The bow of our fragile panga would ride up one wave only to be slammed into the trough, exacerbating pain in my long-suffering back. We held on for our lives, and sometimes the jolts were so sudden our hands would break loose of their hold on the gunwale and slam back down adding pain to our fingers and joints.

Sometimes the waves were so close the bow would slam into the next wave, digging right into it with a scary and painful jolt.

Some wave sets were huge, six, eight feet and more, and if Jesús did not approach them just right, we'd roll from side to side, coming close to capsizing.

I looked into the roiling water, waves furiously moving from east to west. The western lee of the island was straight ahead. A strong swimmer might make it, but not in a storm like this. He would be swept far to the west, where the Baja landfall was many miles away. Plus, as was too often the case in Baja pangas, we had no life jackets so survival would have been iffy at best. If we tipped over, I concluded that it would be best to try to hang onto the boat.

A half hour of terror

It took about a half hour of sheer terror before we reached the lee of the island and safety. We looked at each other and could visibly see the tension slip away. Jesús breathed easier and it was only then when I realized this 12-year fishing veteran had also been very unnerved.

"Señor," he said, once we displayed tentative smiles and tried to relax, "Thank you for cutting your fish. I think five minutes more we would have been in big trouble. We left just in time."

We stayed close to the shoreline down the 12 miles of Cerralvo Island. The sun came out and it seemed peaceful. But ahead we still had about a five-mile storm-whipped channel to cross to get to Punta Arena and the mainland.

We headed into the chop and the waves were large and formidable. I looked back and Jesús made a circle of his forefinger and thumb, meaning, "It's okay; it's tough, but nothing I can't handle." And he handled it expertly, riding the troughs when he could, and turning directly into the larger waves. On really big sets, he even throttled down giving us a smoother ride up and down the roller coaster waves.

A crowd gathered on shore

A small crowd had gathered on shore. It appears most gringos had fished south of the island and did not experience the full onslaught of the chubasco. Someone said that one of the fishermen on the last boat in before us had got out and kissed the ground.

As we told our story to other gringo fishermen, Jesús was relaying our experience to fellow pangeros. About the fish, I heard him tell them, "No se, pero fue mui grande! Mas que 50 kilos," *I don't know how big it was, but it was real big, at least 50 kilos (110 pounds).*

In the spring of 2015, I visited Cuba and went to the village where Ernest Hemingway was inspired to write *"The Old Man and the Sea."* As I watched a few weathered old Cuban fishermen come in, I recollected my 1998 experience in Baja and thought about when I lost my fish. While Hemingway's "Old Man" lost his fish to a mighty predator, I had lost mine to a mighty storm.

During that storm, I learned renewed respect for the strength of the yellowfin tuna, as well as greater admiration for the daring pangeros like Jesús. Most of all, I looked at the fickle Sea of Cortez through more weathered eyes. I will never again be casual about fishing there.

Honeymoon in a Hammock (1999)

By the late nineties it seemed that every second car heading down Baja's Highway 1 had been festooned with brightly colored polyurethane torpedoes–they call them kayaks! Looking like primary-colored hot dogs, some cars boasted two, three or even four, depending on how ingenious the driver is, or how large his family is.

By the decade's end, kayaking loomed as one of Baja's more pleasant diversions, already nurtured by such kayaking legends as Valeria Fons whose book *Keep It Moving* features a trip around the peninsula and Andromeda Romano-Lax whose 1995 book *Sea Kayaking in Baja* features 15 kayaking trips complete with maps.

It's little wonder that Baja California became one of the sport's hottest venues. The 800-mile-long shoreline of the Sea of Cortez has hundreds of coves, reefs and islets all itching to be explored. To make it even better, the shoreline is protected from the huge Pacific swell, is warmer, and is pretty much undeveloped.

Just go in any outdoor store like REI or Adventure 16 and check their pamphlet racks and you'll see what I mean. The words "Kayak" and "Baja" peek out at you from numerous brochures. I'd been all over Baja but had not tried kayaking—until May 1999, that is.

That's when I arrived in Mulegé on Baja's Sea of Cortez, secured a room at the legendary Serenidad Hotel and set out to find the environmentally-conscience kayaking concern Eco Mundo. In addition to their operation on the shores of Bahia Concepcion, at the time they had a small office next door to the Las Casitas restaurant in town. Becky Aparicio and her partner Roy Mahoof, owners of Eco Mundo, had invited me down and I was to meet Becky at the restaurant.

Las Casitas (The little houses) is a legend itself. It's a delightful little five-room rambling hotel/restaurant across from little Hidalgo Park in the center of the village. First opened in 1961 by the daughter of area rancher Don Jose Gorosave, Cuca, and her husband Fred Woodworth, it is still popular.

It was a balmy Sunday evening. Relaxing in the outdoor bougainvillea-shrouded patio with a hot mesquite-fire searing the juices of not only meat but several lobsters as well, it was a wondrous Baja night.

The feeling of serenity was short-lived however as a nearby table of five middle-aged fishermen were starting to feel the effects of margaritas the size of birdbaths.

Soon two women entered and Las Casitas restaurant manager Javier Aguiar Zuñiga introduced me to Becky Aparicio and her friend Sherie who had flown down from San Diego for a visit. I joined their table to discuss kayaking and books.

When a young couple walked in, Becky flagged them over too. "Greg, this is Paul and Tracy from Chicago. They're here on their honeymoon and are staying down at our palapas at Eco Mundo."

"Wow, what possessed you to come kayaking in Baja?" I asked them.

"We had planned to go to an eastern resort and then at the last minute, just weeks before the wedding, saw these awesome photos of Baja in an adventure clothing catalogue. We changed our plans," said Paul. Tracy was holding his arm with the possessiveness of a new bride and smiled sincerely enough to let me know she too thought this non-traditional honeymoon was a pretty slick idea.

Finding Baja from Chicago

It seems they had flown to Mexico City, then on to Los Cabos, rented a car and drove north about 450 miles up Highway 1, an endeavor that required considerable effort on their part. And they were making it a true adventure by seeing other sights along the way.

Soon several of the fishermen had joined us and we moved a couple tables together. There were two or three conversations going at the same time. I marveled at the women's ability to keep all the conversations going. They were talking to me, the newlyweds, two of the more sober men, and at the same time fending off the advances of a couple of the drunks.

One overweight guy was trying to put the make on everyone, even squinting deeply to cast amorous glances at a full-figured potted cactus in the corner. I was waiting for him to put his arms around the plant as its spiny defenses might have made an effective protest. Made for a fun evening.

In the morning, I met Becky at 8 a.m. at the Eco Mundo palapa at Posada Concepcion on the bay south of town. I arrived just as Paul and Tracy were emerging from their palapa to load their little blue rental car. Their plan was to kayak one

Eco Mundo Palapas

more time, go for a hike in the desert, and give Sherie a promised ride to the Loreto Airport on their way south to Los Cabos.

They showed me the palapa in which they had spent their honeymoon. It was open, facing the bay, constructed of straw and clay and thatched roof, and its interior was void of cumbersome furniture save two hammocks.

"Two hammocks," I mused. "That's a hell of a way to spend a honeymoon."

"It's so wonderful here," Tracy replied, "We can live with hammocks for a couple of days."

They got in the kayaks, pushed off, and headed out onto a glassy sea. As they vanished around the cove, Becky prepared me with a life vest, map, dry bag and a simple functional paddle. Joining me would be Sherie and a couple of youthful Brits who also were staying at one of the three Eco Mundo palapas.

We stroked out onto the pea-green water to cross an arm of Bahia de Concepcion (Conception Bay), arguably the most beautiful of the Sea of Cortez. It was low tide and we were headed for a reef. The 19-year-old Brits started at a brisk pace and I found myself racing to keep up. Shortly, I dropped back and sheepishly excused my burst of speed to Sherie by simply saying, "It's a guy thing,"

Young hatchlings on the rocks

We glided over the shallow rocks and circled the exposed reef where pelicans just sat and watched us. Then we headed for a steep, rocky island in the center of the inner bay. There we marveled at young pelicans just learning to fly. We saw several nests and young seagull and pelican hatchlings. The furry little critters looked so vulnerable and out of place on those sharp hard rocks.

The Brits left and Sherie headed back to clean up before her return flight, so I paddled on alone. On the lee side of the island, it was even more dazzling. I could stop paddling and just listen to the silence of the sea. It was so much more peaceful than a noisy panga. On the lee side, I drifted over small kelp beds, crystal-clear water and coral so fine it looked like delicate pasta.

Here were more nests. Furry little seagull chicks were stumbling over the slippery rocks under the watchful eye of mother. It was awesome. As I began to paddle back I noticed the bright green shallow water give way to a deep cobalt blue.

I crossed the channel and paddled along the coast back to Eco Mundo. I was ready to return to Mulegé but Sherie was antsy as Paul and Tracy had not returned from the desert yet and she had a 2:30 flight out of Loreto, about an hour and 20 minute drive away. I decided to wait as in a magnanimous moment the night before I mentioned that if she was stranded I had a car. We waited and waited until finally Becky suggested she go up to the highway and try to flag down a bus.

At the highway we could see the desert trail the newlyweds had taken. No bus, no newlyweds. 12:30. "Let's wait until 12:45," I said not relishing the 3-½ hour round trip.

12:45. No bus, no newlyweds. We headed south. Fortunately, this woman was not only appreciative, but good company. Now married to a La Jolla doctor and the mother of two sons, she has been a Baja buff since her teens.

I got her to the airport at 2:05, time to spare. Heading back, I considered stopping at Eco Mundo to see if Becky had organized a search party for the newlyweds yet, when their distinctive blue rental car passed me heading south. Well, they're okay, but I was curious as to what happened.

Becky said that they admitted just losing track of time, not taking a watch with them.

I wonder though, with spending their honeymoon on different hammocks, maybe they made up for it by getting romantic in the desert. If so, it was worth my long drive.

(2024 Update: I had returned several times at Eco Mundo before Roy and Becky dissolved their relationship and closed their unique ecological hideaway. It was auctioned off in 2007. I enjoyed their hospitality and often think of them when I'm out kayaking elsewhere.)

Birthplace of the Californias (2007)

As the historic Loreto mission appeared on our left, one of the men in our shared airport taxi said with strained apprehension, "And what little village is this?"

My wife and I looked at each other in awe. I decided to give the guy the news, "Uh dude, this **is** Loreto, the heart of downtown, as a matter of fact."

Loreto City Hall

We had just arrived on one of the two new weekly Alaska Airlines flights from Los Angeles (Thursday and Sunday). Alaska's 1½ hour flight now joined Air California's three weekly flights and Aeromexico's daily arrivals (all from Los Angeles) to Loreto, Baja California Sur, Mexico, on the Sea of Cortez about 800 miles south of Southern California.

Loreto, established in 1697, bears the distinction of being the birthplace of all of California. For what was once the capital of the Mexican and U.S. states of California, tourism has still not yet taken off—but it appears all that is about to change.

Snowbirds from the Pacific Northwest (now aided by Alaska Airlines) are pushing into yet another warm locale for their seasonal nests. New houses are sprouting up along the town's northern shoreline, many built by these migratory northerners.

Up to now, about 80 percent of the visitors to Loreto have been Californians who have enjoyed the simple amenities of this small unimposing town of about 10,000 hardy *loreteños.*

Compared to Cabo San Lucas, a burgeoning city with a population of 300,000, and where the Los Cabos Airport disgorges passengers up to a record 239 landings and takeoffs in one day, it's no wonder my taxi mate was confused. I never saw him again, but he would have experienced an incredibly more laidback, quieter time than he might have imagined. That's the Loreto of today.

For years there have been attempts to bring growth to Loreto, and maybe this time it will happen. Back in the 1970s, the Mexican Government Tourism agency, FONOTUR, pegged Loreto for development, along with Cancun and Los Cabos. While the others became internationally famous, all Loreto got out of the deal was a golf course, which suited many Baja aficionados just fine.

It was at a place called Nopolo, seven miles south of Loreto, where construction commenced on a master-planned community, with tennis, golf, and resort hotels, and then the project sat—for about 30 years.

Along with the golf course, only the adjacent Hotel Loreto Presidente became operational. The Presidente later became the Eden Loreto, and after being closed for a while, re-opened last year as the Whale's Inn. Meanwhile a new Camino Real Hotel opened on the other side of the Nopolo golf course about two years ago.

Enter the Loreto Bay Company. The company's Villages at Loreto Bay development has already exceeded $100 million (U.S.) in residential sales in its first 17 months of operation. $30 million of that came in the last four months alone.

The Loreto Bay development, which lines three miles of coastline encompassing 8,000 acres will feature 6,000 homes, a town center, artisan's village, hotels, spas, golf courses and a marina. It promises to be an environmentally friendly development near a very old setting.

(2024 update: The Loreto Bay hotel is now the Loreto Bay Golf Resort and Spa at Baja.)

Over 325 Years Old

Loreto, the only 17th century town in the Californias, came into being over 325 years ago, on October 25, 1697 and is truly the "Historical Capital of the Californias." The Loreto mission "Nuestra Señora de Loreto" (Our Lady of Loreto) became the first of a missional system that colonized and settled not only Baja California but 48 locations all the way up to Northern California.

When the town was wiped out by a hurricane in 1829, the capital of Baja California territory was moved to La Paz and Loreto dwindled in importance.

For years, Loreto remained a laid-back oasis where summer's heat forced a slow, easy pace for locals and visitors alike. California's first city had changed very little until the 1960s when fishermen discovered the place.

Fishermen began going to Loreto to catch dorado (mahi mahi), yellowtail, marlin, sailfish, grouper, red snapper, sierra, rock sea bass, roosterfish, yellowfin tuna, and other species. The pelagic fish are mostly in evidence during the hot summer months when the word "dorado" becomes synonymous with Loreto.

An Alaska Airlines package offered us lodging at either the Camino Real (which I knew to be way south of town),

Loreto Mission, from 1697

or at the Posada de las Flores right downtown. We opted for the Posada, a boutique inn of 15 units right on Loreto's main plaza, a short walk from everything.

It's a delightfully appealing place with its old world architecture blending in nicely in the heart of Loreto. It features a unique rooftop swimming pool with a Plexiglas bottom that is the main lobby's ceiling. With all that charm, we still found amenities lacking and management from mediocre to poor; plus, the central location can get quite noisy.

We took out our frustrations by taking a brisk walk around Loreto. It's a great walking town, and we covered it several times.

The old Plaza Salvatierra which fronts the historic mission and the old *Museo de las Misiones* (museum) next door was inviting. We toured the mission church, noting its only concession to the 21st century being electric fans lining the chapel. The museum is an enchanting visit into the past, complete with fine art and colonial artifacts. A nominal fee is charged.

Whimsically shaped ficus trees shade the plaza and the tourist shops along the Paseo Salvatierra.

We visited Bill Benzinger, owner and founder of the Hotel Oasis, where I usually stay. The Oasis, a charming hotel on the water and a short walk from everything, offers three plans: room only, bed and breakfast, and all-inclusive meals. Founded in 1962, the Oasis is featured in my book *Baja Legends,* and has catered to fishermen for years.

We walked over the other side of the mostly dry riverbed to visit former Canadian Wendy Wilchynski, now owner of the charming Villas de Loreto, a comfortable smoke-free resort that offers nine standard rooms, a poolside casita and a beach house. Book early; they fill fast.

We returned to town along the beach, crossing the water from the river and estuary where pelicans, sea gulls, cormorants and terns shared space with cranes, noble snowy egrets, and majestic blue herons.

There's plenty to do in Loreto, especially for those interested in the outdoors and mini-adventures. Along with fishing, the area offers superb diving and snorkeling. The waters are usually crystal clear with incredible visibility and some 3,000 species of maritime animals, including 800 varieties of fish.

There's kayaking, sailing and whale watching, mountain biking, mule riding, limited shopping (credit cards, even Visa, are not widely accepted in shops and restaurants), and golf. You can rent a car and find a secluded beach or head into the Sierra Giganta mountains that provide a dazzling backdrop to Loreto.

Most popular is visiting the historic Mission of San Javier, California's second (1699) and best preserved. The mission sits in a mountain valley surrounded by trees and orchards originally planted by the padres. These days there is a direct road providing easy access. There are also numerous locations in the area where you can visit ancient cave art and paintings.

Most hotels have packages that can arrange for any activity. In addition, there is Las Parras Tours, which offers Natural History and Cultural Tours (missions), kayaking, cave painting, mule riding, mountain biking, whale watching and sailing. Desert Expeditions offers much of the same.

Paddling South offers extended kayak adventures, and also hosts mountain biking excursions, or divers can check out Cormorant Dive Center.

Guaycura Adventours & Sportfishing has its own fishing fleet and also offers other tours and packages with several hotels.

Arturo's Sport Fishing has everything from two passenger pangas to four passenger mini cruisers. Arturo's offers numerous package deals and a host of ecotour activities.

In addition to the Camino Real (with 137 rooms), and the 140 room Whales Inn at Nopolo, and the others mentioned above, there's the 40 room La Pinta (one of a chain throughout Baja) on the beach in Loreto, the Hacienda Suites at the town's entrance, and the small Las Cabanas de Loreto just opened by wildlife photographers Richard and Jill Jackson.

South of town is the eco-resort Danzante, named for a nearby island. The 10-acre seaside property offers nine hilltop suites with commanding views of the sea.

For dining, excellent fish tacos with all the trimmings are offered by Lulu at her popular McLulu's stand as you arrive in town. Another great taco stand (fish and carne asada) is El Rey del Taco on Calle Benito Juarez. Run by Francisco Garcia and family, it opens when they feel like it (usually in time for lunch), and closes when he runs out of food (by dinner time).

One of the town's landmark restaurants, Café Olé, an institution for 23 years, is downtown next to the Posada de las Flores and offers excellent food, large portions, and reasonable prices. Local expatriates meet there for breakfast and lunch.

Other good restaurants, all informal as is the entire town, are La Terraza (above Café Olé), Playa Blanca (upstairs across the street), Mexico Lindo (very good), Macaws (fronting the beach), El Taste, and El Nido (both for steak), El Canipole, and El Tio Lupe (both near mission).

A new restaurant has in a few short months become a favorite of tourists and the expatriate community as well. Across the plaza from the city hall is Mita Gourmet, a small restaurant opened in November 2004 by Uraguayan restaurateur Juan Carlos Cortes Hillard and his wife Martha.

I was surprised to see cruise passengers in town one day. But there were 100 of them off the *Spirit of Endeavor,* anchored offshore. Cruising CB West departs La Paz to the south and makes several stops on remote islands and at towns like Loreto.

The passengers remarked that it was a wonderful adventurous cruise, the best ever according to some. An occasional small cruise ship of hardy travelers has a much more minimal impact than in Cabo San Lucas where 900,000 of its visitors in 2004 arrived on cruise ships.

For now, the charm of Loreto is that you can do a lot or you can do nothing. Even downtown you'll wake up to the sound of roosters crowing. It's not for the disco crowd, it's a place for introspection and withdrawal. It can get very hot in the summer when even the dogs hardly move. I've always liked the place, even though, and perhaps because, it's grown very little.

In town, lots and houses are being bought by Americans and Canadians, many of whom are integrating into the community rather than creating their own isolationist cocoon. But with a major resort coming in just down the road, who knows what the future will bring?

Maybe my taxi-mate will discover a lot bigger place if he ever comes back.

Yellowtail Highlight Loreto Action (2013)

The Loreto pangero who took us fishing was as old as dirt. Turns out he was a couple of months younger than me – well, that's still as old as dirt. But it seems he should have turned the fishing over to a younger person.

Just outside the Loreto harbor about two dozen small pangas bobbed in the smooth strawberry reflection of an awakening sun, dropping and retrieving their bait rigs, pulling up feisty mackerel for bait, two, three and four at a time. When our white-haired old skipper headed in the other direction, I pointed back. He shook his head indicating he had a better place to make bait. He didn't. He didn't have a better place to fish either. We spent three hours in the unremitting sun yielding only a few bait mackerel—and that was before we started fishing!

Our skipper also chose to ignore the hot yellowtail action north of Isla Carmen to take us elsewhere. Meanwhile my colleagues were pulling in yellowtail until their arms were sore, big ones too—20 pounders.

My fishing partner for the day was Betsy Crowfoot, a very fine outdoor writer/photographer/sailor. Unfortunately we were out of live bait shortly after I finally pulled in one smaller yellowtail (8-10 pounds), Chagrined, we headed back in to be regaled by the outstanding fishing exploits of the others.

We were attending an Outdoor Writers Association of California conference (OWAC), held for the first time in Loreto, Baja California Sur, the 315-year-old birthplace of California.

The mission city of about 10,000 friendly citizens rolled out the red carpet for our small group which included outdoor magazine and newspaper writers along with some radio and TV hosts.

I tried fishing later that week and a helpful skipper with a toothy grin and an upbeat attitude took me to Isla Carmen, where amid other anglers and pangas I caught fish, including a nice 25-30 pounder. The yellowtail action in May was overall excellent. A couple of my colleagues even had to buy more ice chests to spirit their booty home.

Another day about a dozen of us went on an Isla Coronado adventure. We circumnavigated the small island where scores of barking seals and sea lions welcomed us and hundreds of brown pelicans guarded their cliffside nests. We also marveled at those anomalies of nature—the blue-footed boobies, their powder blue webbed feet contrasted against the guano-covered rocks.

We then kayaked from one white-sand island beach to another where we snorkeled in the crystal-clear water with incredible visibility. I spotted several varieties of the area's 3,000 species of maritime animals which include 800 different fish.

Our meetings are full of adventures and some attendees went into the mountains to the remarkably well-preserved San Javier Mission.

Jeaninne Perez, owner of El Caballo Blanco bookstore, invited me to do a book signing and it was great meeting many of my Baja book supporters from the Loreto area.

It's not all play, and among presentations we were treated to an outstanding slide show by Loreto-based wildlife photographer Richard Jackson.

The evening meals mostly offered local seafood, from the clam chowder, squid and scallops at Domingo's to the fire-baked chocolate clams at the Hotel Oasis. We also enjoyed The Palapa's seafood buffet at the Hotel Tripui in nearby Puerto Escondido.

Various hotels provided lodging, including The Oasis, Posada del Cortez, La Damiana, Hacienda Suites, Santa Fe, and Angra. The El Palmar Casas, owned by the Vagabundos Del Mar travel club, hosted a nice wine reception.

Arturo's Fleet provided most of the fishing, and our kayaking adventure was through Sea Kayak Baja Mexico.

On earlier visits to Loreto, I usually headed straight for the Hotel Oasis, founded in 1962 by now 83-year-old Bill Benzinger. It is a charming hotel on the water and a short walk from everything. They have catered to fishermen for years. Today the Hotel Oasis is run by his daughter Ana Gloria Benzinger Davis. She was instrumental in getting our group to town, and lining up the incredible itinerary.

The final dinner, held in the Hotel Oasis patio, was memorable: we watched chocolate clams get baked in rocks, listened to Mayor Jorge Alberto Avilés Pérez's brief welcome, heard an outstanding vocalist, and enjoyed some spirited dancers twirling and spinning in their colorful skirts.

Ana Gloria commented on our conference: "We're pleased that you chose to come to Loreto and that you had a good time. Now you can see all that Loreto has to offer its visitors."

Well, along with everything else, I caught some nice fish – and I met a fisherman older than dirt.

(2022 Update: Betsy Crowfoot is now Betsy Senescu and a Board member of OWAC. And Loreto is still growing.)

Fishing/Golf Tourney in Loreto (2017)

Talk about something new! The flyer from the Villa del Palmar at the Islands of Loreto clearly said "Fishing and Golf Tournament." I'd been in fishing tournaments before, but I had never, ever, swung a golf club, unless you count when I was a kid trying to putt through a windmill.

Also, while I'd fished Baja's Loreto area before, I'd never even heard of the Villa del Palmar Beach Resort and Spa at the Islands of Loreto. So it would be *something new at someplace new.* And what a resort it is!

Located 20 miles south of the historic BCS town of Loreto on the beautiful Danzante Bay, the resort looms out of the desert sand shimmering like a mirage at the water's edge. Bright green fairways fill the arroyos and rocky hillsides to provide an incongruous yet magical backdrop.

For years Danzante Bay was an almost hidden gem just down the road from the village of Ligui and nearby rustic beach camping sites. The modest Danzante Destination Resort that later graced the bay sold its interests in 2014 to the Villa Group, a conglomerate with interests in about a dozen Mexican resort properties.

With such a dazzling landscape, including a natural bay on the Sea of Cortez backdropped by the bright and rugged Sierra de la Giganta mountains, the Villa Group did justice to nature's palette.

The Villa del Palmar at the Islands of Loreto is a luxury all-inclusive beachfront resort featuring 181 spacious suites offering 1, 2, or 3 bedrooms, large terraces and incredible views. There are three restaurants that offer everything from comfort food to fine dining, five swimming pools, two tennis courts, and a 39,000 square-foot spa. There are time shares, villas, and home sites available to purchase, and a day use option is offered. Guests can enjoy a plethora of aquatic activities, and a world class golf course!

Danzante Bay Golf Club

While I can hardly judge golf courses, this one is a dazzler. It made me think of Pebble Beach, but rather than cypress tress gracing the rocky cliffs, think desert. Baja's newest, and already called Mexico's best new course, Danzante Bay Golf Club was designed by Rees Jones who laid out the diverse course over rocky outcrops, native desert arroyos, and sand dunes. With an elevation change of 250 feet, the signature hole is the breathtaking par-3 Hole 17.

While the fishing lured me to this Baja outpost, I was encouraged to try my hand on the as-yet unfinished course (some holes are played twice). Golf pro Danny Garcia was helpful and patient as I kept missing the ball and/or digging up divots. My group only played about half the holes while the more experienced players went 18 for the gold the next day.

To me, hitting the green on the 17th hole seemed as a task as dropping a marble into a paint bucket from a bridge. I didn't even want to waste a ball. Yet, golfers regularly pinpoint that cliff top green which is surrounded on three sides by the frothing sea way down below. My partner Rich Holland of *Western Outdoor News* got his second shot on the pinnacle and close enough to chip in, while Joe Shields of the *Virginia Sportsman* donated a few balls to King Neptune. Sid Dobrin, a principal of Inventive Fishing and University of Florida English professor, just said "Wow," and called it, "Visually stunning."

The 17th hole at Danzante Bay Golf Club

A rewarding final hole is the downhill 18th, a 520-yard par 4. From the cliff top back tees, I could hardly see the fairway!

Winning Tournament golfers were Ignacio Gutierrez (1st) who snagged 4 nights in a Resort Deluxe room; Paul Moreno won the 2nd place $500 (U.S.) prize. Moreno, the COO of the Villa Group, donated the money to Casa Hogar (home for kids with no parents or with serious family problems). Cynthia Valdez won the $200 3rd place honors.

The last of the 18 holes are currently being completed to create a 7,107-yard, par-72 course, that according to Bryan Hendricks, Outdoors Editor of the *Arkansas Democrat-Gazette,* "I can't imagine a golfer not enjoying this course."

Chasing Dorado in Loreto

The golf portion of "The Islands of Loreto Fishing and Golf Tournament 2017 by the Villa Group" attracted only 16 participants, but most of us were after the feisty dorado (mahi mahi) hoping to win part of the $100,000 (MXN) prize.

Each day of the two-day tourney, a dozen teams left nearby Puerto Escondido to fish the sea around Carmen and Danzante Islands. I only fished the second day, having been humbled on the golf course the first day.

Three of our group (Shields, Holland, and myself) left the aptly named Puerto Escondido (Hidden Port) on a boat provided by Wild Loreto for the glassy sea as the sun was rising over Carmen Island. Our skipper Humberto Burgoin Mayoral opted to fish the area north of the island that is often hot for dorado and yielded some small ones the previous day. After a couple of bites and one brief hookup by our team, I landed a 10 pounder that seemed heavier than it was. Maybe I'm just getting old.

Dorado not big enough to be a winner

At weigh-in, there were several in the 10-12-pound range that missed the money. The winning team, Los Mayates, checked in with a 25.3-pound beauty and claimed $100,000 (MXN), about $5,500 U.S. Second place, with a 14.3 pounder, was the Los Primos team, who won $50,000 (MXN), while the third-place honors and $30,000 (MXN) went to Los Compadres del Dorado with a 13 pounder.

It was a Dorado Tournament but a special prize was awarded to the Maros Team from Cabo San Lucas for bringing in a 279 lb. Black Marlin. The huge fish had to be hoisted from a balcony to be weighed to the delight of the considerable onlookers. Team Maros won a free pass to the exclusive Bisbee's Los Cabos Off-shore Tournament to be held this October. According to Captain Rafael Alvarado, the 10-foot marlin took two hours to land.

The 2nd annual Islands of Loreto Fishing and Golf Tournament 2017 by the Villa Group drew twice as many entrants as the previous year. Sponsors included Marina Puerto Escondido, Danzante Bay Golf Club, Danzante Tours, Bisbees, Blue Anchor Restaurant, and Outpost Charters.

Next year's tourney promises to be even better with the golf course completed and a greater awareness of all that Villa del Palmar at the Islands of Loreto has to offer. The spa is top-notch, offering a number of treatments. After swinging that golf club I enjoyed a relaxing back massage.

Guests can fly from LAX to Loreto on Alaska Airlines in less than two hours, and the airport is also served by WestJet from Canada. Highway 1 travelers can access the resort 20 miles south of the historic town of Loreto. I advise all to take time to explore Loreto, the first settlement in the Californias. The resort has regular shuttles to town.

As a long-time Baja Buff, my experience at the Villa del Palmar at the Islands of Loreto was certainly different for me. I personally missed the bouncing dirt roads, the uncertainties of lodging and campsites, the ubiquitous street food, and mingling with the locals. But to a new wave of vacationers, this resort is as good as it gets. I found a beautiful new place, and I tried something new—but I think I'll go back to putting in the windmills and castles –when I'm not wandering around Baja's back roads.

New Port in San José del Cabo (2006)

Changes—big changes—have come to San José del Cabo, that "other" Cabo, the town closer to the Los Cabos Airport.

From downtown San José, a little dirt road used to cross the upper estuary and end at a small beach village called La Playita. There a broad, white-sand beach was home to the *pangueros,* fishermen who pulled their 18 to 20-foot *pangas* up the sandy berm each day. Those Mexican locals and early gringos who settled on that side of the estuary lived in semi-isolation, far removed from the bustling and rapidly developing tourist town of San José. But that was before!

Marina San Jose when under construction

Now progress has stretched across the estuary in such a big way it had been called "the most ambitious single property development in Baja." The 2,000-acre residential resort under construction features two golf courses (Jack Nicklaus and Greg Norman designed), a full-scale marina, restaurants, shops, five-star hotels, and a major housing subdivision with lots, condos and homes available.

As the Puerto Los Cabos marina was being dredged back in early 2006, I watched huge rocks being placed to form the breakwater jetties. The marina, which partially opened in late 2006, now offers 500 slips and can accommodate yachts and boats up to 400 feet. The anxious pangueros were assuaged by the developers as they moved to the harbor that they would no longer have to pull their boats up on the sand bar.

Big development plans

Major developers of Puerto Los Cabos are Jorgé Buch Braniff, of Mexico City, and Eduardo Sanchez-Navarro (Of Corona beer). In an article in *Destino: Los Cabos,* Buch commented on how their development will help the people of the area with jobs, etc., and especially those across the estero whose infrastructure will improve greatly.

Broad new avenues and *glorietas* (traffic circles) now head into the hills beyond the Puerto. Homesites of approximately a half-acre were being sold from the mid-low $200,000 (U.S.) to $4.3 million (yes, U.S. dollars) for an oceanfront lot.

Progress. I still recall driving out to La Playita on a dirt road, where one could find a couple of bodegas, the La Playita hotel and restaurant, and a bunch of pangas sitting on the berm, just waiting for fishermen.

Reminds me of what happened on Playa Medano in Cabo San Lucas. With the opening of the Casa Dorado hotel and the re-imagining of the Hacienda, it became more like Cancun than the Cabo I recall.

Misión La Serena, the most exclusive deeded private residence club in Baja, is being developed on 7.4 secluded beachfront acres. Condos with all the state-of-the-art amenities and electronics gadgetry will run from U.S. $350,000 to $2 million.

In March, Misión La Serena public relations manager Jesús Corral said, "We are currently building the oceanfront units, along with the three-tiered infinity pool and beach club." Corral added that Misión La Serena had sold about 10 percent of their inventory and were scheduled to open at the end of November 2006.

The fresh-water estuary at San José del Cabo has always loomed important to the cape region. Indians lived in the fertile valley that fed the estuary, and the Spanish padres established the area's first mission along its banks. Later Spanish sailors had their Manila galleons stop there to take on water, fresh fruit, vegetables, meat, and hide out from marauding Dutch and English pirates.

In April 8, 1730, Padre Nicholas Tamaral, founder of the mission of Purisima, established the new mission at San José del Cabo. The name San José was given honoring José de Villapuente, a colonization benefactor, with the "del Cabo" (of the cape) added to distinguish it from Comondú, where that mission was also called San José.

The original site of the mission was along the estuary but the mosquitoes drove the padre to resettle inland, first along the right bank of the arroyo some nine miles from the ocean (about where Santa Anita is). As Arthur Walbridge North wrote in his 1907 *Mother of California,* "Here there was an abundance of rich soil, plenty of water, a roadstead not far distant, and a climate that might reconcile one to exile from the rest of the world."

In 1734, there was an Indian uprising in the south and, disgusted at seeing their liberties curtailed by the Catholic padres, the Indians rose up and killed Tamaral as well as the missionaries at Santiago and Todos Santos. In 1753 the mission was moved to its present site downtown.

Until recent decades, San José del Cabo was a much larger town than the other "Cabo" down the corridor, Cabo San Lucas, long the site of a fish cannery and little else.

For years, visitors have extolled the delights of San José. In Arthur North's 1910 book *Camp and Camino in Lower California,* he wrote: "San José del Cabo is a charming and picturesque pueblo, with the inevitable mission and plaza, many sky-blue, flat-roofed adobe residences, attractive gardens, rich soil, much running water, and every conceivable tropical and semi-tropical fruit."

The 1964 *Lower California Guidebook* by Gerhard and Gulick, waxes much the same as North, "San José, with its mild climate, somnolent atmosphere and beautiful surroundings, is certainly one of the most beautiful towns in Baja California....At the mouth of the arroyo below the town is a large fresh water pond (estero) which drains into the sea. There is a clean white sand beach with ideal bathing, since the warm waters of the Gulf and the cold waters of the Pacific join here in just the right combination."

Today's changes to the peaceful area are so momentous and far reaching that environmentalists are howling. They claim that the developers have destroyed thousands of native plants, bulldozed dunes, and are destroying the natural habitat of many species including the osprey. And they argue that a pipeline has even been laid upon a beach where sea turtles nest.

Others mention that while some locals benefit by new jobs and a supply chain created, others were forced to sell their homes in the name of progress. Also, most of the jobs created in Cabo's recent boom have been filled by mainland Mexicans.

Gringos who live across the estuary have been shocked into the reality of the progress. Many echo the musings of Jim (Jaime) Tolbert, owner of Baja Books and Maps, who said, "The Puerto Los Cabos idea as they state it is to develop a community with an 'authentic Mexican village.' Well, we were an authentic Mexican village long before they came along."

Arthur North liked the authenticity so well that back in 1910, he wrote, "It is a frequent saying down in the Peninsula that if a man stops a week at San José del Cabo he becomes a "lotus eater" and only ropes can haul him away."

I suppose that when people invest millions of dollars in a location, it really would be difficult to "haul them away."

The Pearl of La Paz (2020)

It was pearls (perlas) that attracted Hernan Cortes to La Paz but he was unable to sustain his colony of Spanish settlers back in 1535. Until a mission was established there in 1720, La Paz was visited only by temporary pearl-hunters.

La Paz was noted for its black pearls (actually a metallic gray) and the pearls were harvested for over 400 years. One large pearl, a pear-shaped 400-grain "Pearl of la Paz" was gifted by the pearlers to the Queen of Spain.

Until 1874 when diving suits were introduced, local Indians were often forced to free dive to bring up the shells bearing the coveted pearls. In the late 1800s, the beautiful mother-of-pearl shells themselves also began to be harvested and shipped.

By decree of May 11, 1861, La Paz, then with a population of about 800, was named a free port and, along with shipping pearls, was able to receive foreign goods.

In 1868 Russ Browne reported in his book *Explorations in Lower California* that "The pearl fishery has greatly declined for several years past; the oysters having become scarce in the waters of the best fishing grounds, either in consequence of storms or other disturbances."

By 1941 the pearling industry petered out entirely as the pearl oyster which attracted Cortes and hundreds of others disappeared due to over-harvesting and disease.

In 1941 American Nobel Prize winning author John Steinbeck visited La Paz and based his book *The Pearl* on his experience.

Steinbeck became enamored with the town and reported in his book *Sea of Cortez,* "...There is the genuine fascination of the city of La Paz. Everyone in the area knows of the greatness of La Paz. You can get anything in the world there, they say. It is a huge place—not of course so monstrous as Guaymas or Mazatlan, but beautiful out of all comparison....a cloud of delight hangs over the distant city from the time when it was the great pearl center of the world. The robes of the Spanish kings and the stoles of the bishops in Rome were stiff with the pearls from La Paz."

It seems Steinbeck's comment resonated with an interesting story. In August 1883, two divers working for La Paz pearling company owner Don Antonio Justa Ruffo Santacruz found a huge pearl. Ruffo named the gem Carmelaida, in honor of his two daughters, Carmen and Adelaida Ruffo. For many years, he kept the pearl on display.

Mercedes and Don Antonio Ruffo

At some point Don Antonio Ruffo showed the pearl to the U.K. Ambassador to Mexico, who offered to buy it and gift it to Britian's King Edward VII. Instead, Ruffo gifted the pearl to the King himself. They say the King was so impressed with the pearl he had one of the royal jewelers incorporate it into the Royal Crown.

The English jewelers who worked on it named it The Great Lemon *(El Gran Limón).* It is the same headgear that years later the King's granddaughter,

Queen Elizabeth II, wore on official occasions.

The Queen was reportedly curious about the origins of *El Gran Limón.* On her second visit to Mexico in February of 1983 (the 100th anniversary of the huge gem's discovery) she and her husband Prince Philip, while traveling aboard their yacht *Britannia,* made a stop at La Paz as an honored guest of Baja California Sur governor Alberto Andrés Alvarado. After this visit, she went whale watching in Guerrero Negro, before continuing on to Northern California.

The Pearl of La Paz lives on, and not just in Steinbeck's book title, nor as royal jewelry, but in the form of a hotel—and also for many decades, an historic mercantile company.

In 1860 the aforementioned pearler Don Antonio Ruffo Santacruz established La Perla de La Paz, also known as Casa Ruffo, as an important trading house and department store. It was the largest store on the Baja península and offered a wide variety of goods from a kilo of sugar to the finest fabrics and fragrances from around the world.

It also sold hardware tools necessary for the miners of El Triunfo and San Antonio. The grand old store was eventually listed as an *Historical Heritage* in 1986 by Mexico's National Institute of Anthropology.

The over-a-century-old La Perla de la Paz department store was still in existence through the 1990s and I popped in for something every time I was in town. It was a wonderful big colonial store, with thick walls, broad concrete pillars, wide aisles, old yellowing linoleum floor, expansive shelving, and lots of merchandise, from furniture to food to clothing.

Unfortunately, in 2006 it suffered a fire that destroyed most of the building and today only the façade remains standing. The scaled-down department store moved to an adjoining building and the Ruffo family is still prominent in La Paz.

La Perla Hotel

By the mid-1930s there was no place in La Paz (the state capital and largest town) to accommodate anyone. Lodging for distinguished visitors had to be provided by local merchants and politicians.

This led to the government creating a semipublic fund to build a hotel. So the Hotel Perla de la Paz Corporation opened and shares were sold to the citizens. Most of the shares were bought by the Castro and Ruffo families. The Ruffos had early on sold their interest in the hotel but continued to operate their nearby store.

Once funded, by early 1940 construction on what was considered the first modern hotel in the State of Baja California Sur was underway. The legendary Hotel Perla, built in a simplified art nouveau style, opened in March 1940 with 25 comfortable guest rooms and a grand ballroom named "Salon Madre Perla" (The Mother Pearl Salon).

The inauguration ceremony was hosted by its founders: Col. Rafael Pedrejo (then Governor of Baja California Sur Territory), Juan Manuel Castro, Jorge Vonborstel, Miguel Cornejo, Salomon Tuchman, Arturo Canseco and 15 other associates.

Steinbeck was partially prophetic in his reaction: "On the water's edge of La Paz a new hotel was going up, and it looked very expensive. Probably the airplanes will bring weekenders from Los Angeles before long, and the beautiful, poor bedraggled old town will bloom with a Floridian ugliness."

Fishermen now fly in for weekends, but the ugliness projected by Steinbeck is for the most part still on hold. The Hotel Perla, which has graced the Malecon facing the bay for 85 years, hosted most of the important events in the growing city for decades.

Hotel Perla

Following the 1941 attack on Pearl Harbor, a Mexican Air Force Squadron sent to defend Baja California Sur was housed in the Hotel Perla.

By the 1950s the oldest hotel in La Paz had already undergone extensive face-lifting adding two more floors to the previous two. The Hotel Perla quickly became a favorite of American adventurers who drove the difficult route down the peninsula.

The open-air restaurant on the ground floor of Hotel Perla had become the town's gathering place. During my visits there in the mid-1970s, I would sit over coffee and watch the parade of paceños (citizens of La Paz) pass by. In a few days one could meet virtually every tourist visiting the city from that comfortable perch in that outdoor restaurant.

The hotel has undergone welcome renovations several times rendering a more modern, functional, and luxurious facility.

Adolfo Coronado Pasas was the owner of Hotel Perla for decades after he bought it in 1975. His daughter Laura Coronado Pasas was the General Manager, and daughter Isabel Coronado Pasas, the Administrative Manager.

The Coronados did a lot of renovations befitting the historic hotel beginning in the 1970s, including painting it café brown, with lots of terra cotta trim, resplendent with arches, tile and plants. During the year 2000 a five-story tower was added to provide an additional 50 rooms.

The Hotel Perla in La Paz is the oldest, most historical, and for decades was the center of the town's activities.

According to one older guidebook, "The famous Perla Hotel, which has been the meeting place of the town aristocracy and tourists for years, is located right on the Malecón. This venerable hostelry, so inextricable from the lore of La Paz, has had magnificent remodeling and additions of late....Of course, there are any number of hotels and motels, but somehow the La Perla always seems synonymous with La Paz."

In 2020 an investment group acquired the Hotel Perla with plans to morph it into a Hampton by Hilton hotel, giving it an architectural reconfiguration, with a large shopping plaza on the ground level and a totally new presence on to the Malecon.

I've always loved La Paz, but I'll definitely miss the venerable old Hotel Perla.

Unwind in Peaceful La Paz (2010)

When people ask what my favorite place in Baja is, my first question is favorite for what? I have favorite fishing spots, favorite secluded coves, and favorite palm canyons. But to visit over and over again, I've long liked La Paz.

As the capital city of Baja California Sur, it is large enough to find great restaurants, shops, activities, and history. It is still small enough to retain its provincial charm.

I first visited La Paz in the early 1970s, flying down shortly after a divorce, and found magic in that balmy seaside town. It was the warm evenings, warm people, beautiful women strolling the malecón (waterfront walk), pelicans diving for bait fish, and spectacular sunsets. There were just a handful of tourists, mostly Mexicans from the mainland, and the few visiting gringos were friendly. There was also no in-your-face touting, and I quickly felt totally at peace.

During the mid-70s, on two occasions I drove Baja's narrow new Highway 1 to that city just 100 miles north of Cabo San Lucas. Then over the next 35 plus years I visited La Paz numerous times, sometimes flying, sometimes driving, sometimes exploring, researching, or promoting books, and other times snorkeling, fishing, or just kicking back.

La Paz Malecón

La Paz wasn't always so peaceful and welcoming. Back in 1535 the conqueror of Mexico Hernán Cortés attempted to colonize the new land, landing in the northeast corner of La Paz Bay, which they called Santa Cruz.

Cortés had problems supporting the colony. Not only were they harassed by the native Guaycura attacks but found the land too arid to support them. The colony was abandoned and the last of the colonists returned to the mainland in 1536.

Sixty years later, in 1596, the explorer Sebastián Vizcaino set up a colony at Cortés' old site of Santa Cruz. Vizcaino renamed it La Paz (Peace) because at first he found the natives so peaceful. It didn't stay that way, though, as the locals proved anything but peaceful. Once his soldiers started molesting the Indian women, fights started and people on both sides were killed.

From that dubious history, a city grew, and it became the capital of all the Californias in 1829 after Loreto was devastated by a hurricane. Today, with a population of 250,000, it remains the capital of BCS.

By 1950, the pearl fishing that sustained the town for many years had died out, and in recent years the Americans and Canadians who had bypassed the place for the trendier Los Cabos region have discovered the city's charms.

In addition to great snorkeling and diving, there's world class fishing nearby. I've caught marlin, sailfish, dorado, tuna, wahoo, roosterfish, and pargo on trips out of La Paz.

On my 2010 visit I went out with both Fishermen's Fleet owned by David Jones, and Baja Pirates. Another expert is Tailhunter International Sportsfishing run by fellow outdoor writer Jonathan Roldan. Jonathan also has a great restaurant right on the malecón.

Todos Santos booming

On an April 2008 visit, my wife and I took a day trip to Todos Santos, an art colony about 90 miles south. That charming fertile valley by the Pacific has a long history from missionary days and sugar plantations, but today the thick-walled buildings house art galleries and gift shops. Snowbirds from the Pacific Northwest and Canada have been snapping up every bit of land and construction is booming.

Just two years later, in 2010, I noticed that Todos Santos offered even more shopping galleries, restaurants, and services. Todos Santos was awarded the Pueblo Mágico designation in 2006 establishing it as one of Mexico's treasures.

Shops in Todos Santos

My estimation is that the size of the town had *tripled* in just a few years. That's a long way from my first visit where we ate at a palapa restaurant with a dirt floor and chickens at my feet. And that gnarly dirt road that partially went through ranchos from Cabo San Lucas in the 1970s is now paved, widened and traveled regularly by day-trippers from both La Paz and Cabo San Lucas. This trip I was able to revisit Janet Howey and do a book signing at her wonderful bookstore, El Tecolote Libros.

Todos Santos accommodations run the gamut from B&Bs to the trendy Todos Santos Inn downtown. There is also a good value Santa Rosa Hotel, the Hotel California, and on the beach, Posada La Poza. South of town is the outstanding Rancho Pescadero where I stayed in 2010.

La Paz – From Upscale to Funky

Back in La Paz I noted there are still few major resorts like one finds in the Los Cabos region. A relatively new exception wowed me. It is the Costa Baja Resort and Spa on the road to Pichilingue. It's a beautiful upscale place complete with a small marina and golf.

Closer in on the outskirts of town are the La Concha and Marina hotels. Good values are the Araiza Palmilla and Club El Moro nearby. Right downtown are the La Perla (the remodeled original hotel in town), and the Seven Crown. It's a shame that an old favorite of mine, the Los Arcos Hotel has been closed for several years now following a labor dispute.

The old Gardenias Hotel, a few blocks from the water, has been renamed the Bugambillas and has been remodeled. Rooms with new tile and beds are small and still not exciting, but good value. The best value, and more a hostel, is the funky Hotel Yeneka right in the heart of town. The place is so cluttered with souvenirs you could spend a week there and not see all the objects hanging from the rafters and stairways.

There are numerous seafood restaurants, from the Mar y Peña to the Bismark and El Taste as well as popular world-class taco carts. I also enjoyed dinner and a killer sunset at the Roldan's 3-story bayfront Tailhunter Restaurant.

A wonderful culinary surprise in La Paz is the French restaurant La Bohéme. Located downtown on a side street, patio dining in that old colonial building is a delight.

Change is in the Air

It was nice to see some familiar things, because there has been change. Most spectacular is the development of the mogoté, the sand spit peninsula across the bay from town. Condos and a hotel called Paradiso del Mar opened on that low-lying land a short distance but a very long drive away. They take people over there in a 10-minute boat ride from the malecón.

The Grand Baja Spa and Resort just out of town has been remodeled from the old Gran Baja Hotel and 123 beachfront condominiums have been added. There are also new condos at Vista Coral & Marina Estates and La Cocha Pearl, and custom lots and homes have been sold at Moravia Golf & Country Club.

I met the new owners of Allende Books located in an old colonial building at

Independencia 518, between Serdán and Guillermo Prieto. Bruce and Kathleen Bennett offer a lot of books in English and enjoy meeting visiting gringos. Allende Books was originally established by Diane Carmona on Calle Allende. Now on Independencia, the bookstore shares the same historic building with a small B&B called El Angel Azul

Over the past decade the malecón has been widened and art sculptures now grace the walkway at strategic locations. When the sun goes down, the paceños still set off on their evening strolls. The quiet of the balmy evenings is often shattered a bit by young men in cars cruising the route. The tradition has changed a little bit to accommodate a more mobile population.

Nevertheless, the bucolic and easy living of La Paz is a real magnetic pull.

(2024 Update: Allende Books is now at 21 de Agosto in Zona Centro.)

Respite on the Tropic of Cancer (2010)

I found a captivating newer resort in an enchanting old setting, right on the Tropic of Cancer. Actually, that imaginary globe-circling demarcation slices through two of my favorite Baja Sur towns (Santiago and Todos Santos), and this luxury boutique resort I discovered is in El Pescadero, just south of the latter. As the Tropic of Cancer crosses the peninsula just north of Cabo San Lucas, getting there is now an easy drive up the Pacific.

Road Between Cabo & Todos Santos 1975

There the "tropico" slices through the artistic town of Todos Santos that has seen a lot of recent growth. Only 50 miles north of Cabo San Lucas, the area has been slowly inundated with visitors as paved roads are now being widened to accommodate them.

Thus far Todos Santos—the locals are proud to say—remains low key, no high-rise monstrosities blighting the landscape and paving beach access, only simple thatch-roofed buildings and rustic retreats that poke out benignly between swaying palms, shady fruit trees, and fertile green fields.

The Todos Santos /Pescadero area was originally developed by Jesuit padres in 1724 who introduced farming to the local Indians. Juicy mangoes still drop from trees, pleasantly rendering a fruity aroma throughout broad valleys. In the 19th century, mestizos came, planted sugar, built sugar mills and turned out small cones of panocha, a rich, dark brown sugar.

I first discovered the area in the 1970s, when the narrow dirt road wound its way up from Cabo San Lucas and continued north to La Paz. At that time, the main road went through a small farming/fishing community called El Pescadero, about three miles south of Todos Santos. I was enchanted by El Pescadero's few rustic dwellings of mesquite branches and thatch, many buried beneath dazzling splashes of contrasting color – bougainvillea in hues from brilliant magenta to bright coral and orange, along with flaming red carnations. But the town was very small and did not even have a restaurant. That is not the case anymore.

Todos Santos 1975

El Pescadero is slowly growing; the paved road bypasses the original town to create a new village a little to the west of the original. The whole area has been attracting Americans and Canadians who have been building permanent or vacation homes.

Todos Santos itself has become an artist's enclave, and day-trippers from Cabo and La Paz now wander about the picturesque cobbled roads, thick-walled colonial buildings, and old sugar plantations. The old road entering town from La Paz and points north was paved in the early eighties and then in recent years transformed again into a wide four-lane highway. That widening is continuing all the way south to Cabo San Lucas. Unfortunately, with the wider road, progress of the high-rise variety is imminent.

Rancho Pescadero Sets New Standard

Meanwhile, there's Rancho Pescadero, a small ocean-front oasis, tucked away on a dirt road about 1 mile from the highway. As you enter the 15-acre property you know you're somewhere special when you pass the organic garden where herbs and produce are tenderly cultivated for the resort's kitchen.

The 27-room luxury boutique hotel which opened with 12 rooms in December 2009 exudes class and quality in a relaxed, non-pretentious setting. I've spent nights around the world in lodging, and Rancho Pescadero still stands out for its meticulous attention to detail.

Lounging at Rancho Pescadero

It's the brainchild of designer Lisa Harper, former CEO of Gymboree, a Bay Area clothing firm, who with her personable husband, George Lilinoe, a former construction company owner, created the resort right on the broad, sandy beach. George, originally from Hawaii, says, "It's all Lisa, she wanted that 'woman's touch,' she made it special and her ideas have been 'right on.'"

The 'right on' resort features suites that all open up to broad ocean-view terraces. All rooms have Jacuzzi tubs, step-down showers, big sinks, lots of fluffy towels, candles, board games, robes, a pareau, flowers, and feature an attentive staff to ensure every expectation is met.

While my wife attended a Yoga class led by hotel manager Christine Sperber, I grabbed some hotel surf fishing gear and tried my luck. They regularly catch feisty rooster fish (pez gallo) and good-sized sierra from the shore here but I was denied in my only attempt. George, who fishes almost daily, chided me for starting too late. But hey, I was there to relax so I didn't mind.

Then when my wife had a massage, the relaxing pool kept me captive for only so long. So I jumped on one of the hotel bicycles and pedaled around the area, up and down the dusty roads of the farming community. I saw bright melons ripening in the tropical sun, and locals wearing bandanas like Western outlaws while harvesting fat red chiles.

Along the closest road to the beach, I passed a couple small B&Bs and some rudimentary surf camps. If fishing isn't your thing, try surfing. Along that long stretch of beach is a fine beach break at Cerritos, and the popular point break at San Perdito.

I later took a brief dip in the pounding surf, and in the evening we enjoyed the simple beach cabanas and fire pits the hotel provides for its guests atop the dunes. They even supply the firewood.

The hotel's restaurant offers great meals and further spoils its guests with fresh coffee and a fruit plate delivered to your room each morning. At night, gregarious George delights with guitar and hula lessons around a communal fire pit. I'd hate to see the place change.

What concerned me more was the area. I knew the dirt road days for through traffic were gone. But a broad four lane highway can only bring progress, and a few minutes south of El Pescadero the first multi-unit building was rising like a spectral intruder on a broad sandy beach. The local Mexicans told me they don't want their area to become "another Cabo," but with progress comes opportunity. That two-edged sword will likely force them to accept changes. They live in one of the world's most idyllic spots, and up to now their laid-back culture has been one of taking life as it comes.

Almost prophetic, as if he envisioned an El Pescadero area, Henry Miller in his book Tropic of Cancer wrote, "Day by day. No yesterdays and no tomorrows. The barometer never changes..." Of course, Miller wrote that book before determined developers discovered Baja's "Tropico de Cancer."

(2024 Note: Rancho Pescadero Resort and Spa was closed for remodeling in early 2022 and has since reopened larger and even more luxurious.

Beyond the Peninsula

Festivities in Merida, Yucatan

Adventures from Mainland Mexico

My earliest memories of Mexico were in Baja California as a child in the 1940s. We camped on the beach and enjoyed that mysterious land down south. Later, as noted, I acquired a weekend retreat home on the ocean between Rosarito and Ensenada. *(See: A Cantamar Haven).*

I have always had an affinity with Baja and have found the people there among the most friendly and gracious in the world. In addition, the beaches, deserts, missions, villages, out-of-the-way places, and laid-back resorts there have been a constant attraction to me. Thus, I kept returning to those two intriguing Mexican states that occupy the Baja California peninsula.

My affection for Baja led me to the obvious—to see more of Mexico!

So I have. To date I've been in 28 of the 31 Mexican states, plus D.F. (Mexico City), and I've visited more than half of those states several times each.

This section highlights a few of my experiences on the other side of the Sea of Cortez—the **Mexican Mainland.** The first story is a true adventure that I would never want to relive—how I survived a major hurricane in Mazatlan (Hurricane Olivia, 1975).

In addition to that frightening adventure, I am also including a few other articles from a wealth of Mainland experiences in which I have snorkeled in both the Pacific and the Caribbean, caught sailfish and dorado at Zihuatanejo, lazed in Pacific coast villages along the Costa Alegre, and watched the cliff divers at Acapulco.

My wife and I have also explored unique mountain villages in Colima, Guerrero, and Michoacán and spent time in the picturesque silver town of Taxco.

We have traveled all over the three Yucatan Peninsula states of Quintana Roo, Yucatan, and Campeche, where we've explored numerous Mayan ruins from the popular ones at Chichén Itzá, Cobá, Tulum, Uxmal, and Palenque (Chiapas) to rarely visited ones down narrow dirt jungle roads. By touring individually instead of in a tour bus we've been able to see so much more.

We've experienced Day of Dead celebrations in several Mexican cities, including Veracruz and Xalapa, and watched parades and city-wide activities in Oaxaca, even visiting cemeteries with locals honoring their deceased family members. We've also celebrated Mexican Independence Day festivities in various cities.

We've photographed Aztec ruins at Monte Alban, and picturesque net fishermen at Lake Janitzo in Michoacán.

We've done a lot of walking in our explorations. Leila and I have hiked and walked in jungles, hills, deserts, and for miles around various cities like Guadalajara, Mexico City, Taxco, Puerto Vallarta, and colonial Guanajuanto. One day we walked along the shore of Lake Chapala from Ajijic to Chapala. On another ambitious, but miserably humid day, we walked the seven miles over the hill from Ixtapa to Zihuatanejo.

Through the years we've often rented a car and taken off, usually with my wife driving and me navigating. We've driven from Mazatlan to San Blas and Puerto Vallarta, and on one foray from Mexico City we drove to Acapulco, then up the coast past Zihuatanejo, over the mountains and back to Mexico City.

Among various other driving adventures departing from Mexico City, three years ago we drove to San Luis Potosi, Aguas Calientes, and Zacatecas—where we explored a 16th century silver mine (Mina del Eden) under the city streets.

We've had some interesting and intriguing visits to a variety of places in Mainland Mexico—I invite you to visit some of them with us.

Surviving the Storm (Mazatlan – 1975)

I was alone in Mazatlan, and after a night of wild partying thought the fresh air of a fishing trip would change my perspective. So I walked to the dock and found the skipper I'd been with on a previous trip. Soon we were headed out of the glistening harbor. The fresh salt air and small talk in broken Spanish with the skipper and his deckhand actually helped my mood.

I lost a sailfish after a couple of thrilling leaps in the air but managed to catch a couple of nice dorado (mahi mahi).

However soon the sky started turning slate gray and the wind started whipping the waves into whitecaps. Concerned, we headed back. All the boats, even the professional shrimp boats, were making a beeline for the harbor. Something was up.

At the dock, while the weather became more ominous, and the wind stronger and the sky darker, the crew made up some ceviche (fresh diced fish, tomato, onion, lime juice cocktail) from the dorado. After eating my fill, I gave them the rest of the fish and took off. I headed for the Copa de Leche, across from the sea wall at downtown's Olas Altas beach.

People were scurrying around town. Small groups gathered around shops where radios had ceased their usual fast-tempo music to feature an excited announcer. A couple of my Mazatlan friends, restaurant employee René and his girlfriend Linda, were glued to the radio at the Copa de Leche.

"Huricán," translated René. "Ciclón. And now it has turned toward Mazatlan."

Most destructive hurricane in 50 years

It would be hours before we realized the full effect. It turned out to be Category IV Hurricane Olivia, the most destructive force to hit Mazatlan in 50 years, leaving scores dead, thousands injured, and 50,000 homeless, as winds up to over 150 miles per hour sank boats, wrecked aircraft, and literally ripped the city apart.

We watched the waves across the street leaping higher and higher, spilling over the concrete seawall. As evening's darkness enveloped the already-ominous setting, the rain fell harder, and wind whistled through the city streets, swirling debris with abandon.

This was serious. The hurricane was supposed to continue out to sea, but it had turned and was headed directly at the city.

After we helped René move the tables inside and batten down the business, we knew it was time to head for safety. Linda ran to her hotel next door. My lodging, the small Olas Altas (Tall Waves) Hotel, was two short blocks around the south end of the crescent-shaped waterfront, and up a slight hill.

It was hard to run against the overpowering wind. Had I waited too long? The rain beat harder. Halfway there, all the visible lights in town went out. In the darkness, the sound of the howling wind and crashing surf brought fear.

A restaurant occupied the first floor of my three-story hotel. On the right, steps led up to the second level lobby. I ran up just as the manager got a butane lamp going. I felt secure.

Several guests and a few employees stood nearby on that second-floor lobby gazing out the large louvered window at the tempestuous storm. I joined them briefly, wondering what lay ahead. Large waves (olas altas) were careening in at right angles to our hotel. While water splashed over the high seawall in front, we were on high ground and off to the side of the waves' frontal direction.

I ascended one more flight of steps to my ocean front room on the top floor. Sitting on my bed in the pitch-dark room, I felt uneasy as the windows rattled and the wind howled. Sleep was out of the question. I decided to head down to join the others, feeling my way along hallways and down the stairs.

The storm was noisy now, with thumping and crashing of objects unknown outside. Just as I passed stairs to a rooftop, the door above gave way, and timber, bricks, and gallons of water came cascading down.

Water was not the only problem in the hotel. Here and there a pane of glass could be heard shattering.

One such window shattering was followed by the screams of women. The manager and two employees rushed to the source of the screams, an ocean-front room off the lobby where two frightened American girls met them at the door. Their room was drenched, with water coming in from the broken window as well as water surging in from the lobby floor.

As the girls were escorted to an inside room, three other guests joined me in the lobby, a Mexican man and his attractive but frightened wife, and a calm young man I later learned was an American named Mike.

We stayed by the sturdy check-in counter near the front door. Windows were breaking and things outside were smashing around while the wind howled and roared. The young couple held each other. Our nerves had wound us tense but we all smiled at each other, as if for reassurance.

The Eye of the Storm

Soon it became calm, real calm. While the workers tried to sweep away the six inches or so of water that kept cascading from above, the manager took his flashlight outside. I followed. Debris was everywhere. Car windows were smashed. Electric poles were bent to 45 degrees. He picked up a large "A" from the street that had been ripped from his "Olas Altas" sign.

"Muy malo," we both agreed. Our smiles now hinted more at relief than reassurance. How wrong we were! It was the eye of the storm that was passing over the Olas Altas. Little did I realize then that shortly the spinning storm would attack us from the other direction.

It was near midnight, and I'd had a long day. However. just as I reached my room, I realized my mistake. The storm returned with more velocity than before, as it was now directly hitting the hotel's front rather than the hill behind.

No sooner had I reached my room when a deafening roar sent a window crashing toward me. I ran into the bathroom where I still didn't feel safe. I made a dash to the hotel room door but couldn't open it. I pulled and pulled but the force of the wind behind me was so strong the door would not open.

I had to get out of there and kept trying. I finally forced the door open by wedging one knee in and pulling hard. It opened enough for me to slip into the hallway.

Just then a large hallway window gave way and pieces of glass sailed past me on both sides as I ran. Flashes of lightning provided sporadic illumination over the frightening tableau: water, a foot deep; debris, everywhere; bricks tumbling down from above. I finally reached the lobby, and what I hoped was safety.

The entire lobby window gave way

Just as I reached the sturdy counter where the others were huddled, the lobby's entire louvered window section gave way, and the ensuing mighty gust blew five of us out the front door! We scrambled for the safety of the doorway. We hugged and squeezed together, pressing as closely as possible to the wall.

We were outside the building, between the main entrance and the corner where 18 steps led down to the street!

Wind howled in through the large opening where the lobby window used to be, whirled violently around the lobby itself, and then came blasting out the door.

We shuddered and pressed together as debris whirled around us and hurtled down to the street and into the ocean beyond. The door slammed shut with several panes of its glass sent flying. Someone near me screamed. He'd been cut. We all frantically realized one thing—we were trapped outside—the very worst place to be in the middle of a violent hurricane.

The man who screamed was nearest the door, then Mike, then me, and then the young Mexican couple.

Missing Plate Glass Window

Mike hollered, "Our best chance is to quit blocking the door—let it go—and make a run for it. Maybe we can be protected behind the counter."

As wood, glass, bricks, chairs, and desks were being hurtled through the lobby, he added, "The door's going to go anyhow. This guy's cut badly. We've got to try."

Shortly the wind howling through the lobby slammed the door open. I couldn't see if the first two guys made it inside, because the force of the wind and gusting debris forced me and the couple around the bend. A banister led to the street. We desperately grabbed for it, hoping it would hold.

We flattened our bodies against the wall, squeezing the banister. The woman held my arm. We three were so close our heads all touched, and we kept our faces down for better protection.

The large window over our heads gave way and the man yelled. He was cut. Maybe we all were. Who could tell? Due to the many particles of glass and dirt in the air, our eyes were shut. We were drenched. I licked my lips—salt water—or was it blood? All I knew was I was alive. But for how long?

I was sure we three were the only ones left. I couldn't see how the other two could have made it inside. I reasoned that they were swept down the steps behind us in that initial blast. And what of the others inside? Surely their fate was no better than ours.

The wind, water and debris made it impossible to move. We held on and hoped, fearing death from either debris or being washed away. How long could we hold on? How long had we? When will this end? Many things raced through our minds as we hung on for our lives.

Our bodies were like flags!

Most terrifying was the wind. On three shocking occasions gusts of the fury were strong enough to lift our feet up, and our bodies were like flags, almost horizontal. But we held on. I squeezed the banister with an unknown strength, my left hand facing down, and my right hand facing up. But how long would the grip hold?

The entire hotel shook several times. The accompanying noise was deafening. There were cracking noises. I couldn't tell if it was thunder or if the hotel was going to split in two. Flashes of lightning provided occasional light.

We didn't say much. Occasionally a whimper or a brief prayer in Spanish. Occasionally we gave each other a one-or-two-word encouragement.

Finally, after what seemed an eternity, a shout came from inside. A flashlight beam played across the damaged lobby. "Aqui!" I desperately hollered in answer. A voice told us to try and make a run for his light.

The wind had lessened somewhat. I looked to the couple; the man nodded assent. Hand in hand we ran to the light. It was the manager, who then helped us to an inside room. We'd made it!

The room was crowded. The light played on Mike and the other man—they too had made it. Water was a foot deep in the room, but compared to where we had been, it was calm. I sat on the edge of a bed in utter exhaustion. Tears rolled down my cheeks. I was alive! We all sat in shock as the storm abated, each reflecting on the ordeal we had survived.

Soon the manager made the sign of the cross, shook his head, hugged the three of us, and muttered something about "two hours."

The butane lamp helped the woman attend to her husband's cut hand—it was not too serious. The other fellow, a hotel employee, had a towel wrapped around his arm—his hand was half severed, but fortunately he had been able to stop the bleeding. He was among the thousands later whisked off in one of the ambulances that wailed through the city.

We survived a disaster

I looked into the eyes of the couple, Luis and Lydia, visiting from Chihuahua—on their honeymoon! Now our smiles meant many things, relief, exhaustion, and a bond formed by those who survive a disaster. Drenched and leaning against each other, we dozed intermittently until dawn.

Along with being soaked, I was shaking from raw nerves as I returned to my room. There I was welcomed by shards of broken windows littered about, and on the floor – the bathroom door that had been ripped from its hinges. And I had tried to seek refuge behind it!

Salt water covered the hotel room floor, some 60 feet above and across the street from the ocean. I lost all loose belongings not in my secured suitcase that had been banged around the room but was still there. In the center of it I actually found one set of half-dry clothes.

Outside was a shambles: restaurant and hotel furniture all over the street, steel electric lights totally crumpled, reinforced concrete benches smashed, windows broken everywhere, cars demolished, boats sunk, bricks and walls crumbled everywhere, and sirens wailed around the town as ambulances dodged fallen trees and power lines to help those stricken.

I took photos of the devastation, selling one after I returned home to my estimable hometown newspaper, the *Los Angeles Times.* (Oct. 28, 1975).

I looked back up at the Olas Altas Hotel. It really was gutted. How ironic, I thought, a hotel destroyed by its own namesake—"High Waves."

AFTER THE BLOW FELL—Debris on street in Matzatlan where hurricane death toll rose to 27.
Photo by Greg Niemann

Author's Photo as it Appeared in the Los Angeles Times on Tuesday, October 28, 1975

I left Mazatlan the next day. As the taxi dodged the disaster's aftermath enroute to the airport, I was still unaware of the full impact of the storm.

Most boats were sunk, and all 14 of the small airplanes at the Mazatlan Airport had been flipped upside down.

I've been back to Mazatlan several times through the years, and every time I've gone back I stop by the old Olas Altas Hotel, even if it's just to kiss that sturdy banister.

An Uncomfortable City Tour (Mexico City – 1995)

Mexico City is one of the world's largest metropolises with 20-something million people scrambling all over the place. We joined them. We stayed at a centuries-old hotel near the "Zocalo"—in the Mexican heart of the city—away from the tourist area called the "Zona Rosa." Yet even though we discovered the city on our own, we did join the tourists for a day.

Mexico City Zocala

We walked, took taxis, and used the excellent Mexico City subway system (Metro). One day we took the subway to the "Terminal del Sur," and then a public bus over the mountains to the city of Cuernavaca (total round-trip cost about $12.00 for the two of us. Another day we took the subway to Xochimilco where we joined the throngs of people on picturesque boats as we plied the extensive waterways.

To visit the "Teotihuacan" pyramids about 50 miles north of the city, we considered renting a car. Instead, we opted to take a day tour, something we normally avoid.

We were rookies in the "tour" game but should not have been surprised at how captive they can be. We learned! It was our only tour as we generally avoid being shuttled around be others.

I'll never forget that pyramid tour. Our "international" group consisted of a 40ish woman from Stuttgart, Germany whose husband was attending meetings so she was out to see the sights alone. There were two elderly women from California's San Fernando Valley.

A young man from England was seeing as much of the world as possible in what seemed as short a time as possible. There was also a young Japanese couple.

There was a charming young woman from Moscow, Russia who spoke Russian, French and Spanish, but no English. Irena was married to the temporary Argentinean ambassador to Mexico. He previously was ambassador to Russia.

Aside from my wife and I, the tenth member was a 62-year-old man from Quebec, Canada, taking a day off from a working visit. He was able to converse in French with the Russian woman.

Our tour guide Caesar mostly spoke English for our group, reverting to Spanish occasionally for Irena.

Often the German woman looked puzzled. If I could think of the German words I had gleaned from my military service in West Germany, I would help translate. Thus, we set out to conquer the pyramids.

First the bus stopped for 45 long minutes to allow a reciprocal curio shop time to take advantage of our shopping instincts. Captive in that shop full of overpriced handicrafts, we could see the Pyramid of the Sun looming over the distant fields, beckoning our closer inspection.

The tour company stopped at the shop first because vendors at the pyramids would sell us the same items for a fraction of the price, especially if one could haggle. No point in having a busload of tourists "shopped out" when arriving at a paid curio stop.

No haggling in this captive gift shop, however. Only after a very few minor, and pricey, purchases were made were we allowed to continue.

As the bus entered the pyramid property, we noticed a half dozen or so restaurants where we figured we'd be taken for lunch. A lunch stop was planned, but lunch was not included in the price. We were aware tour operators cut deals with restaurants as they did with the curio shop. That's expected and accepted. After all, you're miles from anywhere anyway. But we didn't expect what they had in mind.

The ancient pyramids were outstanding. Five of us climbed both the Pyramid of the Moon and the Pyramid of the Sun, one of the world's largest man-made structures.

My wife is a shopping genius and haggling with strolling vendors, made such good deals at the site the Canadian and the Englishman both gave her money to make their purchases.

Noon had come and gone before we boarded the bus again. We disembarked near some more ruins, a number of curio stands, and a cafeteria where several other busloads of people were filing in and out.

We toured the Temple of the Serpent figuring by the time we rounded these ruins, the cafeteria would be ready to accommodate us. It was not to be. We were hurried back in the bus, with vendors still running after my wife, trying to accept her last and final offer.

Hungry, we rode for an interminable length of time, turning off the toll road, bouncing along secondary roads with enough potholes to preclude resting or napping. We passed scores of restaurants. 1:30 came and went.

I pulled out my map. After lunch we were to visit the Basilica of Guadalupe which was not far from the toll road we took out. Where were we going now? Finally, I saw airplanes. We were now back at the Mexico City airport, having taken an incredibly circuitous route. The bus even weaved in and out of the waiting taxi lanes and finally pulled up in front of the busy passenger terminal.

We had spent over an hour going way out of our way to eat in an airport restaurant where the reciprocal deal obviously was made. It was now 2:20. By now, we were more furious than hungry.

Smiling Caesar proudly led his charges into this second-floor restaurant for a dose of "airport food" only to discover that most of us had bolted for other fare. I wonder what kind of kickback he got for bringing in only four people. The rest of us took off for the food court in front of a blubbering and embarrassed Caesar.

It was a quieter, moodier, afternoon as we were rushed through the "Basilica de Guadalupe" so fast that later in the week my wife and I took the Metro for a more extensive visit.

Sculpture of Juan Diego & Fray Juan de Zumarraga, Mexico City

The next day Irena joined us as we explored Chapultepec Park together, enjoying each other's company despite the language difficulty. We later became pen pals as she practiced English.

(Note: this was before the proliferation of the internet when pen pals meant physical paper).

Earlier, while atop the pyramids, I had taken photos of the Canadian and Brit, which commenced more foreign writing. *(Note: This was before today's super-handy smartphone technology which makes such social contacts handier and more common).*

More Mexico City

We saw a lot during our first visit to Mexico's bustling capital, but we'd been back several times, exploring more and more of the city.

We learned where all the municipal markets were (Mercado de San Juan, La Merced Market, etc.), joining locals in the bustling stalls that sell everything from clothing, tools, produce, butchered meat, and iced-down fresh fish. The markets all have crowded food stalls where a few pesos for lunch will reward you with regional favorites. Some stands are so popular you have to stand to munch your tacos.

We visited the home/studio of Frida Kahlo and Diego Rivera in Coyoacán, the Palacio de Bellos Artes, and museums, parks, and monuments. We spent a lot

Belles Artes, Mexico City

of time walking around the Zocalo and Historic Center, visiting the Cathedral and appreciating the murals in the Palacio Nacional.

On one trip I even spent a day at a writing workshop in the city's San Angel sector. It was presented by the very fine author C.M. Mayo, who had written one of my favorite books about Baja California. (*Miraculous Air,* The University of Utah Press, 2002).

We've flown into Mexico City often, using the city as a jumping-off place, often renting cars to head out to other parts of the country. (My wife usually drives while I try to navigate).

One time we drove to Taxco, down to Acapulco, up the coast to Zihuantanejo, inland to Uruapan, Patzcuaro, and Morelia, and then back to Mexico City. On another occasion we drove to San Miguel de Allende and environs to partake of the Mexican Independence Day (Sept. 16) festivities.

Another time we left the city for the Gulf of Mexico and enjoyed de Los Muertos festivities in Veracruz. From there we went to Xalapa in the hills, and then to Tlaxcala and Puebla. Near Cholula we were visiting some ruins and looked up to see the famous volcano Popocatepetl get quite active and spew ash and smoke into the sky.

You would think after renting and returning enough cars from the Mexico City airport that I'd be better at directions in that area. You'd be wrong. We're fine out on the highways, but sometimes we have to make a few wrong turns when we get back to the city.

But unlike being captive by a tour guide, we usually stop for some good local food *before* we get to the airport!

Route of the Maya (Yucatan – 2007)

It was about the hardest rain I'd ever seen – the downpour was torrential. We had the windshield wipers going full blast and still could hardly see out. Fortunately, we were almost to our destination in the middle of the Yucatan peninsula. We'd left the Cancun Airport under threatening skies and hoped to make it to Valladolid before dark. We almost made it, before the skies unleashed their fury and the darkness settled in.

My wife drove and I navigated as we entered the town with water pooling everywhere. Activity had stopped with the exception of shopkeepers busy with brooms and mops trying to keep as much water as possible out of their shops. I was looking for the El Meson del Marques hotel which I knew should be facing the town's main square (zocalo). Getting to it was another problem. As we drove around the square, I was afraid we'd stall in the deep water.

Spotting the hotel, Leila pulled up to the high curb in front and I removed my shoes and socks, rolled up my pants and waded to the lobby entrance. A hotel employee came out and directed Leila to the secured parking lot behind the hotel, and as we were checking in the heaviest rain abated, leaving the merchants to get the edge in the battle to keep the water out of their shops.

We loved the old El Meson del Marques hotel—for its prime location, the helpful service, and the cozy respite it especially provided that night. The restaurant is excellent, with tables surrounding an enticing courtyard and an extensive menu, including some traditional Mayan meals.

We've been back several times since that memorable rainy night. The rooms have cable TV and telephones; some have bidets and tubs. The swimming pool is especially refreshing after a hot humid day exploring the area. Valladolid is an excellent base for exploration of the archaeological sites and natural treasures of the Yucatan, including Chichén Itzá ruins and several fascinating caves and cenotes.

Back to the Yucatan

We've visited much of Mexico, but out of Mexico's 32 states (including the Federal District), the three states (Quintana Roo, Yucatan, and Campeche) that comprise the Yucatan peninsula have been a particular magnet.

In the Yucatan, we've explored numerous Mayan ruins from the popular ones at Chichén Itzá, Cobá, Tulum, and Uxmal, to some that are rarely visited down narrow dirt roads in the jungle.

Some of those old Mayan sites, like one at Oxkintok, where the state of Yucatan borders Campeche, inspire awe as the somber quiet is disrupted only by chattering birds and monkeys. That jungle site is one of several so tranquil and ethereal it's hard to picture the thousands of people who once occupied a vibrant city there.

The entire Yucatan peninsula is porous limestone and riddled like Swiss cheese. Caves and cenotes (holes full of water) are everywhere. Most caves will have a guide or two sitting around outside to take the occasional visitor inside their dark and perplexing interior labyrinths. The massive Grutas de Calcehtok (near Oxkintok) cave system is considered one of the largest on the peninsula, and occasionally cavers still discover more tunnels there.

Among more frequented caves is Loltun in southern Yucatan near the confluence of all three states. A third option is another large and extraordinary cave, the Bakankanche cave system near the heavily visited Mayan site of Chichén Itzá.

Swimming in Cenotes

There are cenotes everywhere and a swim in one of them will be long remembered. I especially like the Cenote Dzitnup near Chichén Itzá, where a beautiful turquoise pool rests in a vast limestone chamber replete with the requisite stalagmites and stalactites. A small hole in the chamber roof allows daylight and casts a spotlight on the water. It seems mandatory to swim over to it.

Another of my favorite cenotes is in downtown Valladolid. The Cenote Zaci is about 240 feet deep, with a walkway around its 140-foot diameter, and beckons visitors to jump in the cool emerald green waters. It is walking distance from the El Mesón del Marquis hotel on the town zocalo.

The main road from Cancun passes Valladolid and Chichén Itzá on its way to the wonderful old colonial city of Mérida. The toll road is wide, straight as an arrow, and well maintained.

Mayan Woman

Once you get off the toll road, the roads are generally paved and good, but slow. Every small village features at least two "topes" or speed bumps – and you *will* come to a stop before crawling over them. The flip side of driving those secondary roads is seeing Mayan life as it has been for centuries, the thatched housing, unique tricycle taxis, and traditional dress (long white gowns with beautiful elaborate embroidery, and for the men white trousers and straw hats.)

You can fly into Cancun or Mérida with a host of air carriers and remain ensconced at any number of Cancun resorts. But to really experience the Yucatan, try to get out of the large resort areas and enjoy all that the Yucatan peninsula has to offer.

(2024 Update: A modern train system (Tren Maya) is almost totally completed to facilitate getting to much of the Yucatan peninsula.)

Elegant Old Haciendas (Yucatán – 2011)

Imagine stepping out of your private hot tub to relax on an outside bed. You're surrounded by green jungle, chattering birds, and old ruins that poke through the greenery. You're at the back door of your massive upscale suite resurrected from a grand old estate, and after your nap, you can walk down the path, perhaps heading to a masseuse appointment or a romantic dinner in a gourmet restaurant.

Mexico's Yucatán has a lot more to offer than the resort area of Cancun. The peninsula's three states (Quintana Roo, Yucatán, and Campeche) share a Mayan history, and majestic ruins, charming villages, colonial towns, and old hemp and sugar plantations dot the verdant landscape. In recent years, the haciendas of these old plantations have themselves become prime destinations, and deservedly so.

The haciendas were once the impressive estates of sisal (hemp) factory owners who made fortunes supplying natural plant fibers to the rope and twine making industry in the late 18th and early 19th centuries. Many were also sugar farms and cattle ranches.

When synthetic materials replaced natural sisal, most of Mexico's haciendas were abandoned. Many fell into ruin. But for those who like to revel in antiquity, some have been saved and given new life.

A few have been meticulously restored, including five that are part of the Starwood (Sheraton, Westin, etc.) Properties Luxury Collection. There are also several other non-Starwood haciendas, but through the years we'd been accumulating Starwood points for hotel and resort usage.

Each resort hacienda has been totally renovated, and modern amenities (big-screen TVs, private hot pools, and outside beds) are delightfully blended into the old plantation buildings. Gourmet restaurants and creative swimming pools highlight historic brick buildings where old wheels, pulleys and other equipment still lie around.

I like the haciendas for their preservation of a past era, the feeling of romance and history, as well as for the modern amenities and sense of privacy now offered. Plus, they are usually located within striking distance of many peninsula attractions. We enjoyed the first one so much we made it a quest to stay in several others, budgeting our time in each as they can get pricey.

Two non-Starwood haciendas, Hacienda Chichén Itzá and Hacienda Uxmal are owned by Mayaland Resorts.

Hacienda Chichén Itzá

The Hacienda Chichén Itzá is located just a two-minute walk from the famous ancient Mayan city of Chichén Itzá. Recently renovated, the eco-friendly hotel has 44 air-conditioned rooms in cottages sprawled over lush gardens where colorful birds sing their approval. There's a nice swimming pool and a very good restaurant. While not the most luxurious hacienda, its location allows you to walk over to the pyramid's light and sound show after all the busses have headed back to Cancun.

Hacienda Uxmal

The Hotel Hacienda Uxmal, adjacent to the important Uxmal Mayan ruins, has been host to royalty and celebrities. According to the hotel, Queen Elizabeth of England and Prince Phillip, the late Princess of Monaco Grace Kelley and Prince Rainier, Jacqueline Kennedy Onassis, the Shah of Iran, and others are among those who have used Hacienda Uxmal as their base while visiting the Yucatán.

It's a great location to visit the ruins (about 78 kilometers south of Mérida) but is not a real sisal hacienda. It's also near the ruins at Kabah, Sayil and Labná, as well as the Loltun Caves. I found it to be a nice two-story hotel with swimming pool and good buffet meals to accommodate all the bus people it attracts.

Hacienda Xcanatun

The closest hacienda hotel to downtown Mérida, Hacienda Xcanatun was originally constructed in the mid-18th century to oversee livestock and agriculture. It then became one of the most important sisal producing haciendas in the area. After a five-year rehabilitation, it opened in 2000 and is now one of Mexico's Boutique Hotels.

The 18 suites in three buildings are finished with historical millwork and elegant furnishings. The lush nine-acre gardens, quaint on-site chapel, traditional Mayan spa treatments, and outstanding restaurant make this a memorable experience. Hacienda Xcanatun is near the impressive Dzibilchaltun ruins.

Starwood Properties Luxury Collection

All five of the Starwood Haciendas are understated elegance. They offer luxury and privacy in incredibly dramatic settings. It's hard to pick a favorite.

Hacienda San José (Izamal)

Hacienda San José is the closest to the picturesque colonial city of Izamal where horse carriages provide taxi service over the cobbled streets. A 1562 Franciscan

Convent there even attracted Pope John Paul II.

The 15 rooms at Hacienda San José include four Mayan-style rounded stand-alone deluxe huts and one room, #9, which has a spectacular ceiba tree growing in the bathroom right up through the roof.

Many of the rooms have small private pools and hot tubs out back. We got upgraded to a suite next to the chapel, where we had dinner served on our private patio next to our private pool. The main pool includes hammocks over the water. It's an incredibly relaxing experience.

Private Pool, Hacienda San Jose

Hacienda Temazon

Despite their basic similarities, each Starwood hacienda has its own personality. Hacienda Temazon, which has hosted U.S. President Bill Clinton and international celebrities, has a broad dramatic main entrance, a welcoming lobby/restaurant and a vast back garden anchored by a long swimming pool that laps up against what was the hacienda's machine room.

Hacienda Temazon

Its 28 rooms (some with terraces and private outdoor plunge pools) have been created in every building on the property—including what was once the stable. There's also a spa which offers the option of booking massages in the cool room that is the organic entrance to an underground river on the property.

This was our first Hacienda experience and the "wow" factor never left. The restaurant meals were great and after dinner, the Mayan worker would come to our room through the jungle out back to fill and heat our private outside plunge pool.

Hacienda Santa Rosa

The Hacienda Santa Rosa, 65 kilometers south of the Mérida Airport and just past a small village, opens up to a broad field where a delightful pink chapel anchors the property. With lots of soft color and intricate decorative painting—some of it original and all of it created from records of how the house originally looked—this hacienda has a feminine feel.

Hacienda Santa Rosa

Today, Santa Rosa's 11 rooms are furnished with

European pieces and feature privacy and elegance. The swimming pool is built in and around an old building. And workers build bonfires in front of the terrace during dinner time. Room #5 is big and roomy with a private pool and patio. Number #6 is a great room but a bit more public, and the Casa Maya room (a separate thatched house) has a private hot tub and outside bed and hammock.

The Santa Rosa grounds include a garden and the Mayan gardener beamed with pride as he showed us the traditional medicinal herbs and plants.

Hacienda Uyamón

Hacienda Uyamón

The most remote of the Starwood haciendas (about 30 kilometers south of Campeche) is one of my favorites. There are 12 stand-alone rooms dotted throughout its lush setting which are reached by following a geometric 100' long water feature/art installation through the jungle.

A small spa now occupies what was the stable and an intimate swimming pool has been created around elegantly crumbling columns which once supported a roof that's long gone.

The restaurant is top notch, and once we even had dinner under the mammoth ceiba tree with a private bonfire built for us against the adjacent ruins.

The rooms are all private, but a couple of the outside beds and private pools can be seen through the trees from trails (#8, for example). I've stayed in #11 twice and the spacious room opens to a small outdoor grotto type hot pool, and a covered bed on a platform. Deliciously private and romantic.

Hacienda Puerta Campeche

Hacienda Campeche

Finally, there's Hacienda Puerta Campeche, right in old town Campeche, capital of the state of the same name. Not actually a hacienda, it's a series of buildings once used to store sisal. Skylights brighten up the 15 rooms that feature 18-foot ceilings with exposed beams and rafters, comfortable beds, and cool tiled floors. Room #1 upstairs is large and luxurious with private rooftop patio.

The hotel's dramatic pool meanders through the foundations and columns of a flooded building, like an old Roman crypt. An excellent restaurant highlights the hacienda.

While most of the others are isolated, Hacienda Puerta Campeche is right in old town and across the street from the nightly light show highlighting the walled city's ramparts. It's a great walking town, with narrow cobbled streets and brightly colored pastel colonial buildings.

In addition to the ones mentioned, there are other haciendas throughout the Yucatán, some restored for hotels, others for shops or museums, and others well preserved, but not renovated (Hacienda Yaxcopoil, for example, is like stepping back in time). And Hacienda Ochil is not a hotel, but has been carefully renovated for tours and has a restaurant and gift shop.

Staying in a restored hacienda is not for everyone. Most are very old buildings, often in the middle of some very dens0e jungle. Occasionally we have found mosquitoes, flies, and bugs. It's almost like luxurious camping in unbelievably romantic and picturesque historical surroundings.

There are hotels and resorts around the world, but the Haciendas of the Yucatan are in a class by themselves, and definitely among the most unique.

(2024 Update: Starwood Resorts has now morphed into Marriott Bonvoy.)

A Puerto Vallarta Holiday (2022)

We try to make our regular visit to the Mexican Riviera town of Puerto Vallarta in winter, when a chill comes to Southern California. We also enjoy the numerous festivities, like the Dia de Guadalupe processions. Yet another reason is to attend the Wednesday night Art Walk in Old Town Vallarta.

Every Wednesday night, from November to May, a dozen or so art galleries (In December, 2022 there were 16) in Viejo Vallarta (Old Town) stay open late to welcome tourists who wander along the cobbled roads following self-guided maps from one gallery to another. Actually about 30 galleries get into the act by capitalizing on the official participation of their neighbors. Wine and snacks are offered at most, and there are paintings, statues, and other media for everyone's taste. It's a great opportunity to meet the artists as well as other tourists.

The large and sprawling city of Puerto Vallarta grew up around Old Town, an area of narrow cobbled streets, numerous craft and jewelry shops, restaurants, a small shady plaza and the Church of Nuestra Señora de Guadalupe, whose ornate tower crown is a Puerto Vallarta icon.

Not only has the town grown in size since my first visit there 50 years ago (1974), but in class and distinction as well. The widened concrete malecón, or sea

Art on Puerto Vallarta's Malecón

wall, extends along the length of Old Town and is interspersed with eye-catching sculptures. Tourists join the locals strolling the broad seaside walkway at dusk, enjoying snacks or buying mementoes from carts, or catching some social activity at the open-air theater known as Los Arcos (The Arches). From the malecón, cameras click like mad when the sun sets over beautiful Bandera Bay, the largest on Mexico's Pacific Coast.

In recent years the malecón has been extended south to what is known as the "Romantic Zone." Now a pedestrian bridge crosses the Rio Cuale along the beach linking the two sections of town. Previously only two one-way automobile bridges linked the town.

In the middle of the Rio Cuale with pedestrian access from the bridges is the Isla Cuale, a long narrow island with a path linking a few nice restaurants and lots of handicraft stands wedged in and among immense, shady banyan trees, some home to several bright green iguanas. For those who like a little fun leaving the island, there are two pedestrian rope suspension bridges that really bounce you up and down.

Near the river and fronting the beach, several old garden type hotels have been torn down and replaced with large high-rise condo units.

The Romantic Zone is incredibly popular and is the center of most of the town's vibrant nightlife, much of it catering to a gay clientele. There are noisy hotels crammed up against one another, lots of restaurants and two small sandy beaches that can get very crowded. There are many condos and B&Bs for rent in the area, but I'd check the noise factor out first.

While Puerto Vallarta (PV to many) has only been a major tourist destination for less than 50 years, there is evidence of continuous human habitation in the area since about 580 B.C. In 1524 there was a large battle in the area between Hernán Cortes and the Spaniards against over 10,000 indigenous people. Later the Bay of Banderas served as a refuge for the Spanish Manila galleons.

Puerto Vallarta itself was founded in 1851 as Las Peñas de Santa Maria de Guadalupe and became a municipality in 1918 when it was renamed after the former Jalisco governor Ignacio Vallarta. It became a city in 1981 and now has over 175,000 inhabitants.

Liz Taylor and Richard Burton

What put PV on the proverbial map was in 1963 when American director John Huston (there's a statue of him on Isla Cuale) filmed "The Night of The Iguana" in Mismaloya, a small village to the south. During the filming, the extensive media coverage followed Elizabeth Taylor and her extramarital affair with Richard Burton. Their romantic hideout, Casa Kimberley—two small villas in Old Town that share a footbridge between them—is still a tourist destination.

By the late 1960s the Mexican government had invested in highways and an airport, making PV accessible for the first time. At first most tourists were Mexican. Then the Americans started coming.

Over the years hotels have been added, stretching north to the airport and beyond, into the neighboring state of Nayarit. There is now a huge marina welcoming cruise ships all week long, and a second marina farther north at Nuevo Vallarta.

The surge continues northward and Punta Mita, the point at the far end of the bay, has some elaborate five-star resorts. North of Punta Mita along a broad sandy beach called the Costa Azul are a couple of old villages that are slowly being taken over by gringos. The first, Sayulita, still has some charm left, but I was asked to "speak English" in one restaurant obviously owned by expatriates.

The next town north, San Pancho, is still a quiet little Mexican village, with young girls sweeping the dirt roads in front of shops, dogs sleeping under mango trees, and old men watching visitors walk by. But not for long. I saw grandiose plans to totally redo the place in American style, adding a whole hillside of condos.

While PV has obviously been discovered, there's still plenty to do.

In recent trips I've gone out fishing for sailfish and dorado, and once went on a snorkeling excursion where we stopped for lunch on a secluded tropical beach; returning to town we slowed to watch some whales in the bay.

Puerto Vallarta offers evening dinner cruises, an old galleon cruise with fireworks, whale watching trips, jungle tours, dune buggy adventures, bungee jumping, kayaking, golf, parasailing over the bay, banana boats, swimming, and the most recent addition of zip line adventures taking you out over the jungle canopy.

The village of Yelapa

A couple years ago I finally made the boat trip to Yelapa, something I had been putting off for one reason or another since 1974. Yelapa is on the mainland south of Puerto Vallarta, but it could be on the moon for all its accessibility. The small beach village just recently received electricity to connect with the world.

The only way to get there is by water taxi (about $20 U.S. roundtrip) and there are only two boats each day, each of which gives you about three hours there. From the small dock you can walk around the village paths although some are wide enough for tourists on horses and little golf carts that drop off supplies to the handful of little cafes and shops.

At the top of the village a waterfall tumbles out of the jungle into a rock-lined pool and is a relaxing reward for hiking up the path.

Another hike takes you past a lagoon to a broad sandy beach where three or four restaurants on the sand are open for the lunchtime visitors. At the end of the beach is a small rustic hotel, La Lagunita, where thatch-roofed rooms peek out from the jungle.

Yelapa gives one the feeling of stepping back in time, even if it's only an hour boat ride from Puerto Vallarta.

In PV itself, there are hotels everywhere depending on your taste. I like to be downtown where I can walk to everything if possible. One time we stayed at the Westin hotel in the Marina and while the amenities are nice, we found we were hopping on busses every day to go downtown. The city buses that cover the main road in front of all the hotels are inexpensive, seemingly safe, and run frequently. Lots of middle-aged gringos ride the buses.

Closer in, within walking distance (about 1 mile) from Old Town is the Sheraton Buganvilias. Closer yet, is the Buenaventura, and next door to it, the Premiere which is a bit more upscale and adults only.

Fine dining is a PV pastime and I have a few favorites. The Cafe de Artistes is a wonderful restaurant with both a romantic patio and indoor dining. In Old Town, it is across the street from some of the art galleries, so good for Wednesday night.

Two of my favorites are on the Isla Cuale—the River Cafe, and the elegant Le Bistro. Another don't miss is the La Palapa, on the Playa Los Muertos in the Romantic Zone. Right on the sand, we try to lunch there every trip. The walls are covered with photos as I remembered the town from the 1970s.

Puerto Vallarta is seemingly for everyone, and you can cast pretensions aside and dine on the street. I found some excellent shrimp tostadas at a stand called Mariscos del Jefe on the main street a block from the Ley grocery store. The guy's been doling out great mariscos (sea food) from that stand for 38 years.

While the city definitely has been growing, Puerto Vallarta has thankfully retained much of its romantic and enchanting heritage.

Sailfish in Zihuatanejo (2008)

Rounding the point, the returning fishermen throttled back their engines and gentled their pangas and small cruisers into the cozy harbor. Bearing exuberant sunred tourists and dead dark-blue sailfish, one by one the boats gurgled up to the sturdy old concrete dock.

I watched, looking for someone amid the hubbub of the early afternoon ritual on the Zihuatanejo pier.

I spotted him, helping one of his departing passengers onto the dock. Glancing up, he nodded at me in recognition, smiled, and set about to anchor and clean the source of his livelihood, the trim 24-foot panga *Dos Hermanos.*

Deciding to wait, I noted eager young dock boys toting and wheeling heavy sailfish, those unlucky ones not released by the anglers that is, to the photo spot where the vanquished speedsters of the sea would be hung upside down, while their captives would grin and gloat for the folks back home.

Although it had been months since I'd fished with him, Capitán Cheva Ruiz remembered me and approached after his boat was secure. "Gregorio, how you been?" We usually spoke Spanish, but like almost all of Mexico's sport fishermen, he has a rudimentary working knowledge of English.

Capitán Cheva Ruiz

I answered, "Fine. Remember those three sailfish I caught that day?"

He beamed, "And dorado too."

A better memory than me! I'd forgotten the dorado (mahi mahi) so excited was I to land three big pez velas (sailfish) in one day's outing.

Cheva had a booking the next day, but said he'd give that couple to his brother Adolfo in the *Dos Hermanos II* so he could accommodate me. Whether fishing with me solo was easier, or I tipped better, I didn't know. Maybe he just liked me. Regardless, full of anticipation I planned to return the next morning.

A fisherman's dream

Zihuatanejo, or just plain "Z," on Mexico's Pacific coast is a fisherman's dream, and sailfish from 70 up to 150 pounds are abundant. So are marlin. On the week of my last visit in December 2008, someone caught and released a marlin weighing over 400 pounds.

I've matched my personal "hat trick" of three "sails" in one day on other occasions in "Z." If Cheva or Adolfo were both booked, I've fished with the veteran Francisco "Chico" Garcia in the *Rosa Nautica,* or his brother Martín Garcia in the *Marflen* or *Llamorada.*

Fishing is best from December through May when the blue water current is generally close in and pelagics including sailfish, marlin, tuna, wahoo and dorado abound. I've only had a couple poor trips in "Z" usually when the water was roiled from recent storms.

I release my sailfish after a couple of quick photos, but occasionally one will swallow the hook and die, whereupon I give him to the skipper, who will sell it or take it home to his family.

There are numerous Mexican destinations known for good fishing: Los Cabos and the East Cape in Baja California, and Mazatlan farther north on the mainland, but Zihuatanejo is my favorite. I'm not alone. *Sport Fishing* magazine listed "Z" in second place out of the world's top 20 sailfish destinations.

There are several fishing tournaments including a major Catch and Release Sailfish Tournament and an annual fly fishing one run by my outdoor writing colleagues Gary and Yvonne Graham of *Baja On The Fly*. Their contestants catch big sailfish, roosterfish (pez gallo), and tuna by casting a fly rod to fish that have been "teased" close in by live bait. For more info on this or other tournaments or to line up a day of fishing in advance, Zihuatanejo-based Ed Kunze can help.

Boats vary in size and comfort, although going solo I've found the smaller pangas quite effective. Skippers usually troll four or five lines, using stout Fenwick or Sabre rods with Penn International 30 and 50 reels. They experiment to see which colored lures draw the most action that day and they also sew bait fish onto large hooks.

Game fishing involves a lot of sitting and watching. Leaving port, you delight in seeing the tropical sky brighten, and the awakening sun paint a swath of tangerine and crimson across distant peaks. Alongside the boat, porpoises frolic in your wake. Turtles rise to the surface like dark rafts and then gently kick their webbed feet to slide back to the mysteries of the deep. Sometimes a whale might startle you by breaching nearby.

Adolfo Ruiz heading to harbor

Birds are more than a curiosity as their squawking presence and dashing dives indicate boils of bait fish, brought to the surface by larger fish. Large concentrations of birds all circling, chattering, and diving will quickly draw several boats of fishermen, all intent on disrupting the food chain.

When a fin is spotted, the capitán will quickly and deftly circle to draw hooked offerings in front of the game. The hours of ennui from scanning the sea quickly become adrenalin-pumping action as the clip snaps from the outrigger and line starts whirring off the reel.

You allow your fish to run before setting the hook and tightening the line. Then as you raise the rod, the large sailfish will make a dramatic leap high in the air. Down with the rod, and you quickly trying to pump line back. Again and again. You gain. The fish gains. The agile 100-plus pounder clears the water again and tail

Sailfish in Zihuatanejo

dances for several yards. Finally, after an exciting 20-30 minutes, the fish tires and allows you to bring him in.

The capitán pulls him aboard briefly for photos. You're elated from the heady experience and your muscles are sore from the battle. You're also in awe of your adversary who impudently flutters his trademark erectile dorsal fin as he swims away.

Zihuatanejo and Ixtapa

Zihuatanejo has long been a fishing village and still retains much of its old charm, which is saying something because its sister town Ixtapa, about seven miles north over a hill was created specifically for tourism. The first of Ixtapa's 13 major hotels opened in 1975 along the two-mile long Palmar Beach. Ixtapa has a marina where fishing boats can also be secured among the yachts bobbing in its 450-acre harbor. Nearby are well-manicured golf courses.

The towns are totally different. There are no golf courses in Zihuatanejo, nor any high-rise hotels, nor fancy harbor. The town fronts the quaint Playa Principal (Main Beach) and more intimate Playa Madera, while farther down the ten-mile horseshoe-shaped bay is the broad Playa La Ropa, home to several nice low-key getaway hotels. On the point before La Ropa beach is the upscale Casa Que Canta hotel, its five-star amenities sprawling down the rocky promontory.

I prefer the friendly Brisas Del Mar hotel on the Playa Madera, a small beach fronting other comfy bungalows and inns like the Bungalows Ley next door. A concrete path has been built on the rocks connecting that beach with Main Beach. I can slip out of my hotel room and walk along the path to the historic fishing dock in 15 minutes. My well-rested wife usually greets me there when I return in the early afternoon.

We enjoy December, where along with great fishing, village celebrations include the Christmas posadas and the Day of Our Lady of Guadalupe (Dec. 12), when the townspeople really fiesta. They dress their young children in traditional costumes, and neighborhood groups carry "their" floral-bedecked float in procession to the church where special masses are conducted. There's plenty of food, music, dancing and fun. Celebrations are a regular part of Mexican life and seem both reverent and vibrant in a village like Zihuatanejo.

Humid in summer

With "Z" on the Pacific north of Acapulco, the weather is hot and humid much of the year but most of the rain and stickiness occurs from June to October.

Cruise ships have discovered the beautiful round bay of Zihuatanejo and its accompanying town; more and more of them stop there each year, anchoring and lightering their passengers ashore. Their intrusion has forever changed the town, adding additional seafood restaurants and trinket shops along the beach, but "Z" has resisted better than most locales and managed to stay the course.

The locals won a big victory in 2007 by thwarting grandiose plans for a major harbor to better accommodate the ships. "It would have destroyed our town," one shop owner told me. "We want them, but there was no need to change what they come here for."

Besides fishing, there are other tourist and sporting activities in the Ixtapa-Zihuatanejo area, including horseback riding, snorkeling, diving, kayaking, banana boats, parasailing, catamarans, day trips to idyllic Las Gatas beach across the bay, and even swimming with dolphins. Along with clothing and trinkets, there are silver shops and several art galleries in both "Z" and Ixtapa.

Main Beach Zihuatanejo

If you like a major high-rise resort type place, go to Ixtapa. There are a number of nice restaurants there and typical resort amenities. But if you prefer a more independent trip, like wandering around a small town and nosing through the maze of a bustling Mercado Central, "Z" is for you.

We go to "Z" about once a year, even if it's just for a few day "fix." All we seek is one dinner at the world-famous Coconuts, one dinner at the Kau Kan restaurant on the hill overlooking the bay, a day for me to go fishing, and perhaps two or three lunches at Any, one of our all-time favorite restaurants.

Restaurante Any (La Casa de Pozole) is a small authentic Mexican restaurant replete with thatched roof in the heart of downtown. Their food is typical of the State of Guerrero, including tamales and a mouth-watering pozole, a thick soup made of hominy and chicken or pork (instead of menudo's tripe). What makes it special is the plate load of goodies that accompanies it. Founded by Felipe and Rogelia Mejia in 1988, the restaurant is now run by their children Liza and Ana Maria "Any" Mejia and brother-in-law Jose. They now have a second restaurant in Ixtapa.

Among Zihuatanejo hotels, I've found Brisas Del Mar. with its view, patio hammocks, in-room jacuzzis, and great proximity, hard to beat. *(2024 note: Brisas del Mar is now called Hotel Aura del Mar. The Hotel Bungalows Madera one block away is also nice and a good value.)*

For dining, it's downtown's Coconuts restaurant for its enchanting patio and tasty coconut shrimp, or Kau Kan's view, mango shrimp salad and stuffed lobster.

Throw in the incredible tamales and pozole at Any, and I won't even mention additional places, like our favorite stand in the public market.

Plus, there are plenty of sailfish—including some I've caught before.

Mexico's Second City (Guadalajara – 2013)

The trio of guitarists enthusiastically belted out the melodious "Gua-da-la-ja-ra, Gua-da-la-jaaaa-raaaa," drowning out city noises and reminding the appreciative street-side diners where they were—in Mexico's second city, the birthplace of the country's iconic music, mariachi.

With broad sombreros, tight pants and spangled jackets, mariachi groups are everywhere in the Guadalajara area, from fancy restaurants to small cafes with a few outside tables of local "Tapatios" (What a person from Guadalajara is called).

It had been 25 years since I'd been to the charming capital city of Jalisco, and while all the character and friendliness remained intact, much had changed – including a huge new Expo Convention Center, and the massive Millennium Arch 2000. At 52 meters (150 plus feet) the bright yellow landmark arch spans a busy roadway.

I was comforted with the familiar in the historic Centro area where broad shaded sidewalks face parks and plazas, cathedrals, classical buildings and monuments. Anchoring one plaza is the venerable Degollando Theater (1856) which continues to provide performances including the current Ballet Folklorico.

The city center (centro), est. 1531, is also home to several museums, government buildings (Palacio de Gobierno, Palacio Municipal), and the Plaza de Armas that recognizes important Tapatios. We reveled in the bustling central market (Mercado Libertad) where we were surprised to find the entire second floor was dedicated to homeopathic medicine, herbs, and even brujeria (witchcraft). The comprehensive

Picturesque carriages in downtown Guadalajara

market offers amulets, herbs, spices, and concoctions for every possible ailment.

Our favorite dining surprise came at a busy shop called Croissants Alfredo. We found the soft, doughy croissants so delicious we returned a few days later. Baked on premises, they are fresh and piping hot, plain or stuffed with chocolate, cream, pineapple or cajeta (caramel). Croissants Alfredo is on Facebook.

We rode the public busses from our hotel to Centro and beyond, even to the villages of Tlaquepaque and Tonalá. Most busses cost about $.50 even for the long one hour, 20-minute ride to Tonalá. Some rides were direct; others we had to change busses but the drivers were very helpful, reminding us where to get off.

From Centro one day we walked to Calle Independencia where we caught the Macrobus, which commands a special lane in the middle of the highway. We headed north, past the City Zoo, to the end of the line. The line ends there because the city ends there, at a huge chasm (the Barranca de Oblatos) with a muddy river (Rio Grande de Santiago) way, way down below, over 1,700 feet straight down. We hiked around lookouts and miradors, marveling at how abrupt the landscape changes from a busy city to a beautiful and pristine canyon.

Tlaquepaque

One day we took the bus to the artist enclave of San Pedro Tlaquepaque where we saw our first gringos in three days. It was just a handful of non-Latinos at that, though there were numerous Mexican tourists.

Tlaquepaque has matured nicely, with fine art galleries (Gallery Sergio Bustamante, for example) and antique shops joining the more than 200 stores and factories that sell items made from pewter, talavera, copper, leather, stonework, and wrought iron. A six-block pedestrian street has been beautified with public art and bronze statues.

El Parian is a peaceful square dating from 1878 featuring outdoor dining. Street vendors are everywhere and a couple of guys played on the xylophone all afternoon.

The main plaza, Jardin Hidalgo, features a kiosk made of quarry stone topped with a talavera tile cupola, and faces the 200-plus-year-old Sanctuary of Our Lady of Solitude. Nearby is Plazoleta Juan Pablo II (Pope John Paul II Square) where a bronze statue of Latin America's papal favorite is revered.

We found one of our favorite meals in the bustling Mercado Municipal Benito Juarez where we squeezed onto a bench seat among the locals at one of the numerous food stalls and enjoyed a delicious pozole lunch.

Tlaquepaque is a suburb of Guadalajara on the southeast and you can also take a taxi from your hotel or join a tour where it is the most popular destination. Once in town you can join a Walking Tour where the highlights are pointed out.

Tonalá

Farther to the east at the edge of the Guadalajara metropolitan area is the artist and artisan village of Tonalá, where almost every citizen is somehow involved in pottery or handicraft production or marketing.

Shops were just opening as we walked from the bus stop to the city center, but it was quickly apparent that this town was an organized delight. Wedding dresses dominated the shops on one block, and pewter the next. Riots of colorful flowers were featured on one block, and children's dolls the next.

The picturesque plaza fronted the church and the market. As the expected rain began we sought shelter in the public market and enjoyed lunch on outdoor tables covered by tarps overhead. Even so, more rustic mariachi groups strolled by between raindrops to assure the local diners that they were still part of the Guadalajara experience.

We didn't realize until later that Thursdays and Sundays are market days when artisans convene upon the town with their pottery, stoneware, and other handicrafts. We missed that by a day.

Guadalajara has two seasons, the wet one (June, July, and August), and the dry one (the rest of the year). We were there in July, which might explain the dearth of tourists. Most of the rain came in the evening or at night when the skies would open up with booming thunder and a dazzling display of lightning. We just waited out the storm that day in Tonalá.

There are a lot of retired Americans and Canadians living in the Guadalajara area, and most of those are in the communities of Lake Chapala and Ajijic about 40 kilometers south of town. The picturesque shallow lake there provides a restful backdrop to the artist and expatriate colonies. On our previous visit we went down there to wander cobbled streets and note the walled enclaves of the gringos but were not in the mood to be among a bunch of English-speaking expats this time.

Things to do:

Outside of exploring Centro Guadalajara and the villages of Tonalá and Tlaquepaque on your own like we did, there are several options available to make the most of this area.

Guadalajara City Tour—Perhaps the best value and comprehensive day trip is the Guadalajara City Tour where for 390 pesos (about $27.00) a walking tour of the historic Centro area is provided before an air-conditioned bus whisks you to both Tonalá and Tlaquepaque (about 7 hours total).

Tapatio Tour—An open deck bright red bus offers tourists a birds-eye view of the downtown area and Tonalá and Tlaquepaque.

La Caladrias—If you really like the open feeling hire a Caladria (horse and buggy) for an hour or so and clip-clop around the parks and plazas.

Tequila Express—The town of Tequila about 80 kilometers away is the heart of Mexico's tequila country. The Tequila Express tour ($100 US) is a full day outing into the Valle de Tequila (one of Mexico's Pueblo Magicos) which along with seeing how the fiery liquid is made, includes a fiesta with mariachis and folkloric show.

In the Guadalajara area there are numerous hotels, including the larger chains. The town of Tlaquepaque also offers several smaller inns and B&B's. Choose from the Casa de las Flores, the Casa de Rotoño, the Casa Campos, or the Villa de Ensueño, all a short stroll from the heart of town.

I enjoyed Guadalajara more this time around. The absence of in-your-face tourism was most appealing and we were able to meet many friendly Tapatios. While it is a big city (1.5 million) it is a pleasant contrast to burgeoning Mexico City and environs (18 million). Plus, they've got the world's best croissants.

Mask Makers of Mexico (Pátzcuaro, Suchitlán, Comala – 2008)

"I think it's this way," I said as we trudged up the narrow, cobbled Suchitlán road. The house where the internationally known mask carver toiled had initially eluded us. Then a local old woman had pointed in the direction of the hill.

"It has to be one of these houses. The road ends in jungle farther up the hill."

What had led us on this quest for yet another Mexican mask? The living room wall of our Baja home was already covered with them.

Leila and I were in the state of Colima, Mexico, way up on the slopes of the Nevado del Colima volcano, which at 13,845 feet, towers over the area and the neighboring states of Jalisco and Michoacán.

We had driven up the narrow road from the charming small state capital of Colima, past the picturesque village of Comala, to Suchitlán, a small artisan's village. We had heard that a Señor Herminio Candelario was a master mask carver who sold his creations at excellent prices.

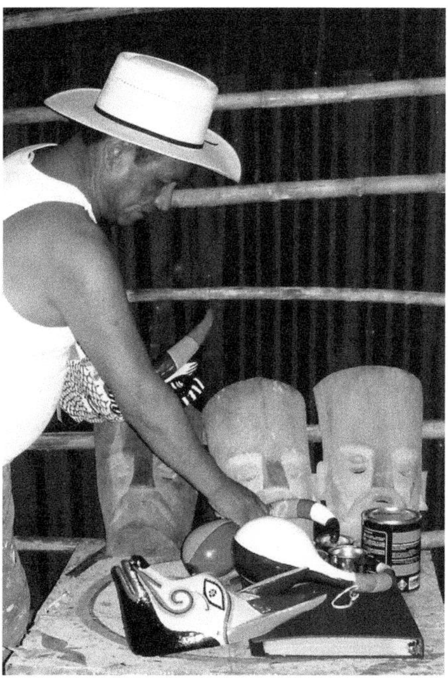

Señor Herminio Candelario in shop.

An old tradition

Masks are found in many native cultures, and even in some contemporary ones. We've picked up numerous masks through the years, including some from places as diverse as China, Japan, Bali, Spain, Argentina, Brazil, Jamaica, and New Zealand. Venetians have been using elaborate and graceful masks since the 13th century for Carnival and other annual ceremonies.

Our collection contains masks constructed from every conceivable material: wood, glass, paper, cloth, beads, feathers, metal, tin, leather, animal hide, goat horns, even tree bark.

In Mexico, masks are generally carved from a soft wood, like a Palo Bofo or Red Cedar. They're still used in numerous celebrations, from local village parades and festivals to national holidays and Christian holy days as integral parts of rituals and dances.

Masks in Latin America date back at least some 3,500 years. They were used in Mexico by native priests to summon the deities and were worn during sacrificial rites.

In attempting to indoctrinate the Indians, the Spanish who arrived in the 1600s took advantage of powerful existing images and were savvy enough to incorporate much of the indigenous customs, including the use of masks, in their attempt to spread Christianity.

To this day masks in Mexico are popular and are used in many current rituals. I've seen young children display a combination of awe and fear as a group of masked and costumed men danced their way into a Zihuatanejo church ceremony.

The mystery a mask provides extends beyond the religious. Form-fitting masks which cover the whole head offer disguise and create intrigue among Mexico's "lucha libre" wrestlers.

Mexican masks often incorporate both human and animal features, with jaguars, alligators, dogs, fish, snakes and lizards interwoven with a human face. Devil masks have long been popular in numerous celebrations and, like most masks, are designed for specific dances.

The use of masks eventually grew beyond their original purpose. The trend of creating masks for sale and collection rather than strictly for ceremony began in the early 1900s, and now is a cottage industry all its own.

The beautiful hand-carved wooden masks of Mexico have enjoyed resurgence in the last few years and certain antique shops and antiquities dealers can't get enough of them.

Searching for masks

We've been collecting for years, and our "mask" searches have led us on many a merry chase. Once in Guadalajara we heard about a mask shop near Ajijic. So we took a bus there. Upon arrival we were told "it's just down the highway." We started walking and kept walking along the dusty roadside along the north shore of Laguna Chapala in the summer heat. No shop. Through the village of San Antonio. Still no shop. "It's down there, not far, but before you get to Chapala," someone said. Finally, we see it in the distance on the outskirts of Chapala. Our reward for that long, over five-mile, sweaty morning walk was a boarded-up shop that *at one time* did sell masks!

Acapulco Mask Museum

In Acapulco we visited the Casa de las Máscaras museum a short walk from the old Fort San Diego. The museum houses an amazing cultural collection of over 3,000 high quality masks made by artisans both historic and contemporary, not only from the mask-making State of Guerrero, but all of Mexico.

On another trip, Leila and I visited the Museo Rafael Coronel in Zacatecas which offers a fascinating display of their over 3,000 Mexican masks.

Señor Candelario of Suchitlán

Thus, we found ourselves searching for Señor Candelario. While visiting Colima, capital of the state of the same name, we had heard about Señor Candelario of Suchitlán. We were compelled to visit.

The road in the shadow of the great volcano finally levels a bit when it approaches the verdant village. Walking up to the Candelario residence we noted the skies darkening and a woman rushing out of a house to take laundry off the lines before the drizzle. To her right a thatched shelter rested on a bush-shrouded ledge overlooking a small rivulet.

"Hola! Buscamos por Señor Candelario, Herminio Candelario," I inquired of her.

"Si, si, es aqui," she said. Smiling, and with her hands full of the family's clothes, she nodded toward that small rustic shed just past her now-empty clotheslines. We walked to the broad open side facing the foliage and met the artist. He wore a white Panama hat, paint-splattered pants and tank-top, and a broad grin. Wood shavings littered the hard earth floor, and a restful trickle from the stream just below completed the ambiance of this remote workshop.

After he proudly displayed his wares, we opted to buy one he had completed rather than returning for a special order. He then autographed the multi-hued beauty we had selected, and we paid $40.00 U.S. for it.

We celebrated with an outstanding lunch at Los Portales de Suchitlán, a large and very popular Sunday afternoon kind of place on an old coffee plantation.

Artisans near Pátzcuaro

It was a different ending on another excursion a year or so later. We were in Pátzcuaro, a small colonial city in the inland State of Michoacán. Named one of Mexico's Magical Towns, it rests in a valley on the shores of Lake Janitzo where fishermen with huge butterfly nets provide numerous photo opportunities.

We drove around the lake visiting pleasant villages along the way, one of which, Tocuaro, was noted for artisans and mask makers. We stopped where a small sign outside a home said "Mascaras de Danza, vende." On the broad shady tiled patio in front of the house, Felipe Horta Tera and his son Victor Hugo were busily carving and painting masks.

There were beautiful, elaborate creations and took many hours of painstaking detail. When we asked how much for one beautiful piece, we rubbed our hands in anticipation of a super bargain when he answered "Cuatrociento cincuenta (Four hundred fifty). At the time the peso was about 10 to 1, which meant that for about $45.00 we would possess a real work of art. Then we realized he meant "dollars," which was surprising because no place in the state of Michoacán ever quoted in dollars, not even the hotels. But that's what he meant and we decided we didn't want it that badly.

That evening in downtown Pátzcuaro, we sat in the plaza across the street from our Hotel Mansion Iturbe, a 14-room restored 17th century mansion. There we witnessed another spectacle involving masks. A group of young performers were dancing for a small gathering in the park with the Danza de los Viejos (Dance of the Old Men).

Danza de los Viejos, Pátzcuaro

Commemorating Huitzilopochtil, the god of fire and battle, the dancers with straw hats and bright clothing wore wooden masks painted white with ruddy pink cheeks. Leaning on canes and assuming the hunched backs of the elderly, they increased their tempo as they danced round and round.

Watching them tapping with their canes, we realized that perhaps that day we didn't add another gem for our wall, but we were able to see masks used in their original purpose. Nobody can take that away from us.

For those interested in Pázcuaro, in addition to the Hotel Iturbe, another wonderful old hotel is the Hotel Posada La Basilica, on a hill where you can see across the red tiled roofs to the historic lake beyond.

For Suchitlán and Comala, there's the Best Western Ceballos on the town square (wake up to sound of church bells.) Also out of town is the large Hotel Maria Isabel resort.

Sampling Mexican Culture

Day of the Dead

The Day of the Dead (Oaxaca – 2010)

It was a chilly night, and quite late as Leila and I approached the cemetery. Lights from numerous candles and a few flashlights cast eerie illumination on the very dark hillside reserved for the dead. The cemetery, however, buzzed with activity as the living came to visit. People moved about, their shadows seeming to make the stone markers dance with life.

We entered and joined numerous small groups who had crammed this rural village cemetery in their celebration of death. We too had candles, sweets, and flowers to dispense among assorted headstones of the visitors' loved ones.

It was November 2, the Day of the Dead, (Dia de los Muertos), an important holiday throughout Mexico where the living pay homage to the departed. And we were among the locals in a village cemetery on the outskirts of Oaxaca.

Religious observances in Mexico are often a curious blend of Indian tradition and symbolism, Spanish pomp, Roman Catholic ceremony, and Mexican bravado. This special brand of folk Catholicism is tolerantly accepted by the prelates in Rome.

No holiday better exemplifies this unique composite of customs than Mexico's deep-rooted Dia de los Muertos. After Christmas and Easter (which are also observed with some cultural blending), it is Mexico's third most important holiday.

Celebrated over November 1 and 2, it combines Halloween (31st), All Saints Day (1st), All Souls Day (2nd) and the Day of the Dead. Predating the arrival of the Spaniards, the ancient holiday was based around the Indians' beliefs that the dead returned once a year to be fed.

Even today, the holiday is a happy time to welcome the souls of the dead who come back to visit. To greet them, the Mexican people flock to cemeteries (panteons) where headstones of deceased relatives have often been previously cleaned by children and surviving relatives.

Food and offerings are laid out and graveside parties and picnics are held by the loved ones of the deceased. Of course, after the spirits have enjoyed the food, the family members are free to indulge.

In many homes throughout Mexico, family altars (ofrendas) are prepared, and favorite photos of the deceased are displayed, along with flowers (usually marigolds), food, liquor and often a specially prepared Pan de los Muertos (bread).

Cakes and cookies in the shape of skulls and skeletons abound; papier-mâché skulls and cross bones along with spindly black-and-white wooden skeletons (calaveras) replace balloons as decorations. Most famous is the Calavera Catrina which depicts a female skeleton dressed in a big dress and a dapper hat.

Many believers look for signs that the spirits did come: a few crumbs where there weren't any before, a glass that had tipped over, or a wind that had blown a candle out. Those signs tend to reinforce the beliefs.

Celebrations throughout Mexico

We've attended several of these celebrations, in Baja and in mainland Mexico. This recent year, we were in Oaxaca, a charming colonial city in Southern Mexico that is arguably the most famous Day of The Dead destination where cemetery visits are offered to two different cemeteries.

Along with the several crowded Oaxacan area cemeteries, numerous processions, parades, and festivities took place, in all the churches, in the plazas, and throughout the streets. It also seemed every home or business had prepared an elaborate ofrenda, adding colorful displays throughout the city.

We started the night at the main city cemetery where food stands were set up outside, live music could be heard from blocks away, and locals danced among the mausoleum crypts. Candles were omnipresent and the flickering flames lent a surreal image as throngs of people moved in and out of the shadows.

Now in this little village several miles outside of town we wandered about the spooky graveyard. Many families were keeping vigil, some quietly, alone in their thoughts, and others in a party mode. They seemed to appreciate our attendance and interest.

"Es mi papá," one teenage girl told me, pointing to a grave covered with food and flowers. Her mother told us about him, and how long ago since he had passed away, and reminded us that he was a "very good man." But the time for tears was clearly long gone and a contented happiness infused with pride brought him back for her.

At another grave, a woman was adding a few bottles of Tecate to a growing pile of tamales, chocolates and fruits. "This was his favorite beer," she told us about her deceased husband. "He loved his Tecate."

Some members of another large family group had a card game going as they sat above a grave in flickering candlelight.

Family member holding vigil

The observances and scope of Day of the Dead activities vary by area and municipality. The colonial city of Pátzcuaro in central Mexico also holds substantial events in honoring their departed. We noted the celebrations were more subdued in some cities (Veracruz, Xalapa, and Tlaxcala).

Baja California is not especially renowned for Day of The Dead celebrations. Tecate, and La Paz, (Baja Sur), are two that have events to mark the celebration. In most cities you will know when you're in the vicinity of a cemetery, however. You will usually find street vendors selling flowers, food, decorations, and small "calaveras," those little wooden skeletons.

Traffic sometimes gets backed up in Tijuana in front of Panteón Jardín on Calle Benito Juarez (2nd Street/Calle Segundo) where the shortcut from the Ensenada toll road dead ends (no pun intended) into the cemetery. Tijuana also offers graveyard tours.

Rosarito's Katrina Fest

To honor the Day of the Dead and the Calavera Catrina, the city of Rosarito hosts a family-friendly event on November 1 and 2 called "Katrina Fest" (spelled with a "K"). In addition to typical Day of the Dead festivities, the event includes art demonstrations, food, and music. The free event takes place in the Municipal Art and Culture Institute (IMAC) in Rosarito at Abelardo Rodriguez Park, starting at noon and running until midnight.

Oferta in Oaxaca restaurant

Nowhere else in the world but Mexico is death celebrated with the same light-heartedness. Mexicans laugh and joke about death and from childhood learn that life and death are a pair.

Mexican comedian Hector Suarez says that laughing at death does not mean Mexicans aren't afraid of it. "Mexicans fear death," he said, "so they want to be death's friend. They think that if they are his friend, he won't do anything to them. That is why a Mexican plays with death."

According to one Mexican anthropologist, "In terms of its impact on society, the Day of the Dead is the most important celebration of the year. It is a day for joy, a day for sadness. It is a ceasefire, when people are expected to forgive each other. It gives people an inner strength. It is sad to see a relative die, but it is not so sad if you have this belief."

Guadalupe – Mexico's Major Celebration

If there was ever a country that enjoys fiesta time, it's Mexico. It doesn't take much for workers to lay down their tools, pick up a beer, and crank up the music. There are all types of Mexican parties, and for those who prefer a more reverent occasion, you might enjoy my favorite, December's La Dia de Nuestra Señora de Guadalupe (Day of Our Lady of Guadalupe).

Other celebrations

Religious holidays like Guadalupe join the secular parties like birthdays, Halloween, and Mexican Independence Day (September 16). Among Christian holidays, Easter and Christmas are obviously recognized but there are so many others. For example, on Nov. 1-2, there's the aforementioned Day of the Dead (Dia de los Muertos), where families hold vigil at the cemeteries of their departed loved ones. *(See Day of the Dead story above).*

Catholic saints are revered throughout Mexico. Children are often named for their birthday's patron saint. Villages are named for saints and the villagers generally have a big celebration on that saint's day every year.

For a traditional birthday (Mañanitas) party I've stood in a driveway before dawn with family members when a group of mariachis blasted awake the honored señora.

While honoring mother is widely accepted, the biggest birthday by far is a girl's coming out, her 15th birthday (Quinceañera), a tradition so embedded the cost can set papa back a small fortune. I've attended a few of those, from a laborer's relatively simple backyard affair to one in a rented ballroom downtown Tijuana where hundreds of guests danced to a live band and enjoyed a sit-down catered dinner. A Quinceañera is often more lavish than a wedding (boda).

Mexican celebrations typically are very social affairs. Many people come into towns and villages from rural areas just to participate. The festivities will often include food, market stalls, vendors, balloons, fireworks, solemn processions, the Church, lots of kids, and loud, constant music. If there's two things most Mexicans love, it's kids and loud music.

December 12 – La Dia de Guadalupe

The most cherished religious holiday in Mexico is December 12, La Dia de Nuestra Señora de Guadalupe, when gala parties and processions honor the Señora who became Mexico's iconic religious symbol. Guadalupe is the very symbol of Catholicism in Mexico and commemorates the miracle in December 1531 that is credited to have occurred on the hill at Tepeyac, now a northern suburb of Mexico City.

There in the early days of Spanish rule, the story goes, an Indian peasant named Juan Diego saw an apparition—a lady who identified herself as the Virgin of Guadalupe. She asked Juan Diego to go to the bishop and tell him about her; she also requested a church be built on the site. It is said the local bishop however requested proof.

Juan Diego went back, and the sky again turned brilliant, and the lady reappeared. She told him to take the nearby roses to the bishop. Behind him he found a rose bush growing. He cut them, placed them in his cloak and returned to the bishop, saying he had brought proof as roses were not known to be in that area. When he opened his cloak however, it featured a miraculous image of the lady, now universally known as Our Lady of Guadalupe.

That miracle at Tepeyac helped the Spanish introduce Catholicism to the indigenous Aztecs and was pivotal in entrenching the religion. The fact that one of their own, a poor Indian, was the witness paved the way for converting the previously recalcitrant Indians.

While the likeness on the cloak has been duplicated literally millions of times on every item imaginable, I've seen what the Church recognizes as the original cloak. It is prominently displayed high on a wall at the Basilica of Guadalupe at Tepeyac, above a moving walkway for the faithful to behold and to pay homage. It is one of the most visited Catholic shrines in the world.

Guadalupe Parade, Puerta Vallarta

The December 12 event is recognized throughout Latin America and, as Mexico's most honored commemoration, is celebrated in every city and town.

Traditionally, young children are dressed up for the part. Little boys are attired like Juan Diego in loose fitting garments, a peon's straw hat and a mustache (bigote) drawn by mama's eyeliner. Little girls wear simple white dresses.

The festivities which often include dancing, contests, food, and music, are highlighted by the numerous processions. Various groups are formed, sometimes by neighborhood, or by unions, or companies, or even large families, and they each create their own procession clogging city streets and terminating at the various churches throughout the city or village where special masses are held.

A typical procession features marching drummers and trumpets, dancers in native costume, a single float usually depicting Juan Diego and the Lady of Guadalupe, and lastly the entire group, generally carrying candles and/or singing. It's a colorful and moving event, and in the larger towns there are so many processions, they start several days before December 12. In the meanwhile, busses are rerouted and everything comes second to the tradition.

One time in Tijuana, detoured by a Guadalupe procession, we discovered one street totally devoted to food booths. We were soon sitting among little mustachioed "Juan Diegos" munching tacos when a TV crew noticed a couple of "gringos" in their midst. I suppose our brief interview was aired on the local television that night.

Zihuatanejo child made up like Juan Diego.

In Zihuatanejo on one December 12 our attention alternated from costumed townspeople marching by in processions to a wooden stage on a street corner that featured continuous entertainment. Traditional dancing, singing, and lots of food made the entire day a fascinating glimpse into Mexican culture.

Enterprising photographers posed little Juan Diegos on donkeys, or against a backdrop of the Tepeyac scene set up alongside the Our Lady of Guadalupe parish church.

One group of dancers wore some very scary straw costumes, more sinister versions of the Straw Man from the *Wizard of Oz.* They danced in formation and then split up and accosted and cajoled bystanders. They tantalized the delighted spectators by shaking and vibrating their loose straw costumes. Unfortunately, they were so real I noticed the mascara mustache of one little boy begin to run.

Last year, we even left for Puerto Vallarta a few days earlier than originally planned to catch the Dia de Guadalupe celebrations there. The processions, one after another for days, were colorful and fascinating. But what really caught our attention was the food, much of it from various Mexican cuisines. We ate off the streets for three days. We found Pozole as good as they make it in Guerrero, and Oaxacan pollo (chicken) mole tamales wrapped in banana leaves that melted in our mouths. Add crepes and incredible pastries and I was sorry to see the vendors pack up and leave. One tamale lady gave us her dates (Dec. 1-12) and location for the coming year. Pretty tempting.

After the intense early December Guadalupe celebrations, you'd think that would be enough party for a long time, but the time-honored Christmas Posadas immediately follow – nine more days of festivities leading right up to Christmas.

And then, of course, following that is New Year's, and then Three Kings Day (Jan. 6), and so on throughout the year. Did I mention that Mexicans love their fiestas?

Holiday Tamales and Posadas

Mexican get-togethers usually include food, and often the preparation of food can be a social event itself.

Christmas tamales have become such a Mexican staple that many families will often have three generations of women crowding the kitchen to stuff the masa (corn dough) with meats (pork, chicken, or beef), cheeses and /or chiles, and of course the favorite of many, the dulces (sweet tamales) where fruits, spices and other confections take the place of the meats.

Tamales

Steaming hot tamales which you have to unwrap like little presents have evolved into a very special holiday treat for Mexicans on both sides of the border, as they are also popular among Mexican-Americans.

Because they require so much time to prepare, they are usually only made a few times a year in very large batches, thus the crowd in the kitchen. After stuffing them they are wrapped in corn husks before steaming. Some areas of Mexico, like Oaxaca in the south, might use banana leaves instead of corn husks. I fell in love with the moist and flavorful Oaxacan-style tamales.

Tamale recipes vary depending on the ingredients, but you start with the masa (corn dough). While some families prepare the masa from scratch, many others buy the prepared masa from restaurants or grocery stores that prepare it in abundance every season. There are numerous recipes available on preparing the various stuffings.

Tamales are so popular in certain areas of the United States that they are widely offered in December. Southern Californian tamale-lovers can get their fix in the

Coachella Valley where all sorts of different tamales are available at the International Tamale Festival in Indio. Always held on the first weekend in December, it is rated by Food Network TV as one of the Top 10 All-American Food Festivals.

Almost every year we join 125,000 other tamale-loving festival goers in Indio to sample every type of tamale imaginable. There are over 50 booths covering the five-block event, but none more popular than perennial winner Grandma Lupe's (Lupe Coronel), where lines over two hours long begin forming before the 10 a.m. daily opening. Lupe's are good but I personally prefer some of the other booths where the chile/cheese tamales and a couple of different "dulces" are offered.

The Tamale Festival also features a parade, a carnival, folkloric dancing, entertainment, and more. The tamale is king, and some families and various individual groups also have booths as they join restaurants in providing and selling the succulent traditional fare.

There's much more to Mexican holiday food than tamales however, and south of the border traditions also often call for Buñuelos, Three Kings Bread, Atole, and Ponche.

Las Posadas in Mexico

Christmas preparation in Mexico takes place during the nine days preceding Christmas Eve (Nochebuena). This period of nine days is called the Novena and every night children perform "las posadas," reenactments of the journey made by Jesús' parents, Joseph and Mary.

In the posadas, children walk through the streets of their neighborhood in a colorful procession, singing, carrying lit candles and holding statues of both Mary and Joseph. They symbolically ask neighbors for a place to spend the night. This request is denied twice, but at the third house they are invited to enter where treats have been prepared.

The host family (the host honors are rotated) has a crèche scene set up along with other Christmas decorations. There's usually a piñata for the kids, some Christmas Buñuelos (sweet fritters made from a mixture of water, flour, lard, eggs, and sugar), and Ponche (a kind of punch, made by boiling sugar cane, walnuts, cinnamon sticks and different fruits together. Sometimes it's spiked for the adults.

A posada is celebrated each night of the Novena and finally, on December 24, the devout attend the local church for midnight mass.A traditional Mexican Christmas is thus a solemn affair.

Gifts and presents for the children are withheld until January 6, the Dia de los Reyes (Day of the Three Kings). That day which ends the Christmas season commemorates the day the three wise men presented their gifts to the baby Jesus. However in many Mexican locations these days, formal tradition is eschewed and gifts are also exchanged on December 25.

On the Dia de los Reyes, a traditional sweet holiday bread called a Rosca de Reyes which is shaped like a wreath and decorated with candied fruit is sliced and served. A little plastic baby Jesús doll is baked into the bread and tradition states that whoever gets the piece of bread with the doll in it has to provide food for the next party, that of *Candleria* or *Candlemas* day on February 2.

Poinsettias Bloom in Mexico

Throughout history, Mexico has made numerous gifts to its big neighbor to the north. Tomatoes, avocados and chiles all came from Mexico, and the state of Baja California alone has contributed fish tacos, Caesar salads, and margaritas. The U.S. has received many Mexican sons and daughters, and even, following the Mexican-American War – the gift of the entire state of California.

The most colorful gift that wended its way north is the flaming red poinsettia, that ubiquitous holiday plant that entices Christmas shoppers in malls and supermarkets everywhere. The poinsettia, which blooms in December, lends a festive air to homes and businesses on both sides of the border. And its origins are as Mexican as mariachi music.

Native to the area around present-day Taxco, the Aztecs cultivated the plant they called Cuetlayochitl (Cuetlaxochitle in some references), using the sap to control fevers and the bracts (modified leaves) to make a reddish dye. The plant was so popular that even Montezuma had them caravanned into Mexico City as they could not be grown in that high altitude.

After the Spaniards arrived in the 17th century, a group of Franciscan priests that settled near Taxco began using the red flowers for the Fiesta of Santa Pesembre (Feast of the Holy Manger), the first known holiday usage.

The Poinsettia Legend

What is a Mexican tradition without a supporting legend? The poinsettia legend has a poor Mexican girl named Pepita walking with her brother (or cousin, versions vary) Pedro to Christmas Eve services at the village church where people made gifts to the Christ Child. She was sad as she had no gift.

Pedro said consolingly, "I am sure, Pepita, that even the most humble gift, if given in love, will be acceptable in His eyes."

So Pepita knelt by the roadside and scooped a handful of common weeds and tried to fashion them into a presentable bouquet. In the chapel, Pepita placed the makeshift bouquet at the foot of the Nativity scene. Suddenly the weeds burst into beautiful red blooms and all who saw were certain they had witnessed a miracle. From then on, the flower in Mexico became known as the *Flor de Nochebuena,* or Flower of the Holy Night (Christmas Eve).

The botanical name is also colorful (for Latin) and the plants were named

Euphorbia Pulcherrima Wild (pulcherrima means most beautiful) by German botanist Wilenow who was dazzled by their color. So as the Mexicans have their name for the flower, and the scientists have their identifying moniker, how did Americans come to know it as the *poinsettia*?

Enter John Roberts Poinsett. Born in South Carolina in 1779, Poinsett became a special agent to South America, served in his state legislature, and was a member of the U.S. House of Representatives before heading to Mexico as special envoy. He was the first American ambassador to Mexico (appointed by Andrew Jackson) and was later a Unionist in rebel South Carolina. His outstanding career also included serving as Secretary of War under Martin Van Buren (1837-1841).

But Poinsett is best known for the flower that bears his name. An accomplished botanist, in 1825 he sent some of the brilliant flowers from Mexico to his own nursery in South Carolina, and also to other friends and American horticulturalists—and they thrived. As the plant became more popular, historian and horticulturalist William Prescott was asked to give the plant a popular name. He chose *poinsettia*, honoring Joel Poinsett's contribution.

A little-known fact is that Poinsett was also the person who introduced the American Elm to Mexico, with the end result being a literal swapping of botanical gifts

Over 100 varieties today

The present-day poinsettia has been hybridized greatly in the U.S. and Europe from the original Mexican plant. Today there are over 100 varieties, with varying heights, colors (red, pink, white), bract width, and flowering habits.

Today 90 percent of all poinsettias are grown in the United States. They are commercially grown in all 50 states, with California top producer. One of the world's largest commercial growers is the Paul Ecke Ranch in Encinitas, California which grows over 80 percent of the U.S. wholesale market. In fact, 90 percent of all flowering poinsettias in the world got their start at Paul Ecke Ranch in north San Diego County.

The Ecke Ranch originated in 1902 when Albert Ecke started growing poinsettias in Eagle Rock, now a community of northeast Los Angeles. In 1909, he and his son specialized in poinsettias. They moved to Encinitas in 1923. Paul Ecke poinsettias are known for huge, giant bloom centers and a unique single stem presentation.

In the U.S., December 12 has been designated National Poinsettia Day and the flower represents 85 percent of all potted plant sales during the holiday season. Hundreds of millions of dollars' worth of poinsettias are sold during the brief six-week season.

The cost of a poinsettia is determined by the number of blooms. Red rules as 74 percent of all Americans prefer that color to white (8 percent) and pink (6 percent). Women purchase 80 percent of America's best-selling potted plant.

In the large supermarkets, poinsettias are as ubiquitous at yuletide as candy at the checkout counter, except because of the size and brilliance, the poinsettias are much more obvious and shopping carts quickly get filled with them.

I don't know what use the Mexicans made of the American Elm, but without their *Flor de Nochebuena*, the holiday season just wouldn't be the same for millions of Americans.

Mariachis – The Tempo of Mexico

The uplifting sounds and homey folk lyrics of mariachi music has become an integral part of the Mexican culture and history. Indeed, it appears the entire Mexican psyche is interwoven with the brassy and bold tempo produced by sombrero-clad men in tight-fitting pants, frilly shirts, and waist-length jackets.

Visitors to Baja restaurants quickly become aware they're in a different culture when, along with the cervezas, frijoles and *totopos* (chips), they're treated to ear-splitting renditions of "Rancho Grande" or "La Cucaracha."

Depending on the restaurant's acoustics and size, the experience can range from a bombardment of the aural canals to a lovely, romantic interlude on a seaside patio, like at La Fonda, where strains of "Coo coo coo, La Palo-o-o-oma" can caress the waves below.

Mariachi is Mexico's main contribution to the music world, and has entertained diners, motivated dancers, and serenaded lovers for many years.

The origins of mariachi go back to pre-Cortes days when Indians played music with rattles, drums, reed and clay flutes and conch-shell horns. The Spaniards brought their violins, guitars, harps, horns and woodwinds and the blending of the cultures also brought about the blending of the music. One of those music forms was the mariachi, and as no one can agree on the etymology of the name, its meaning has been lost to history.

Mariachis

But the music has lived on, its modern form evolving in Guadalajara, Jalisco, in the 19th century. Early mariachi groups there consisted of the *vihuela* (a high-pitched round backed guitar), two violins, and a *guitarrón* (a deep voiced guitar which took the place of the harp). Today, a complete mariachi group generally has two trumpets, six to eight violins and a guitar, along with the vihuela and the guitarrón.

Forms of mariachi vary by region and include the *son jalisciense, son jarocho,* and the *jarabe*, a medley of dance pieces. (Jarabe Tapatio, or the Mexican Hat Dance, is a notable jarabe).

Whenever there's a special occasion in Mexico you can be assured that mariachis are present. Mariachis often participate in the courtship process, and the *serenata* (serenade) has become a touching and uniquely Mexican experience.

Las Mañanitas is a melodious birthday song, and it is traditionally sung early in the morning intended to awaken the recipient. Once I helped a friend plan one for his mother and we all gathered at dawn in the driveway below her window as the Mariachis woke up the Los Angeles neighborhood. For my Mexican-American friends, it was another occasion for a party, and tequila and beer quickly supplanted coffee and juice. Those inclined to pass out hardly made it until noon.

An interesting mariachi audition

On another occasion, I hired a Mariachi band in the Baja lobster village of Puerto Nuevo. This is what I wrote about the incident in my first book, *Baja Fever:*

> *Mariachi music wafts through the now-cobbled streets as musicians stroll from restaurant to restaurant along with purveyors of freshly cut flowers and trinkets made of seashells.*
>
> *Leila and I will never forget that summer weekend in 1985 when we went to the village to hire a mariachi group. We were throwing a party in Cantamar about two weeks hence.*
>
> *Several groups of musicians lounged in the shade of a tree near the end of the main road, down about where a market is today. We were introduced to the leader of a group who would be willing to come to Cantamar on that date. We began negotiating how many hours they'd play, how much per hour, etc.*
>
> *As we were closing in on a deal, they proudly offered to let us hear them. We agreed. So Leila and I stood, our arms around each other, in the middle of the dusty dirt road, while this mariachi group serenaded us in the hot August sun. Quickly a crowd gathered out in the road while these guys just kept playing and playing. Their enthusiasm won us over. That we felt special amid a group of gringos didn't hurt either.*

Puerto Nuevo is not the only Baja venue for mariachis. They are everywhere: Rosarito Beach Hotel, Festival Plaza (El Museo Bar), Rene's, and many more restaurants and night spots from Tijuana to Cabo San Lucas. Each spring, La Paz hosts a Mariachi and Tequila Festival.

And in Guadalajara, Jalisco, where it all began, each September there is a Mariachi and Charro Festival which attracts some 50 mariachi groups.

A world of mariachi

Today there are mariachi groups in such diverse worldwide places as Aruba, Canada, The Netherlands, and Germany. There are numerous groups in the United States, including the Mariachi Los Cabos of Salem, Oregon, which performs through the Pacific Northwest. California, naturally, has plenty of mariachi groups.

The music of Mexico is everywhere

One of California's most famous mariachi restaurants is the La Fonda de los Camperos on Wilshire Blvd. in Los Angeles where two alternating bands have performed seven nights a week since 1969. A touristy place, diners long remember the loud music reverberating from both a balcony and the main floor. Traveling groups, like Mariachi Esmeralda (based in Montebello) bring the classic Mexican music to venues throughout the Southland.

In San Diego, the Baja Brewing Company features the Mariachi Del Mar. The group also plays at El Torito in Chula Vista. In Orange County, mariachi groups entertain at Plaza Garibaldi in Anaheim (Mariachi Espuelas de Mexico), Tlaquepaque Restaurant in Placentia, and the El Mariachi Restaurant in Orange.

At the El Mariachi Restaurant in San Clemente unfortunately you won't find a mariachi group. There is a live harp player who provides pleasant background music, but no mariachis. It seems too many customers complained when they had a mariachi group in there as with trumpets blaring, and a lot of "ayy-yii-iiing" in the small space it was just too loud.

If you like "loud" with your meals—well, that's another reason to go to Baja!

Semana Santa in Mexico

"Semana Santa," or "Holy Week" that precedes Easter Sunday (Domingo de Pascua) is one of Mexico's most important religious celebrations, and Baja Californians are just as eager to celebrate as are the rest of their countrymen.

Holy Week is the time of the year when Christians throughout the world commemorate an important part of their faith, the death and resurrection of Jesus Christ. For the many Christian families in Baja California, the rest of Mexico, and most of

Latin America for that matter, the celebrations are centered on religious activities.

Although Holy Week is primarily a reverential time for reflection and worship, it is also a time for Mexicans to vacation. Children generally get two weeks off from school. Many companies shut down for that period so that their employees can spend time with their families. And traveling seems to be a high priority, especially to local beaches.

Throughout Mexico beaches tend to fill up all week. From Playas de Tijuana, and all along the Baja coast to Rosarito, Ensenada, and beyond crowds engage in a party atmosphere, splitting their time off with the religious ceremonies. So don't be surprised if you see more local tourists in these locations during Holy Week.

On our April honeymoon some many years ago, Leila and I drove from Mazatlan to Puerto Vallarta on the Mexican mainland. When we discovered all along the way that every beach was crammed with partying Mexicans we realized just how much they take advantage of the week. It was hard to find hotel rooms in the entire area.

It is still much the same in Baja California and throughout Mexico as many locals get out of town to go camping or picnicking in the mountains, beaches or deserts.

Many observe the week following Pascua as part of this vacation period as well. Numerous Mexicans will take 10 days to two weeks for vacations, especially government employees, making it difficult to complete business during those days. If you are doing banking or interacting with government offices be sure to confirm their holiday schedule. Businesses around Mexico during this popular vacation period can be short staffed.

Of course, adding to the crowds of locals are hordes of gringos from across the border. After all it is Spring Break time for many and students use this same time to put on their party faces.

What this means for travelers to Mexico is to plan early, make reservations where you can, and expect to see crowds, especially in the resort areas like Cancun, Puerto Vallarta, Rosarito, Ensenada, and San Felipe.

There are numerous celebrations, both secular and religious, surrounding Holy Week and many have been around for centuries, arriving in Mexico with the Spanish,

As a case in point, back in the 1800s Mexican novelist and National Poet Guillermo Prieto (1818-1897) wrote:

> From Holy Thursday to Easter Sunday throngs of people danced through the streets, in a movable feast of popular cuisine. Thirsty revelers guzzled aguas frescas, refreshing waters flavored with pineapple, melon, tamarindo, and chia seeds, dispensed by women from palm-frond and flower-decorated stands. Holy Week also marked the traditional start of Mexico City's ice cream season, these frozen treats made with ice carried down from the slopes of Popocatépetl.

To Christians, Semana Santa celebrates the last days of the Christ's life. Pascua is the celebration of the Christ's Resurrection. It is also the end of the sacrifices of Lent. Considering Mexico is almost 90 percent Catholic there is little surprise as to why it is so reverently celebrated.

A Week of Celebrations

Semana Santa begins on Palm Sunday (Domingo de Ramos) and ends Easter Sunday (Pascua or Domingo de Resurección). Some of the religious celebrations that occur during Semana Santa are:

Palm Sunday (Blessing of the Palms): Catholics gather in churches for the blessing of palm fronds or crosses or other figures made from palms. Some of these palms are burned and saved to be used during next year's Ash Wednesday.

In front of most churches are palm leaf vendors, and churches so crowded many have to stand outside.

Jueves Santo (Maundy Thursday): It commemorates the Washing of the Feet and the Last Supper. On this day a sacred oil and balsam mixture called the Chrism, for use in the sacraments, is consecrated.

Viernes Santo (Good Friday): Passion plays are staged in many of the Catholic parishes as a reenactment of the Via Cruz (The Way of the Cross). Many parishes will also host processions and hundreds of people, many in traditional robes, can be seen parading around in the streets, usually carrying an effigy of Christ and the cross, near the parish. The celebration usually reaches its climax with a simulated crucifixion.

Sabado de Gloria (Holy Saturday): This day includes a vigil and a solemn mass in most parish churches.

Domingo de Resurección or Domingo de Pascua (Easter Sunday): For Mexican Catholics this is considered the most important day of the year. They are expected to attend Mass and churches usually are full. In many areas there are also religious processions, vigils, and other reenactments on Easter Sunday itself.

Combining the decidedly Christian holiday with vacation time, many churchgoers admit that they can fit both into the week. One young student admitted: "You can go to the beach on some days, and spend Good Friday and Easter Sunday in church. Those are the most important days after all."

In addition to the religious and time off activities, many families take the opportunity to visit their home cities, so along with the party goers, roads everywhere are more crowded than usual.

What about Eggs and Bunnies?

In case you might be wondering, where's the Easter Bunny and hiding Easter Eggs? Many Mexican families do get into American-type activities. So you likely will see children searching for the coveted Easter Eggs in their yards or public parks.

But one Mexican version of the Easter egg tradition is not hiding the eggs as much as breaking them. Called cascarones (eggshells) they are hollowed-out chicken eggs filled with confetti or small toys and brightly colored. The fun is derived from breaking the egg over someone's head and watching the confetti shower. Some people think that the confetti shower brings good luck and good fortune but for children the pleasure is simply breaking the eggs and enjoying the ensuing flutter of colors.

It's not common, however, to see the Easter Bunny in Baja. You'll see a lot of people in church, a lot of people at the beach, and if you see a grinning kid approaching with a colorful egg, be prepared to be showered with confetti.

In a Mexican Bank (2006)

Next time you have a need to go inside a bank in Mexico just close your eyes and listen. Over the surprisingly quiet murmur of the typical large crowd you will hear, "bam, bam," then a few seconds later some more "bams," and not a minute will go by when you don't hear several more "bams."

If you opened your eyes you'd see the source of this seemingly never-ending pounding. It's bank clerks and officers gone crazy with their stamp pads. It seems like every single piece of paper or document that comes across their desks must be stamped and signed.

Perhaps these clerks would rather be doing something more physical, because they appear to be taking out their aggressions on those poor pieces of paper. "Bam," into the stamp pad for more ink, then "bam" onto the piece of paper thus changing an innocuous form into an official document.

Well, not quite official yet, as the stamped form first must be signed, and this is where bankers really get to strut their stuff. I've never seen a signature (firma) of a bank officer that didn't have the flourish of some "very important person." They usually scribble something really small and then make concentric circles that get larger and larger until they cover the whole lower half of the page. Some signatures are so ornate they would put John Hancock's elegant Declaration of Independence signature to shame.

Other "identifying marks" are merely large scribbles covering the freshly inked stamp with a mark that looks large a large ampersand or a musical clef symbol. And the women are just as creative with their signatures as the men are.

The constant stamping and proprietary signatures are the icing on the cake, as it were. There's a lot more going on at a Mexican bank, and most of it is frustrating for Type A personalities which many Americans seem to be. Most Mexicans seem to stoically and quietly endure the long lines, the waiting, and the inefficient bureaucracy without getting ruffled. So what if it takes half a day just going to a bank to make a deposit or withdraw money? Big deal!

To most Americans it is a big deal, wasting half a day just to exchange some money.

Dollars common in tourist areas

Many tourist areas, especially along the gold coast between Tijuana and Ensenada, deal in the U.S. Dollar. In fact, it's rare to see a peso except maybe as change. Thus, many tourists there do not need to change their dollars. I always have some on me anyhow, because the exchange rates will vary and more often than not you'll pay less using pesos. Also, many small establishments cannot readily make change from any but the smallest bills, whether dollars or pesos.

There are currency exchange booths in most Mexican tourist locations. Called Casa de Cambio (House of Change) they usually give a good rate, almost always better than the hotels which generally render the worst exchange rates. They're quick, efficient, and you can compare with other competing places as they prominently display the constantly fluctuating rates. Make sure however, that they have a sign that says "No Comision," as commission can skew the deal. The government, however, advises that tourists bypass these booths and go to a bank.

There are a number of these Casas de Cambio in the U.S. border towns like San Ysidro. Also, the Costco in Chula Vista has a Casa de Cambio booth and many Baja travelers make it a point to stop there.

In most cases the banks offer the best current rate, often a little better than the Casa de Cambio, and a whole lot better than the hotels. Restaurants, markets and shops will take your dollars at rates that vary all over the place, from an insult to surprisingly good.

Mexico has numerous banks (Bancomer, Banamex, Serfin, Banco Scotia, etc.) and these generalizations apply to all of them.

You'll note the tellers tend to look alike—mostly attractive young women with bright red lipstick and long black hair combed straight back and tied in a ponytail. Plus they all wear their bank's uniforms. One Tuesday I was in a Bancomer branch and noticed all the tellers were wearing white blouses and smart dark gabardine suits. The next day, at the same branch, the same women were all wearing neat mauve suits with striped mauve and blue matching blouses.

And the men at the desks? Surprise, surprise, no uniform at all, not even a suit. Just a dress shirt of their choosing and slacks. Although in some banks men all wear a standardized suit.

Obliged to grab a number

Let's say you're going to a non-tourist area and want to get pesos. You enter a bank and see a crowd of people standing, sitting, and shuffling around. There are several different lines for different windows offering various transaction. First, you want to make sure you enter the correct line, perhaps by asking a guard the simple word "cambio."

In many cases you're obliged to grab a number. When you get #106 and the screen flashes that they're serving #52, you turn around, walk out, and find the nearest Casa de Cambio.

If you brave the line and finally get called, hold out your $300.00 U.S. cash or whatever, and say "cambio." Your first hope is that the teller can handle it and not send you to wait for a specialized teller who "makes change." If she takes it, she'll count it out, grab some papers, write all over them about this difficult transaction, stamp them with a flourish, add her ornate signature and send you and your paperwork to another location.

There you present your papers to another clerk, often a man, who will peruse the paperwork, stamp and sign them again, count out the appropriate pesos for you, hand you the money along with a receipt, and then file the documents.

Other caveats are the denominations and condition of your U.S. bills. Larger bills, like hundreds, often pay at a better rate. And never try to present any old, slightly torn, ripped, or even marginally defaced bills. This is true in many countries and before any trip outside the U.S., I have my U.S. banker carefully count out only new, crisp, clean bills.

Years ago, in a small Mexican village I went to the only bank in town to get more pesos. Out of 10 $20.00 U.S. bills the teller returned three of them to me because of slight tears. One had a little writing on it.

Identification needed

At one bank in the Yucatan, the teller took my money and asked me for picture I.D. As my passport was in a hotel safe, I meekly offered my California Driver's License. She accepted it and then said she needed a copy. I figured she'd make one, but no, she sent me to a desk at the far corner of the bank, where a man on the phone had a copy machine behind his desk. Meanwhile the teller, the line behind me, and I, waited for the man to finish his phone call.

When he hung up, he took my driver's license, made a copy, handed both to me, and I dutifully returned to the patient clerk, who then filled out a form *in triplicate* with my name now on it, stamped all three copies, scrawled her mark on all three, filed one with the copy of my license somewhere, and the other somewhere else, and slid one copy for me through the glass opening—along with the correct amount of pesos.

All that to change money? The guys in the Casa de Cambio street booths have the right idea. It's called simplicity! If you think changing money in a bank is fun, try some more complicated transactions.

Now if you really want to avoid the bureaucracy of the banking system, the ATM is the answer. ATM rates are the same as the banks, which is the daily international exchange rate. The only caveat is the ATM fee and the fee set by your bank, if any. Obviously the more money you draw out at one time, the lower percentage that fee equates to.

ATMs are now everywhere in the world and a whole lot better than messing with travelers' checks, the one-time standard for foreign travel and now all but extinct. ATMs also prevent you from carrying too much cash and are a whole lot less frustrating than dealing with a Mexican bank.

(2024 note: Now I use credit cards as much as possible, rendering cash less important. For the little I need, I might hit a Casa de Cambio first, or use an ATM, minimizing any possible bank experience.

These days, most banks in Mexico (And throughout much of the world) want copies of your passport, so I generally carry a couple of copies with me.

Some ATMs in Mexican tourist areas offer your cash in dollars which just means you'll likely pay more everywhere. What's the point? Also, I never use a solitary ATM, preferring one in a good secure location that affords privacy, like those near the entrance to a bank. (Don't worry; you don't need to go inside.)

Epilogue

Broad ocean view appeals to many prospective Baja homeowners.

Buying a Home in Mexico (2014)

For many people, buying an oceanfront home in Malibu or San Clemente (or anywhere in Southern California for that matter) can be prohibitive. In recent decades more and more opportunists have flocked to Mexico to buy properties better suited to their financial means—not to mention the active lifestyle, sense of adventure, cultural and learning experiences, salubrious climate, and convenient location that comes to those who seek Baja California for their retirement or vacation homes.

According to the 2014 *Expat Insider* report, Mexico is one of the world's most popular expat destination. The survey showed that 91% of the expatriates living in Mexico are pleased with their life there, and 44% added they would like to stay in Mexico for the rest of their life.

It's no surprise therefore that the greatest number of Americans outside the United States live in Mexico; in fact the 2010 Mexican census reported that 738,103 Americans live there.

Some reports indicate that over 1 million Americans have bought homes in Mexico, which is likely because many do not live there full time. Baja California is the most popular Mexican venue for vacation and/or second homes. The northern Baja coast primarily attracts Californians due to its accessibility and strong gringo presence (The U.S. dollar is as common as the peso, and English is widely spoken).

However, it is more typical for people from the Pacific Northwest and Canada to migrate farther south in Baja. Places like San Felipe, Mulegé, Loreto, La Paz, and the entire Cape region fill up each winter with snowbirds. You'll notice lots and lots of Oregon and Washington license plates down there.

What created this exodus besides better affordability? For starters, the aging baby boom generation is out actively searching for retirement havens. The widely publicized drug wars that were mostly outside tourist areas have generally abated. And the pristine beaches and laid-back lifestyle have beckoned.

But the real start was way back in 1973 when Mexico created the Fideicomiso for foreigners.

The Fideicomiso

Previous to 1973, foreigners could not own Mexican beach property. Article 27 of the 1917 Mexican Constitution prohibited foreigners from acquiring fee simple title to residential real estate in areas referred to as "restricted" zones. These restricted zones refer to any land within 50 km. (31 miles) of any coastline or 100 km (62 miles) of either border. Included in this zone is the entire Baja Peninsula.

A lot of us who purchased property there previous to that either built on leased land from a Mexican landowner or settled on Ejido land. Both were iffy propositions too. An owner might die and their disputes could, and did, tie up properties; in some cases the new owners did not wish to honor the rights of the lessees. That happened at Campo Lopez, and then again in a community south of Ensenada. As noted earlier, it even happened at Cantamar where I owned a home for 45 years. Over time most of those disputes have been settled amicably.

Homes on leased land do have advantages though; they are generally less expensive to buy and to maintain, are in good locations, and you can sell your rights with the new owner assuming the lease.

The Fideicomiso is basically a Mexican bank trust and when it was created in 1973 it started the land boom for foreigners wanting to purchase vacation or retirement homes in Mexico. This Fideicomiso provided a legal, simple and safe circumvention of the constitutional provisions. The trust places legal title in the name of a Mexican bank under a permit from the Secretary of Foreign Relations, so the bank may administrate the property on behalf of the buyer/beneficiary, who enjoys exactly the same rights of ownership as a Mexican national.

Originally set up for 30 years, it was later expanded to an additional 30 years (30 + 30), and through the years continued to get more liberal. Today a trust can be obtained for a period of 50 years and then renewed multiple times thus establishing perpetuity for owners of rights in Mexican properties.

A foreign seller can assign these rights to a buyer, or the buyer may obtain a new trust permit, as he or she prefers. There is a one-time cost of currently a little less than $2,000 U.S. for the permit and registration, and bank trust administration fees range from about $200 to $750 U.S. annually.

Title insurance, as is secured in the U.S., is generally available through both Mexican and U.S. companies and should be obtained wherever available.

Ejidos

As I mentioned earlier, be wary of an "Ejido" (Eh-hee-do) as ejidal property can be iffy. More than 50% of all land in Mexico is ejidal, or communal land, meaning it is government property dedicated to the service of a community. Certain provisions in the law now allow ejidos to be converted into private property, but until the conversion process is complete, it may be risky. The ejidos elect officers and what has happened in some cases is that those officers have sold or leased land to foreigners to build homes. I have known some ejido dwellers who are happy with their decisions, and I have known others who had it end in disaster.

Anyhow, why settle on an ejido when today the Fideicomiso is so omnipresent?

In Mexico the licensing and regulation of agents and other professionals is spotty, but there are numerous competent real estate people who can assist you. You will find familiar chain Real Estate brokers like Century 21, RE/Max, and others. Choose your broker carefully; confirm that the agent you are considering is an active member of the Mexican Association of Real Estate Professionals (AMPI). AMPI members operate under a code of ethics and are affiliated with the U.S. National Association of Realtors (NAR) and the Canadian Association of Realtors (CREA).

Make sure you use a title company to obtain a valid transfer of title, and make sure an escrow company (third party) handles the transfer. Check the references of all who might be involved in the transaction. Land America and Commonwealth Land Title are both reputable American companies used in Baja.

Property taxes for residential properties are just over one-half percent (0.65%) of the assessed value.

Insist upon a binding arbitration clause as lawsuits can be costly and time consuming. It is far better for the parties to agree ahead of time to resolve any possible dispute through binding arbitration.

In the old days buying Mexican property was an all-cash deal, though with a substantial down payment, sometimes sellers would carry a mortgage. Now several U.S. finance companies offer numerous possibilities for the Mexican market. A lot of the new developments also assist with the financing. Another option is the use of self-directed IRA accounts for Mexican property acquisitions. Properties purchased with IRA funds are intended to be for investment properties only, not for personal use. It's great for rental income.

There are many condominiums and/or residential developments that specialize in selling properties to Americans. They are very familiar with the Fideicomiso and offer reputable escrow and title companies you will need to buy a home in Mexico. They basically can safely walk you through your purchase.

If you're seriously interested, just go on down there and look around. While you may find a number of listings online, seeing the actual home, development, or location is important.

When you look out at the blue water and see dolphins frolicking, and whitewater crashing, you can imagine sipping margaritas on your deck before you head out for mariachis and a fresh lobster dinner. The change in pace might just do you some good.

(Ed note: This article was written a decade ago, but the basic information is mostly the same today. Still, always check before committing.)

Writers Inspire Travelers to Baja (2019)

Some months ago, Baja enthusiast and fellow author David Kier (*Baja California: Land of Missions*) threw out this tickler via the Baja Nomad Forum:

"Who were the Baja Book Authors who inspired you to travel south?"

He added: "...perhaps it is time to remember those explorers, travelers, and authors if you are at an age where it was books and paper maps that gave you a clue as to what great adventures could be found just south of our border."

He continued: "Vote for the one you got information or inspiration from."

The results in, I was pleasantly surprised to have been named and found myself among some great company. While I had been visiting Baja California all my life, I noted that several of the other finalists definitely had inspired me to further explore the fascinating peninsula.

The results:

1) **Gene Kira**
2) **Erle Stanley Gardner, Ray Cannon, David Brackney (AAA), and Graham Mackintosh (tied).**
3) **Tom Miller, Greg Niemann, and Walt Peterson (tied).**

We are just a few of the hundreds of writers who have covered or written about Baja California over the years.

It is difficult not highlighting such classic guidebooks as **Gerhard & Gulick's** *Lower California Guidebook,* or any of **Harry W. Crosby's** books which are of incredible importance to Baja California historians.

I was personally inspired also by **Marvin and Aletha Patchen** *(Baja Adventures),* and *The Baja Feeling* by **Ben Hunter.**

Likewise, you might consider the outstanding contributions of **Cliff Cross, Joe Cummings, Fred Hoctor, Fred and Gloria Jones, Fernando Jordan, Joseph Wood Krutch, Max Miller, Choral Pepper, Gary Graham,** and **Walt Wheelock** to name a few.

I am familiar with the works of those also cited in the Baja Nomad poll and here are some brief sketches of those also honored:

#1 Gene S. Kira

When it comes to fishing books, *The Baja Catch* by Gene Kira and Neil Kelly (1988) is a must. The large format book is organized well and includes maps of all the hot spots. From my campsite I could look out over a reef, read about what kind of fish are there, and wade out and catch them. Very impressive fishing guide which we dog-eared from extensive use.

Kira's solo novel *King of the Moon* about a small Baja fishing village coping with difficult times is a classic story.

Following his novel, Kira emerged with the epic book about Ray Cannon in *The Unforgettable Sea of Cortez.* The year 2000 winner of the Outdoor Writers Association of California (OWAC) Book of the Year honors, it is massive in size and scope.

Kira also gave me research and marketing advice when I was writing my books, and I appreciated when he later wrote:

"Greg Niemann's *Baja Legends* brings to life the lore and mystique that makes Baja California the place we love. This vivid old timer's story book must be considered required reading for all who fancy themselves as 'Baja experts.'"

#2 Ray Cannon

Ray Cannon was probably more responsible for increasing tourism in Baja than any other person during his prolific years as a writer for *Western Outdoor News.* Originally invited to Baja in 1947 to write about fishing potential by the governor who later became Mexican President Abelardo L. Rodriguez, Cannon fell in love with the land and spent most of his remaining years there.

His regular fishing column inspired generations of aficionados and led to his landmark book, *The Sea of Cortez* published by Sunset Books in 1966. The former Hollywood actor/director/writer had also written *How To Fish the Pacific Coast.*

#2 Erle Stanley Gardner

Beginning in the 1930s, Erle Stanley Gardner wrote the popular Perry Mason mystery series. By the 1950s and '60s, Gardner was extremely successful with radio and television shows. He also developed a love for Baja California and wrote the *Land of Shorter Shadows* about Baja in 1948.

Erle Stanley Gardner

His appetite for remote Baja not satisfied, Gardner organized numerous trips into the interior of the peninsula, traveling by airplane, helicopter, experimental motorcycles and even by horses and mules. During the height of his popularity, he penned six more Baja-related books: *Hunting The Desert Whale* (1960), *Hovering Over Baja* (1961), *The Hidden Heart of Baja* (1964), *Off The Beaten Track In Baja* (1967), *Mexico's Magic Square* (1968) and *Host With The Big Hat* (1969).

He was the first outsider to view numerous cave paintings, even having one—the Gardner Cave—named after him. On some trips, Gardner brought in archeologists to validate the significance of their finds.

Due to his own popularity, Gardner's journeys through Baja California brought enormous attention to a previously neglected region. After he died in 1970, his ashes were scattered over his beloved Baja countryside.

#2 David Brackney (AAA)

The Automobile Club of Southern California has been publishing wonderful guides and maps since 1927, and I never made a trip south without their most current map and guide. Brackney's *Baja California,* published by Wilderness Press (July 2001) is a 500-page paperback that is way more comprehensive than earlier versions.

#2 Graham Mackintosh

In an age when all the world's continents had been explored, there are those would-be adventurers who might decry that it's all been done. Not Graham Mackintosh. Born in London of an Irish mother and Scottish father, Mackintosh with his flaming bright red hair was a teacher looking for adventure. So he decided to walk around the rugged and inhospitable coastline of Baja California.

As Mackintosh said, "I had never done anything adventurous in my life. I wasn't fit. I knew nothing about the desert. I couldn't speak Spanish. I had no money. With my red hair and fair skin I was probably the last person in the world to go traipsing around a sun-baked wilderness."

But he did it anyway and survived to write *Into a Desert Place* (1988). The book won several awards in England and a legion of fans among Baja buffs.

Mackintosh followed up his magnum opus with *Journey With a Baja Burro,* (Sunbelt, 2000), *Nearer My Dog To Thee,* (2003) and *Marooned With Very Little Beer* (2008), both by Baja Detour Press. His adventures have made him one of the most popular modern Baja authors.

Graham is still romping and kayaking around Baja, mostly in the Bahia de los Angeles area. His current adventures have resulted in several photographic eBooks, including four about paddling south to La Paz, and several about kayaking with his stuffed bears which definitely appeal to the young and young at heart.

#3 Tom Miller

Tom Miller, who held numerous saltwater fishing records, had a trailer home near Ensenada before building a palm-thatched hideaway south of La Paz. For three decades he covered all of Baja which resulted in over 1,000 articles for outdoor publications and his weekly column in *Western Outdoor News.*

His original book, prominent because of the maps overlaid on NASA space photos, was *The Baja Book* (1973.) *The Baja Book II* came out in 1982 and *The Baja Book III* in 1989, becoming an indispensable Baja guide.

My personal favorite Tom Miller book is his 1982 *Anglers Guide to Baja California,* a practical, easy-to-follow guide highlighting where the fish are, what kind of fish, and how-to-catch-em. I referred to it often on my trips into the remote regions of the peninsula.

Known as "Mr. Baja" to hundreds of thousands through his books, articles, radio and television work, Miller also wrote *Eating Your Way Through Baja* in 1986.

Shirley Miller (Mrs. Baja) was a columnist for *Western Outdoor News,* co-author of *The Baja Book,* and founder of Mexico West Travel Club. A long-time friend, in proofing *Baja Legends* for me she made numerous **helpful** suggestions.

#3 Walt Peterson

Walt Peterson was deservedly singled out in the poll for his *The Baja Adventure Book* (Wilderness Press, 1987). The large format paperback has it all: adventure activities, how to get there (including topographical maps, charts, and detailed information). I always kept mine in the front seat and was rewarded by being led to many an adventure I never knew existed.

I wish I had room for brief sketches on so many other authors and contributors who have inspired me. No question, Baja is an inspiring kind of place.

Baja Book Reviews (2019)

Books about Baja California are still being written and will continue to inspire legions of future visitors to that enchanting place called "Baja." In recent years I have written a few reviews of some of them. Here are reviews about two fascinating books:

Oasis of Stone
Visions of Baja California Sur

Photographs by Miguel Ángel de la Cueva

Text by Bruce Berger (2006)

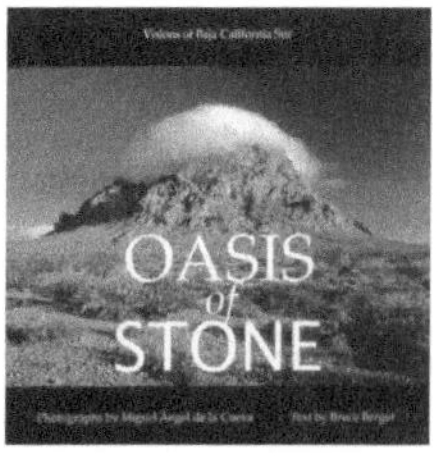

Oasis of Stone is a visual treat so powerful its photographic images linger long after the book is closed. Also captivating are some of the mental images created by the phrasing in the enlightening text. This book is appealing, so appealing you really want to go there to see the harsh, compelling, and forbidding land for yourself.

Baja California Sur, the southern half of the Baja peninsula and the most sparsely populated of Mexico's 32 states, is a veritable fantasyland of rocky headlands, parched desert, wild mountains, tumbling streams, foggy coastlines, unique vegetation, and a plethora of wildlife that thrive in the dry deserts, barren highlands, tropical oases, and the ocean depths.

I've been to BCS numerous times, hiked to waterfalls and petroglyph sites, snorkeled in the gulf, and explored some out-of-the-way places. I've taken photos too, but after perusing the dazzling array of photographs by Miguel 'Angel de la Cueva, I don't think I'd show mine to anybody.

The close-up photos of the flora and fauna are outstanding, but the photos of the land itself: mountain canyons, cobbled beaches, undulating sand dunes, crunchy salt flats, craggy peaks, all captured with incredible lighting give the book its most captivating feeling. De la Cueva capitalized on the sun's dazzling and myriad spectacle, rendering the inviting geology in soft early light, robust late afternoon, and the muted hues of morning fog.

De la Cueva has been documenting the landscape of Baja California Sur since 1998, and, not surprisingly, has garnered numerous awards for his efforts. This is not a photographer on assignment, but one who is truly and deeply enamored with his subject, and it shows. He is founder of Planeta Peninsula, an organization dedicated to advancing the understanding and protection of the natural habitats and cultural traditions of BCS.

Those quality photos needed someone with that deep respect for Baja California Sur to write the accompanying text and captions. By far, the best person for the job was selected. Bruce Berger, who spends much of each year in the state's capital, La Paz, is the author of *Almost an Island,* an excellent chronicle of over 30 years in Baja, and *Sierra, Sea and Desert,* which covers the area's biosphere reserve.

His captions are succinct, but the text is sheer delight, proving that "well-written" need not be stranger to "informative." Consider this observation, "The scarcity of water in Baja California Sur has the ironic effect of making the plants more visible, rather than less. They cannot hide between the masses of each other. At the center of the clearing each needs for the collection of water, they stand visually heightened, immobile, as if born to be seen in the round."

Or this, "Long after Western technology scarred other parts of our planet, the lands of Baja California Sur remained untouched. Isolated, a creature of drought, the peninsula was a cactus among landscapes, embraced by empty space, its spines on guard."

The book is simply organized into four sections which cover geology, fauna, flora, and the arrival of man. It is a hard-bound coffee table book, but one that you might refer to time and again, perhaps to review the nesting habits of a rare bird, to marvel at the buds on the weird cirio tree after a rain, or to wistfully enjoy the beauty of an estuary illuminated by a dazzling sunset.

Published by Sunbelt Publications of San Diego, *Oasis of Stone* is as solid as its subject matter.

—Reviewed by Greg Niemann

Baja's Wild Side

By Daniel Cartamil (2017)

Baja's Wild Side: A Photographic Journey Through Baja California's Pacific Coast Region is a treasure of a coffee table book by Daniel Cartamil. You need not be a Baja Buff to appreciate some of the finest photos of Baja anywhere. I have been through most of the area covered and yet my first reaction was what an incredible artistic eye the photographer displays.

My old photos of the area were merely record-keeping shots compared to the artwork in *Baja's Wild Side.* Now I want to go back to the area and see what I missed. Daniel Cartamil, Ph.D, a marine biologist from Scripps Institute, amassed the amazing set of photos (Over 100 of them in the book) during his 10 years studying sharks in Baja California.

An avid conservationist, Cartamil chronicles the fragile environment and breathtaking nature of one of the most remote areas in North America.

The book is arranged in four chapters, or subsections, based on the geography of the state of Baja California, starting in the south with Bahia Sebastion Viscaino & Inland. Chapter 2 covers The Wild Coast, a little visited section along the Pacific from Santa Rosalillita to El Rosario. Chapter 3, The Valley of the Boojums, features the flora and fauna of the central inland section, and the Gold Coast and High Sierra is covered in Chapter 4.

Cartamil offers unique views of the most traveled section, that along the northern Pacific coast, including a dramatic photo of the "Redeemer Upon the Hill," a massive statue of Jesus just south of the Calafia point.

From fishing villages to a lightning strike while camping along the coast, the images are memorable and inspiring. They make you want to head for the wilds of Baja—like real soon.

Published by Sunbelt Publications and with a foreword by author friend Graham Mackintosh, *Baja's Wild Side* really is a collectible work of art.

—Reviewed by Greg Niemann

The Legacy of Books

In closing, it is obvious that even in this digital age, books, real books, have a significant impact on travelers to Mexico, and more significantly, Baja California.

Without question, the internet is very much alive and important today in bringing travelers up to date on weather and road conditions, lodging and dining options, and much more. There are several forums and boards specifically for those in Baja California.

But books endure. Writers today, through resplendent photography, precise and compelling prose, and tedious historical research, still continue to inspire travelers to that intriguing land called Baja California.

About the Author

An accredited business communicator (ABC), Greg Niemann was a communications manager and publications editor with United Parcel Service for over 34 years, retiring in 1995. Niemann was president of both the Los Angeles and Orange County chapters of the International Association of Business Communicators (IABC) and was named Communicator of the Year by that organization.

He worked for UPS as a teenager in 1957-58, and then served in the U.S. Army in what was then West Germany. He returned to UPS as a Hollywood delivery driver, went to college at night and earned a BA in journalism from California State University, Los Angeles. Promoted into management, Niemann edited the company magazine in Southern California and later coordinated the editing of numerous company publications.

Since retirement, he has been a newspaper columnist and still contributes regularly to several publications. Presently Niemann is on staff of the *San Clemente Journal,* writing the award-winning South of the Border column and other articles. He is a regular contributor to the online *Baja Bound Bulletin*, and pens the History column for the print/online *Coachella Valley Independent.*

A long-time member of the Outdoor Writers Association of California (OWAC), he served on that organization's Board of Directors for several years. Niemann's books include *Baja Fever, Baja Legends, Palm Springs Legends, Big Brown: The Untold Story of UPS*, and *Las Vegas Legends.*

The memoirs brought out in *Baja Fever: Journeys into Mexico's Intriguing Peninsula* created a loyal following of Baja fans. The popular *Baja Legends: The Historic Characters, Events and Locations That Put Baja California on the Map* won an award from the Outdoor Writers Association of California, and is currently in its sixth printing.

Palm Springs Legends: Creation of a Desert Oasis has been one of the top sellers in all Coachella Valley bookstores and is now in its seventh printing. *Palm Springs*

Leila and Greg Niemann, December 2024

Legends won the First-Place award for Niemann in OWAC Book of the Year competition.

Big Brown is in several languages worldwide, and *Las Vegas Legends* was a 2012 finalist in *ForeWord Review* Book of the Year competition.

A popular speaker, Niemann has presented numerous slide shows and/or book signings at venues including Barnes & Noble, Costco, Discover Baja Travel Club; Distant Lands Travel Club, BookExpo America, and the Los Angeles Times Festival of Books.

Niemann is a fourth generation Californian whose great grandfather at one time published the *Pomona Progress and Independent* and also penned a book about gold mines in Baja California. He and his wife **Leila** reside in southern California. They travel as much as possible and **for many years** also enjoyed their weekend home in Baja California, Mexico.

Additonal Reading

The accompanying books and reference materials will help the reader learn more about Baja California.

Books:

Allen, Col. D.K. *Field Notes of Lower California* (San Vicente Basin) (International Company of Mexico, 1887)

Ames, Bette and Knox, Wilma. *Through Baja by RV* (Travel Treasures, 1975)

Automobile Club of Southern California. *Baja California* (Los Angeles: Guidebooks and Maps from 1940s to present)

Baegert S.J., Johann Jakob. *Observations in Lower California, a 1771 report* (Berkeley and Los Angeles: published by University of California Press, 1952)

Bairstow, Lynne. *Los Cabos & Baja* (Fodor's: Macmillan Travel, 2000)

Bales, Mike. *Launch Ramps of Baja California* (Torrance: Launch Ramp Publications, 1992)

Bancroft, Hubert Howe. *History of California, The Works of HHB,* (Santa Barbara: Wallace Hebberd, 4 Volumes, 1969)

Bancroft, Margaret and Griffing. *Flight of the Least Petrel* (New York: Putnam & Sons, 1932)

Barber, Bruce F. *...Of Sea and Sand* (Chula Vista: Black Forest Press, 2003)

Barbosa, Lupita E. and Barron, Martin E. From Velicata to San Diego: Fr. Junipero Serra (Tijuana: Luz Y Arte Editorial, 1984)

Bassett, Theda Lucilla. *Sea of Cortez Dancing* (North Salt Lake, Utah: DMT Publishing, 2002)

Belden, L. Burr. *Baja California Overland* (Glendale: La Siesta Press, 1968)

Benchley, Peter. *Girl From the Sea of Cortez* (Doubleday, 1982)

Berger, Bruce. *Almost An Island* (University of Arizona Press, 1998)

Berger, Bruce, de la Cueva, Miguel Angel. *Oasis of Stone: Visions of Baja California Sur* (San Diego: Sunbelt Publications, 2006)

Blaisdell, Lowell L. *The Desert Revolution: Baja California, 1911* (Madison, Wisconsin: University of Wisconsin Press, 1962)

Blanco, Fierro (Walter Nordhoff). *Journey of the Flame* (New York: The Literary Guild, 1933)

Bolton, Herbert Eugene. *Rim of Christendom* (New York: Macmillin & Co. 1936)

Botello, Judy. *The Other Side* (San Diego: Sunbelt Publishing, 1998)

Boyle, T.C. *The Tortilla Curtain* (Penguin Books, 1995)

Brenton, Tadeo. Ed. *Baja California Yearbook* (Ensenada: Las Californias Publishing, 1963)

Brenton, Tadeo. Ed. *The West Coast of Mexico* (San Ysidro: Grace Loftin, 1969)
Brow, Dix. *Sea of Cortez Guide* (Western Marine Enterprises, 1970)
Brow, Dix. *Boating in Mexico* (Aztec, 1976)
Browne, J. Ross. *Explorations in Lower California* (New York: Harper & Bros., 1868)
Browne, J. Ross. *J. Ross Browne: His Letters, Journals and Writings* (Albuquerque: U. of New Mexico Press (Edited by Lina Fergusson Browne, 1969)
Buffum, E. Gould. *Six Months in the Gold Mines* (Los Angeles: Ward Ritchie Press, 1959)
Bush, Wesley A. *Paradise to Leeward: Cruising the West Coast of Mexico* (New York: D. Van Nostrand, 1954)
Cahill, Rick. *Border Towns of the Southwest* (Pruett Publishing, 1987)
Cannon, Ray. *The Sea of Cortez,* (Sunset Magazine, Palo Alto: Lane Book Co., 1966)
Cannon, Ray. *How To Fish The Pacific Coast* (Sunset, Palo Alto: Lane Book Co.)
Carroll, Richard. *The Motor Camper's Guide to Mexico and Baja California* (Chronicle Books, 1975)
Carmony, Neil B. and Brown, David E. T*ales From Tiburon, An Anthology of Adventures in Seriland* (edited by Southwest Natural History Association, 1983)
Carter, Pel. *Trails and Tales of Baja* (Southwest Arts Foundation, 1967)
Cartamil, Daniel. *Baja's Wild Side* (San Diego: Sunbelt Publications, 2017)
Cepek, Dick and Wheelock, Walt. *Rough Riding* (Glendale: La Siesta Press, 1968)
Conover, Ted. *Coyotes* (Vintage Books, 1987)
Coyle, Jeanette and Roberts, Norman. *A Field Guide to Plants of Baja California* (La Jolla: Natural History Publishing Co., 1975)
Crosby, Harry. *Cave Paintings of Baja California* (San Diego: Sunbelt Publications, 1997)
Crosby, Harry. *Antigua California* (University of New Mexico Press, 1994)
Crosby, Harry. T*he King's Highway in Baja California* (San Diego: Copley Books, 1974)
Crosby, Harry. *Last of the Californios* (San Diego: Copley Books, 1981)
Crosby, Harry. *Gateway to Alta California* (San Diego: Sunbelt Publications, 2002)
Crosby, Harry, James Britton. *The Beauties of Tijuana* (San Diego, Britton, 1964)
Cross, Cliff. *Baja California* (HP Books, 1974)
Crow, James T. *New Baja Handbook for the Off-Pavement Motorist in Lower California* (Bond/Parkhurst Books, 1973)
Cummings, Joe. *Baja Handbook* (Moon Publications, 1992)
Davidson, Ed, Orcutt, Eddy *San Diego: A Brief History* (San Diego: San Diego Trust & Savings, 1939)
Del Postigo, Manuel. *Leyandas y Relatos Bajacalifornianos* (Tijuana: Edicioness ILCSA, 2004)
Demaris, Ovid. *Poso Del Mundo* (Little, Brown & Co., 1970)
DeMente, Boye. *Insiders Guide* (Phoenix Books, 1975)

Doyle, Mike, *Morning Glass* (Three Rivers, CA: Manzanita Press, 1993)
Dunne, S.J., Peter Masten. *Black Robes in Lower California* (Berkeley & Los Angeles: University of California Press, 1952)
Eiler, Dorothea M. *Baja Gringos* (Bristol Publishing, 1993)
Ellsberg, Helen. *Los Coronados Islands* (Glendale: La Siesta Press, 1983)
Ellsberg, Helen. *Dona Anita of El Rosario* (Glendale: La Siesta Press, 1985)
Enea, Sparky. *With Steinbeck in the Sea of Cortez* (Sand River Press, 1991)
Espinosa, Rik. *Espinosa's Guide to Baja* (Roundtable Publishing, 1989)
Espinoza, Anita Grosso de. *Reflections* (Tijuana: Arte y Publicidad Grafica, 1994)
Fischer, Paul. *Adventure to Land's End* (ARS Publications, 1975)
Fisher, Richard, D. *National Parks of Northwest Mexico* (Sunracer Publications, 1988)
Flying Samaritans. *2002-2003 Handbook* (Tucson: Samaritanos Voladores, 2002)
Fodor. *Mexico's Baja* (Fodor's Travel Publications, 1987)
Fogel, Daniel. *Junipero Serra, the Vatican, and Enslavement Theology* (ISM Press, 1988)
Fons, Valerie. *Keep It Moving* (Seattle: The Mountaineers, 1986)
Francez, Padre James Donald. *The Lost Treasures of Baja California* (Black Forrest Press, 1996)
Gardner, Erle Stanley. *Land of Shorter Shadows* (New York: Morrow & Co. 1948)
Gardner, Erle Stanley. *Hunting The Desert Whale* (New York: Morrow & Co. 1960)
Gardner, Erle Stanley. *Hovering Over Baja* (New York: Morrow & Co. 1961)
Gardner, Erle Stanley. *The Hidden Heart of Baja* (Jarrods Publishers, 1964)
Gardner, Erle Stanley. *Off The Beaten Track In Baja* (New York: Morrow & Co. 1967)
Gardner, Erle Stanley. *Mexico's Magic Square* (New York: Morrow & Co. 1968)
Gardner, Erle Stanley. *Host With The Big Hat* (New York: Morrow & Co. 1969)
Garrison, Chuck. *Offshore Fishing; Southern California and Baja* (Chronicle Books, 1981)
Gerhard, Peter and Gulick, Howard. *Maps of Baja California* (Glendale: Arthur Clark Co., 1962)
Gerhard, Peter and Gulick, Howard. *Lower California Guidebook, 4th Ed.* (Glendale: Arthur Clark Co., 1970)
Gerhard, Peter. *Pirates on the West Coast of New Spain* (Glendale: Arthur Clark Co., 1960)
Gessner, Lotti. *Hotel Cabo San Lucas—The Man Behind the History* (Los Cabos 1999)
Goldbaum, David. *Towns Of Baja California: a 1918 report* (Glendale: La Siesta Press, 1971)
Goldman, Edward. *Plant Records of an Expedition to Lower California* (Smithsonian Institute, U.S. National Museum,1916)
Gotshall, Daniel W. *Marine Animals of Baja California* (Western Marine Enterprises, 1982)
Gudde, Erwin G. *1,000 California Place Names* (University of California Press, 1947)
Gulick, Howard E. Nayarit, *Mexico – A Travelers Guidebook* (Glendale: The

Arthur H. Clark Co., 1965)
Hager, Anna Marie, editor, *The Filibusters of 1890* (Los Angeles: Dawsons, 1968)
Hall, Douglas Kent, *The Border: Life on the Line* (New York: Abbeville Press, 1988)
Hambleton, Enrique. *La Pintura Rupestre de Baja California* (Mexico City: Fomento Cultural Banamex, 1979)
Hancock, Ralph, Haller, Ray, McMahan, Mike, and Alvarado, Frank. *Baja California* (Los Angeles: Academy Press, 1953)
Hale, Howard. *A Long Walk To Mulegé* (Pinkerton Publications, 1980)
Hanson, Victor Davis. *Mexifornia: A State of Becoming* (San Francisco: Encounter Books, 2003)
Harris, Richard. *Hidden Baja* (Berkeley: Ulysses Press, 1998)
Hazard, Ann. *Cartwheels in the Sand* (San Diego: Renegade Enterprises, 1999)
Hazard, Ann. *Agave Sunsets – Treasured Tales of Baja* (Solana Beach: Renegade Enterprises. 2002)
Higginbotham, Patti and Tom. *Backroad Baj*a (Something's Fishy Publications, 1996)
Hittell, Theodore H. *El Triunfo de la Cruz – The First Ship Built in The Californias, an 1880 report* (Printed by California Historical Society, 1984)
Hoctor, Fred. *Baja Haha* (San Diego: Backside Press 1984)
Houghton Mifflin Publishers. *Baja Peninsula – Insight Pocket Guide* (New York: 1995)
Howey, Janet & Moore, Lee. *The Todos Santos Book* (Todos Santos: El Tecolote Libros, 1998)
Hugh, Don A. *Solo Below, A Guide Book to Lower California* (AAA Publishing, 1958)
Humphreville, Michael. *In the Shadow of the Volcano* (San Diego, Sunbelt Publications 2006)
Hunter, Ben. *The Baja Feeling* (Brasch & Brasch, 1978)
Hunter, Jim. *Offbeat Baja* (Chronicle Books, 1977)
Jackson, Everett Gee. *It's a Long Road to Comondu* (Texas A & M Press, 1987)
Janovy Jr., John. *Vermillion Sea* (Houghton Mifflin, 1992)
Johnson, William Weber. *Baja California* (Time-Life Books, 1972)
Jones, Fred and Gloria. *Baja Camping* (Foghorn Press, 1994)
Jones, Jack. *Baja* (Fawcett Gold Medal, 1982)
Jordan, Fernando. *El Otro Mexico* (La Paz: State of Baja California Sur, 1976)
Kier, David, *Baja California Land of Missions* (El Cajon: M & E Books, 2016)
Kira, Gene. *The Unforgettable Sea of Cortez* (Torrance: Cortez Publications, 1999)
Kira, Gene. *King of the Moon* (Valley Center: Apples & Oranges, 1996)
Kira, Gene and Kelly, Neil. *Baja Catch* (Valley Center: Apples & Oranges, 1988)
Kirchner, John A. Baja *California Railways* (Golden West Books, 1988)
Klink, Jerry. *The Mighty Cortez Fish Trap* (A. S. Barnes & Co., 1974)
Krutch, Joséph Wood. *The Forgotten Peninsula* (New York: William Sloane, 1961)
Krutch, Joséph Wood. *Baja California and the Geography of Hope* (Sierra Club, 1967)

Kulander, Charles. *West Mexico, From Sea to Sierra* (La Paz Publishing, 1992)
Landeros, Alberto Tapia. *En El Reino de Califia Universidad Autonoma de Baja California* (Mexicali:1998)
Langewiesche, William. *Cutting for Sign: One Man's Journey along the U.S.-Mexican Border* (Vintage Books, 1995)
Largent, R. Karl. *The Baja Conspiracy.* (New York: Dorchester Publishing Co., 2002)
Lingenfelter, Richard. *The Rush of 1889 – Baja California Gold Fever* (Dawson Books, 1967)
Lonely Planet, *Diving & Snorkeling Baja California* (Vic. Australia: Lonely Planet, 1999)
Lucas, Lois. *Baja Sand Castle* (LBL Publishing, 1984)
Mackintosh, Graham. *Into a Desert Place* (England: Unwin Hyman, 1988)
Mackintosh, Graham. *Journey With a Baja Burro* (San Diego: Sunbelt Publications, 2001)
Mackintosh, Graham. *Nearer My Dog To Thee* (San Diego: Baja Detour Press, 2003)
Mackintosh, Graham. *Marooned With Very Little Beer* (San Diego: Baja Detour Press, 2008)
Makabe, Lori. *Best Places: Baja* (Seattle: Sasquatch books, 2003)
Martinez, Pablo L. *A History of Lower California* (Mexico, D.F.: Editorial Baja California 1960)
Martinez, Ruben. *Crossing Over* (New York: Henry Holt & Co., 2001)
Mathes, Dr. W. Michael. *Las Misiones de Baja California* (University of San Francisco)
Mathes, Dr. W. Michael. *A Brief History of the Land of Calafia: the Californias, 1533-1795* (La Paz: Patronato Del Estudiante Sudcaliforniano, 1977)
Mathes, Dr. W. Michael. (Transcriber) *The Capture of the Santa Ana at Cabo San Lucas: November 1587* (The Accounts of Francis Pretty, Antonio de Sierra and Tomas de Alzola)
Mayoral, Francisco A. Fierro. *Remembranzas de un Bajacaliforniano* (Tijuana: Talleras fGraficos, 1963)
Mayo, C.M. *Miraculous Air* (Salt Lake City: University of Utah Press, 2002)
Mayo, C.M. *Sky Over El Nido* (Athens: University of Georgia Press, 1995)
Meigs, Peveril and Sauer Carl. *Lower California Studies: Site and Culture at San Fernando de Velicata* (Berkeley: University of California Press, 1927)
Mexicali Tourist Guide (Mexicali: Baja California, 1997)
Miller, Max. *California's Secret Islands* (Ballentine Books, 1959)
Miller, Max. *The Cruise of the Cow* (E.P. Dutton & Co., 1951)
Miller, Max. *Land Where Time Stands Still* (New York: Dodd, Mead & Co., 1943)
Miller, Mikel K. *I Love Baja* (Little Books World, 2010)
Miller, Tom. *Eating Your Way Through Baja* (Baja Trail Publications, 1986)
Miller, Tom. *Anglers Guide to Baja California* (Baja Trail Publications, 1982)
Miller, Tom and Baxter, Elmar. *The Baja Book* (Baja Trail Publications,1974)

Miller, Tom and Hoffman, Carol, *Baja Book II, Baja Book III* (Baja Trail Publications, 1989)

Minch, John, Minch, Edwin and Minch, Jason. *Roadside Geology and Biology of Baja California* (Minch and Assoc. 1998)

Morrison, Wilbur H. *The Adventure Guide to Baja California* (Hunter Publishing, 1990)

Murray, Spencer. *Cruising The Sea of Cortez* (Palm Desert: Desert Southwest, 1963)

McDonald, Marquis & Oster, Glenn. *Baja: Land of Lost Missions* (The Naylor Co., 1968)

McDonald, Paula. *Crossing the Border Fast and Easy* (Borderline, 1992)

McMahan, Mike. *There It Is: Baja* (Brooke House, 1973)

McMahan, Mike, Hancock, Ralph, Haller, Ray, and Alvarado, Frank. *Baja California* (Academy Press, 1953)

Navarre, Monty and Merrick, Harry. *Baja Traveler* (Airguide Publications, 1974, 1988)

Niemann, Greg. *Baja Fever* (La Crescenta: Mountain 'N' Air Books, 1998)

Niemann, Greg. *Baja Legends* (San Diego: Sunbelt Publications, 2001)

Nordhoff, Walter (Blanco, Fierro). *Journey of the Flame* (New York: The Literary Guild, 1933)

North, Arthur Walbridge. *The Mother of California* (San Francisco & New York: Paul Elder & Co., 1908)

North, Arthur Walbridge. *Camp and Camino in Lower California* (Rio Grande Press, 1910)

Nunis, Doyce B. Jr., (Editor). *The 1769 Transit of Venus: The Baja California Observations of Jean-Baptiste Chappe d'Auteroche, Vicente de Doz, and Joaquin Velazquez Cardenas de Leon* (Los Angeles: Natural History Museum of L.A. County. 1982)

O'Neil, Ann and Don. Loreto, *Baja California – First Mission and Capital of Spanish California* (Studio City: Tio Press, 2001)

Otterstrom, Kerry G. *Mulegé* (Mulegé: AMAC Impresos, 1992)

Palacios Roji, Alma. *Tijuana-Ensenada* (Tijuana: Litografica Limon, 1981)

Patchen, Marvin and Aletha. *Baja Adventures* (Baja Train Publications, 1981)

Patchen, Marvin and Aletha. *Baja Outpost* (San Diego: Sunbelt Publications, 2002)

Pendleton, Don. *Baja Blitz* (Worldwide Gold Eagle, 1993)

Pepper, Choral. *Desert Lore of Southern California* (San Diego: Sunbelt Publications, 1999)

Pepper, Choral. *Baja California: Vanished Missions, Lost Treasures, Strange Stories Tall and True* (Ward Ritchie Press, 1973)

Peterson, Walt. *The Baja Adventure Book* (Wilderness Press, 1987)

Peterson, Walt. Peterson, Michael. *Exploring Baja By RV* (Wilderness Press, 1996)

Peterson, Walt. *Diving and Snorkeling Baja California* (Lonely Planet, 1999)

Phillips, Norman. *Baja Highway One* (Four Wheeler Publications, 1974)

Phleger, Marjorie. *Pilot Down, Presumed Dead* (Harper & Row, 1963)
Pierce, Paul Panther. *A Baja Love Song* (Baja Trail Publications, 1985)
Polk, Dora Beale. *The Island of California – A History of the Myth* (University of Nebraska Press, 1991)
Pourade, Richard F. *The Explorers: The History of San Diego* (San Diego: Copley Press/ Union Tribune Publishing Co., 1960)
Pourade, Richard F. *The Call To California* (San Diego: Copley Press/Union Tribune Publishing Co., 1968)
Pryor, Alton. *Little Known Tales in California History* (Roseville: Stagecoach Publishing, 1997)
Redmond, Jennifer Silva. *Honeymoon at Sea* (RE:Books, Toronto, 2023)
Reseck, John Jr. *We Survived Yesterday: Kayaking From San Diego to Cabo San Lucas* (Griffin Publishing, 1994)
Reveles, Daniel. *Enchiladas, Rice, and Beans* (One World/Ballentine, 1994)
Reveles, Daniel. *Tequila, Lemon, and Salt* (San Diego: Sunbelt Publications, 2005)
Rice, Larry. *Baja to Patagonia* (Fulcrum Publishing, 1993)
Richmond, Doug. *Baja* (Bagnall Publishing, 1970)
Robinson, John W. *Camping and Climbing in Baja* (Glendale: La Siesta Press, 1983)
Roberts, Norman. *Baja California Plant and Field Guide* (La Jolla: Natural History Publishing Co., 1989)
Robertson, Tomas. *Historical Notes on Baja California* (Ensenada: San Miguel, 1972)
Robertson, Tomas. *Baja California and its Missions* (Glendale: La Siesta Press, 1978)
Rocha, Dr. Ernesto Sosa. *Resena Historica de la Pesca en el Puerto de San Felipe* (San Felipe: 2000)
Romano-Lax, Andromeda. *Sea Kayaking in Baja* (Wilderness Press, 1993)
Rovirosa, Lic. A. Salazar. *Cronologia de Baja California* (Mexicali: 1957)
Sadil, Scott. *Angling Baja* (Frank Amato Publications, 1996)
Salvadori, Clement. *Motorcycle Journeys Through Baja* (Whitehorse Press, 1997)
Sanborn, Don. *Mexico Travelogue* (Sanborn Travel, 1974)
Schwartz, Elizabeth Maul. *Troubled Sea* (San José: Authorss Choice {ress, 2000)
Scott, Annette. *Cruising and Sketching Baja* (Northland Press, 1974)
SCORE and HDRA, *Off-Road Racing Handbook* (1987)
Secretaria de Educacion Publica. *Baja California; Historia y Geografia* (Mexicali: 1993)
Senterfitt, Arnold. *Airports of Baja California* (1966)
Shedenhelm, W.R.C. *Rockhounding in Baja* (Glendale: La Siesta Press, 1986)
Simmons, James C. *Castaway in Paradise* (Dobbs Ferry, N.Y.: Sheridan House, 1998)
Smith, Don. *The Baja Run: Racing Fury* (Troll Associates, 1976)
Smith, Jack. *God and Mr. Gomez* (Readers Digest Press, 1974)
Smith, J. P. (Jimmy Jr.). *The Grinning Gargoyle Spills The Beans* (El Cajon: Baja Source, 2001)
Smith, Kacey. *Baja GPD Guide* (Denver: Lizard Lady Publications, 2000)

Smothers, Marion, *Vintage Baja* (In One Ear Publications, 1993)

Snyder, John Otterbein. *The Trout of the San Pedro Martir, Lower California* (University of California Press, 1926)

Stanton, Larry. *Glory Days of Baja* (Culler & Sons, 1996)

Stanton, Larry. *Arriba Baja* (Templeton, CA: Templeton Publishing, 1999)

Statler, Ruan L. *El Gringo Invisible* (Carlton Press, 1988)

Steinbeck, John, and Ricketts, Edward F. *The Sea of Cortez: A Leisurely Journal of Travel and Research* (Viking Press, 1941)

Steinbeck, John. *Log From the Sea of Cortez* (New York: Penguin Books, 1941)

Steinbeck, John. *The Pearl* (Viking Press, 1947)

Stephens, Bascom A. *Annual Publication of the Historical Society of Southern California* (Los Angeles: 1888-1889)

Stephens, Bascom A. *The Gold Fields of Lower California* (1889)

Sundby, Edie Littlefield. *The Mission Walker* (W Publishing, Thomas Nelson, 2017)

Sunset staff. *Sunset Travel Guide to Baja California* (Palo Alto: Lane Books, 1971)

Swain, Bernie. *Bounding Around Baja* (Santee, CA: Caballero Publishing, 2004)

Swain, Bernie. *Mi Baja. No Hurry, No Worry* (Santee, CA: Caballero Publishing, 2002)

Thomson, Donald A, and McKibbin, Nonie. *Gulf of California Fishwatcher's Guide* (Golden Puffer Press, 1981)

Tijuana Map and Guide (Tijuana: Turismo del Estado, 1969)

Tilton, Willis G. *Baja California: The Last New Frontier* (Central OK Printing, 1971)

Timberman, O.W. *Mexico's Diamond in the Rough* (Los Angeles: Westernlore Press, 1959)

Tobias, Jens. *The Gold of Northern Baja* (Tobias, Las Vegas, 2023)

Tomson, Tommy. *Jesuit Gold of Lower California* (Vantage Press, 1983)

Urrea, Luis Alberto. *Across The Wire* (Doubleday, Anchor Books, 1993)

Urrea, Luis Alberto. *The Devil's Highway* (Little Brown, 2004)

Venegas, S.J., Padre Miguel. *Obras Californias* (Introduction by Dr. W. Michael Mathes, University of San Francisco, 1978)

Venegas, S.J., Padre Miguel. *A Natural and Civil History of California* (2 Volumes), 1758 (Reprinted Library of Congress, 1966)

Vogel, Randy. *Climbers Guide to Valle Azteca, Baja California* (Bonehead Publishing, 1995)

Warren, Sam. *Having Fun in Tijuana* (Warren Communications, 1988)

Warren, Roger. *Red Lights of Baja Mexico* (Warren Communications, 1992)

Washburn, Elizabeth H. *Assault on Baja* (Fred Press, 1966)

Waterman, Jonathan. *Kayaking the Vermilion Sea* (Touchtone, Simon & Schuster, 1995)

Wayne, Scott. *Baja California, A Travel Survival Kit* (Lonely Planet, 1985)

Weber, Msgr. Francis J. *The Peninsular California Missions 1808-1880 (Three reports translated and annotated)* (Los Angeles: 1979)

Werschkul, Dave. *Saints and Demons in a Desert Wilderness* (Pacific Grove, CA

Xlibris Corp. 2003)
West, Carolyn and Jack. *Cruising the Pacific Coast* (Sea Publications, 1966)
Wheelock, Walt. *Beaches of Baja* (Glendale: La Siesta Press, 1968)
Wibberley, Leonard. *Yesterday's Land: A Baja California Adventure* (Ives Washburn, 1961)
Wilde, Jocelyn. *Bride of the Baja* (Pocket Books, 1980)
Williams Jack. *Baja Boaters Guide* (2 Volumes) (H.J. Williams Publications)
Williams, Jack and Williams, Patty. *The Magnificent Peninsula* (Publishers Press, 6th Edition, 1998)
Willoughby, Lee Davis. *The Baja People* (Dell, 1983)
Wong, Bonnie. *Bicycling Baja* (San Diego: Sunbelt Publications, 1988)
Wortman, Bill and Orv. *Bouncing Down to Baja* (Los Angeles: Westernlore Press, 1954)
Young, David. *Millions Want To* (Tucson: Three Flags Publishing, 1963)
Zwinger, Ann. *A Desert Country Near the Sea* (Harper & Row, 1983)

Publications and Newsletters:

Baja Almanac: California Norte and *Baja Almanac: California Sur* (Baja Vision)
Baja Bound Insurance, Baja Adventures, www.bajabound.com
Baja California (Robin Cox, Editor, AeroCalifornia)
Baja Explorer Magazine (Landon Crumpton, Publisher, 1991, 1992)
Baja Life Magazine (Baja Communications Group, Eric Cutter, Publisher, 1994-2000)
Baja Times (Roberta Ridgley and John Utley, Editors, 1979-1994)
Baja Traveler Magazine (Landon Crumpton, Publisher, 1988, 1989)
Baja Traveler (Mayte Rodríguez Cedillo, Editor/Publisher, 1999-2000-2001)
Chubasco (Vagabundos del Mar, Fred and Gloria Jones, Editors)
Discover Baja (Lynn Mitchell, Editor, Discover Baja Travel Club, Hugh & Carol Kramer)
El Calendario de Todos Santos (Grupo de Cabo L. Bruce S. de R.L. de C.V., 2000)
El Correcaminos (Los Cabos, Lloyd Kahn, Editor, 2000)
Mexico's West Coast Magazine (Grace Loftin, Editor)
Mexico West Travel Club (Shirley Miller, Publisher)
Pacific Discovery (California Academy of Sciences, 1965)
San Felipe Magazine (Bruce Barber, Editor, October 1991)
San Felipe Newsletter
Sea of Cortez Review (Jennifer Redmond, Editor, San Diego: Sunbelt Publications, 2000)